NEW DIRECTIONS IN MACROMODELLING

CONTRIBUTIONS
TO
ECONOMIC ANALYSIS

269

Honorary Editors:
D. W. JORGENSON
J. TINBERGEN†

Editors:
B. BALTAGI
E. SADKA
D. WILDASIN

ELSEVIER

Amsterdam – Boston – Heidelberg – London – New York – Oxford
Paris – San Diego – San Francisco – Singapore – Sydney – Tokyo

NEW DIRECTIONS IN MACROMODELLING

Edited by

ALEKSANDER WELFE
Chair of Econometric Models and Forecasts
University of Lodz, Lodz, Poland

2004

ELSEVIER

Amsterdam – Boston – Heidelberg – London – New York – Oxford
Paris – San Diego – San Francisco – Singapore – Sydney – Tokyo

ELSEVIER B.V.
Radarweg 29
P.O. Box 211, 1000 AE Amsterdam
The Netherlands

ELSEVIER Inc.
525 B Street, Suite 1900
San Diego, CA 92101-4495
USA

ELSEVIER Ltd
The Boulevard, Langford Lane
Kidlington, Oxford OX5 1GB
UK

ELSEVIER Ltd
84 Theobalds Road
London WC1X 8RR
UK

First edition 2004

British Library Cataloguing in Publication Data
A catalogue record is available from the British Library.

ISBN: 0-444-51633-6
ISSN: 0573-8555 (Series)

⊗ The paper used in this publication meets the requirements of ANSI/NISO Z39.48-1992 (Permanence of Paper).
Printed in Great Britain.

Working together to grow
libraries in developing countries

www.elsevier.com | www.bookaid.org | www.sabre.org

ELSEVIER   BOOK AID International   Sabre Foundation

Introduction to the Series

This series consists of a number of hitherto unpublished studies, which are introduced by the editors in the belief that they represent fresh contributions to economic science.

The term 'economic analysis' as used in the title of the series has been adopted because it covers both the activities of the theoretical economist and the research worker.

Although the analytical method used by the various contributors are not the same, they are nevertheless conditioned by the common origin of their studies, namely theoretical problems encountered in practical research. Since for this reason, business cycle research and national accounting, research work on behalf of economic policy, and problems of planning are the main sources of the subjects dealt with, they necessarily determine the manner of approach adopted by the authors. Their methods tend to be 'practical' in the sense of not being too far remote from application to actual economic conditions. In addition, they are quantitative.

It is the hope of the editors that the publication of these studies will help to stimulate the exchange of scientific information and to reinforce international cooperation in the field of economics.

The Editors

Contents

Introduction to the Series   v

Preface   ix

List of Contributors   xiii

Chapter 1. Modelling Volatility and Its Implication for European Economic Integration   1
Stephen G. Hall

Chapter 2. Causality and Exogeneity in Non-stationary Economic Time Series   21
David F. Hendry

Chapter 3. A Small Sample Correction of the Dickey–Fuller Test   49
Søren Johansen

Chapter 4. Inflation, Money Growth, and $I(2)$ Analysis   69
Katarina Juselius

Chapter 5. Recent Advances in Cointegration Analysis   107
Helmut Lütkepohl

Chapter 6. The Use of Econometric Models in Economic Policy Analysis   147
Grayham E. Mizon

Chapter 7. Bayesian Comparison of Bivariate GARCH Processes. The Role of the Conditional Mean Specification   173
Jacek Osiewalski, Mateusz Pipień

Chapter 8. Modelling Polish Economy: An Application of SVEqCM   197
Aleksander Welfe, Piotr Karp, Piotr Kębłowski

Chapter 9. Optimal Lag Structure Selection in VEC-Models   213
Peter Winker, Dietmar Maringer

Subject Index   235

Preface

There is no exaggeration in saying that the development of econometrics cannot be separated from macromodelling. The first macromodels attempted to empirically verify mathematical models of the business cycle proposed by Ragnar Frisch and Michal Kalecki, but mainly in John M. Keynes's *The General Theory of Employment, Interest and Money* (an excellent historical review can be found in the work by Bodkin *et al.* (1991). It is astonishing that Keynes himself was initially very hesitant about such efforts as shown in his critique of Jan Tinbergen's study presenting a model constructed for the League of Nations. It should be added, however, that at a later time Keynes modified his attitude to the construction (and application) of macroeconometric models. The attractiveness of Keynes' theoretical proposals was huge; as a consequence, for over three following decades macromodels were Keynesian-oriented and models based on alternative paradigms started to be constructed much later.

Already during World War II the immense potential of econometric models for practical application in the simulation of alternative economic policies and forecasting was observed. A powerful impulse in this direction was given by the pioneering works by Lawrence R. Klein that brought forward a series of models for the United States (Klein, 1950). The largest of the models then, the Klein–Goldberger Model (Klein and Goldberger, 1955), contained 20 endogenous and 43 predetermined variables (19 of them being exogenous). This was, of course, a Keynesian-type model, but to a large extent it also drew on John R. Hicks' and Oskar Lange's proposals. From early 1953 it was used to prepare forecasts for the US economy. It turned out that forecasts generated using this model were definitely superior to the competing projections. These findings triggered a huge interest not only in multi-equation models but also in econometric modelling itself. In a relatively short period of time macromodels were built for most developed countries of the world, becoming a commonly used tool for macroeconomic policy analyses. Concurrently, the research in the production, investment and consumption functions gave birth to many discoveries within the theory of econometrics. Also, the multi-equation models themselves, as well as problems in estimating their parameters and analysing their properties inspired many advances (Haavelmo, 1943; Koopmans, 1949; Theil, 1958).

Unfortunately, the intensive work conducted in the 1960s and 1970s on macromodels that were constructed not only for academic purposes but also to meet the needs of governmental agencies and private companies had its negative consequences as well: specification of equations was not sufficiently based on theory, parameter estimations did not meet theoretical requirements, the simplest estimation methods were typically employed and simultaneity bias disregarded, analyses of models' properties allowing for their stochastic nature were usually neglected. This approach was reflected also in the term: 'empirical model', which intended to justify the model's weak connection with economic theory and the compromise resulting from empirical research.

The second half of the 1970s brought a surge of criticism expressed by Lucas (1976), Hendry (1980), Sims (1980) and Leamer (1983). Each of their stimulating studies addressed a different aspect of econometric modelling (or actually macromodelling).

The 'Lucas critique' caused rational expectations to be introduced into the modelling of economic agents. Paradoxically, estimation problems of models with rational expectations aroused even larger interest. Important qualifications raised by Leamer, and especially Hendry, consolidated in the 'common awareness' of modellers the need for scrupulous and adequate testing of economic hypotheses. Perhaps, the most difficult to absorb was Sims' critique.

Around the same time the work by Granger and Newbold (1974) was published, devoted to the problem of spurious regression that had been originally noted 50 years earlier by Yule (1926). Quite soon unit root tests were developed, proving that an overwhelming majority of stochastic processes generating macroeconomic time series were non-stationary. It was, however, the concept of the cointegration of variables, presented for the first time probably in the work by Granger (1984), that charted the right course toward solving the non-stationary variables' modelling problem, and the Granger Representation Theorem (e.g. Engle and Granger, 1987) provided theoretical foundations for constructing systems of equations for non-stationary series. The essential conclusion resulting from the theorem is that only reduced rank systems of difference stationary variables can be represented in the vector autoregressive (VAR), vector equilibrium correction (VEqCM) and moving average (MA) forms. Cointegration of variables is, therefore, a prerequisite for the existence of a long run equilibrium, and vice versa long run equilibrium implies cointegration. In this way, cointegration theory has underpinned the synthesis of error correction propagated by the LSE School and of VAR models advocated by Sims. This opened entirely new possibilities of interpretation, but in the first place it provided theoretical grounds for thorough testing of economic hypotheses and for building macroeconometric models. At the same time non-trivial problems in parameter estimation appeared, especially in testing the size of the cointegrating space. A satisfactory solution to the latter question was proposed by Johansen (1988).

Undeniably, cointegration theory is one of the major achievements in the field of time series analysis and the unceasing interest in this field of research proves that many questions are still to be answered.

Traditional macromodels are built using quarterly or monthly data; macroeconomic data published at higher frequencies are few. An exception is statistical information describing financial processes, and especially transactions at the Stock Exchange. In this case, samples may include thousands of observations. Hence, it is not surprising that such samples have inspired many researchers, producing specific problems that need to be solved, but also unique opportunities for statistical analyses. It was exactly the research in financial processes that triggered rapid development of new classes of models, and especially the ARCH models, originally used by Engle (1982) to model inflation. This justifies the claim that high-frequency economic data have created another field, very important for the development of econometrics.

This volume discusses many important issues, but for obvious reasons the book is not comprehensive, forecasting is probably the most important omission. The chapters have been sequenced in alphabetical order determined by authors' names. Some chapters focus solely on methodological issues, some combine theoretical and applications, and others only deal with the application of specific macromodelling strategies.

All authors participated in the Macromodels International Conference (www.econometrics.uni.lodz.pl/macromodels) that was brought into being by Professor Wladyslaw Welfe in the year 1974 and organized in Poland on an annual basis since then. Initially, the conference was actually the only forum, where econometricians from the former East-European countries could regularly meet their colleagues working outside the socialist bloc. Although, this situation changed after the Berlin Wall collapsed, the Macromodels remained an important meeting. The following conferences, and especially the most recent one, the 30th, held in Warsaw between December 4 and 6, 2003, have proved that interest in macromodelling continues to be strong, which promises optimistic prospects.

Aleksander Welfe

References

Bodkin, R.G., L.R. Klein and K. Marwah (eds.) (1991), *A History of Macroeconometric Model-Building*, Hants: E. Elgar.

Engle, R.F. (1982), "Autoregressive conditional heteroscedasticity with estimates of variance of United Kingdom inflations", *Econometrica*, Vol. 50, pp. 977–1008.

Engle, R.F. and C.W.J. Granger (1987), "Co-integration and error correction: representation. Estimation and testing", *Econometrica*, Vol. 55, pp. 251–276.

Granger, C.W.J. (1984), "Co-integrated variables and error correction models", Working Paper, Department of Economics, University of California, San Diego.

Granger, C.W.J. and P. Newbold (1974), "Spurious regressions in econometrics", *Journal of Econometrics*, Vol. 2, pp. 111–120.

Haavelmo, T. (1943), "The statistical implications of a system of simultaneous equations", *Econometrica*, Vol. 11, pp. 1–12.

Hendry, D.F. (1980), "Econometrics – Alchemy or Science?", *Economica*, Vol. 47, pp. 387–406.

Johansen, S. (1988), "Statistical analysis of cointegration vectors", *Journal of Dynamics and Control*, Vol. 12, pp. 231–254.

Klein, L.R. (1950), *Economic Fluctuations in the United States, 1921–1941*, New York: Wiley.

Klein, L.R. and A.S. Goldberger (1955), *An Econometric Model of the United States, 1929–1952*, Amsterdam: North Holland.

Koopmans, T.C. (1949), "Identification problems in economic model construction", *Econometrica*, Vol. 17, pp. 125–144.

Leamer, E.E. (1983), "Let's take the con out of econometrics", *American Economic Review*, Vol. 73, pp. 31–43.

Lucas, R.E. Jr (1976), "Econometric policy evaluation: a critique", in: K. Brunner and A.H. Meltzer, editors, *The Phillips Curve and Labor Markets*, pp. 19–46, Amsterdam: North Holland.

Sims, C.A. (1980), "Macroeconomics and reality", *Econometrica*, Vol. 48, pp. 1–48.

Theil, H. (1958), *Economic Forecasts and Policy*, Amsterdam: North Holland.

Yule, G.U. (1926), "Why do we sometimes get nonsense correlations between time series? a study in sampling and the nature of time series", *Journal of Royal Statistical Society*, Vol. 89, pp. 1–64.

List of Contributors

Numbers in paranthesis indicate the pages where the authors' contributions can be found.

Stephen G. Hall (1), Tanaka Business School, Imperial College, London SW7 2AZ, UK

David F. Hendry (21), Economics Department, University of Oxford, Manor Road, Oxford OX1 3UQ, UK

Søren Johansen (49), Department of Applied Mathematics and Statistics, University of Copenhagen, Universitetsparken 5, 2100 Copenhagen O, Denmark

Katarina Juselius (69), Institute of Economics, University of Copenhagen, Studiestræde 6, 1455 Copenhagen K, Denmark

Piotr Karp (197), Chair of Econometric Models and Forecasts, University of Lodz, 41 Rewolucji 1905r. Str., 90-214 Lodz, Poland

Piotr Kębłowski (197), Chair of Econometric Models and Forecasts, University of Lodz, 41 Rewolucji 1905r. Str., 90-214 Lodz, Poland

Helmut Lütkepohl (107), Department of Economics, European University Institute, Via della Piazzuola 43, I-50133 Firenze, Italy

Dietmar Maringer (213), Chair of Econometrics, Faculty of Economics, Law and Social Sciences, University of Erfurt, Nordhaeuser Strasse 63, D-99089 Erfurt, Germany

Grayham E. Mizon (147), Head, School of Social Sciences, Murray Building, University of Southampton, Southampton SO17 1BJ, UK

Jacek Osiewalski (173), Department of Econometrics, Cracow University of Economics, ul. Rakowicka 27, 31-510 Kraków, Poland

Mateusz Pipień (173), Department of Econometrics, Cracow University of Economics, ul. Rakowicka 27, 31-510 Kraków, Poland

Aleksander Welfe (197), Chair of Econometric Models and Forecasts, University of Lodz, 41 Rewolucji 1905r. Str., 90-214 Lodz, Poland

Peter Winker (213), Chair of Econometrics, Faculty of Economics, Law and Social Sciences, University of Erfurt, Nordhaeuser Strasse 63, D-99089 Erfurt, Germany

New Directions in Macromodelling
A. Welfe (Editor)
© 2004 Published by Elsevier B.V.
DOI: 10.1016/S0573-8555(04)69001-8

CHAPTER 1

Modelling Volatility and Its Implication for European Economic Integration

Stephen G. Hall

Tanaka Business School, Imperial College, London SW7 2AZ, UK

Abstract

This chapter utilizes a relatively new technique, which allows the calculation of large conditional covariance matrices, to analyse three areas relevant to the development of the European Monetary Union. The technique is called orthogonal GARCH and it uses a principle component representation to avoid the problem faced by most multivariate GARCH techniques, where the number of parameters rises rapidly as the size of the system increases. The chapter then uses this approach in three exercises: first, it considers the correlation of shocks within the core countries of the European Union. Second, it examines the role played in foreign direct investment (FDI) by exchange rate uncertainty, in particular the effect of the changing correlation between Sterling and the Euro or US FDI is investigated. Finally, a standard VAR decomposition is performed for shocks hitting the core European countries, this is then extended to the case where the structural residual covariance matrix may be time varying.

Keywords: volatility, European integration, GARCH

1.1. Introduction

The starting point for this paper is the observation that structural change is endemic in economic data and relationships. Indeed the very notion of economic integration or alternatively transition implies the occurrence of structural change as the integration takes place. Yet most econometric techniques and analysis proceed on the basis of applying a model which assumes structural stability. In many cases this may be viewed as a reasonable approximation, but when we are actually interested in the issue of change itself it is obviously inappropriate to apply a technique which excludes the possibility of observing change. The purpose of this paper is to summarize three pieces of recent research which all exploit a relatively new way of modelling a changing conditional covariance matrix. This technique makes it possible to model quite large changing covariance structures in a very parsimonious way. All three papers focus on the issue of European integration, although in rather different ways. The first paper by Hall and Yap (2003) simply considers the changing correlation between GDP and exchange rates within Europe. The second paper, by Barrel Gottschalk and Hall (2004), considers the impact of exchange rate volatility on foreign direct investment (FDI) flows from the US into Europe and the final paper by Hall (2003) considers the implications for a VAR analysis of the interrelationship of GDP within Europe if we again allow for a time varying correlation structure.

The structure of this paper is as follows: the next section outlines the basic technique of orthogonal GARCH and its place in the general ARCH literature. The next three sections outlines the three pieces of analysis and finally some conclusions are drawn.

1.2. System GARCH

The standard univariate GARCH model is now very well known, but this model suffers from the obvious drawback that it can only be used to produce a measure of the conditional variance of a process. If we are interested in understanding the complete conditional distribution of a group of variables then we need to extend the basic GARCH framework to a multivariate context, so that we may consider complete conditional covariance matrices. A number of studies have already used this extension and a number of alternative specifications exist in the literature (Kraft and Engle, 1982; Bollerslev et al., 1988; Hall et al., 1990; Hall and Miles, 1992; Engle and Kroner, 1995).

Essentially, we are interested in building a model of a complete conditional covariance structure of a set of variables. So consider a set of n variables Y that may be considered to be generated by the following VAR process.

$$A(L)Y_t = e_t$$

This varies from a conventional VAR model as we assume that

$$E(e_t) = 0 \quad \text{and} \quad E(e_t e_t') = \Omega_t$$

So that the covariance matrix is time varying. We then make the standard ARCH assumption that this covariance matrix follows an autoregressive structure. Estimation of such a model is, in principle, quite straightforward, as the log likelihood is proportional to the following expression:

$$l = \sum_{t=1}^{T} \ln|\Omega_t| + e_t' \Omega_t^{-1} e_t \qquad (1.1)$$

and so standard maximum likelihood (or quasi maximum likelihood) procedures may be applied. The only real difficulty comes in the parameterization of the process generating Ω_t; the natural extension of the standard GARCH formulation very quickly begins to generate huge numbers of parameters. If we define the VECH operator in the usual way as a stacked vector of the lower triangle of a symmetric matrix, then we can represent the standard generalization of the univariate GARCH model as

$$\text{VECH}(\Omega_t) = C + A(L)\,\text{VECH}(e_t e_t') + B(L)\,\text{VECH}(\Omega_{t-1}) \qquad (1.2)$$

where C is an $(N(N+1)/2)$ vector and A_i and B_i are $(N(N+1)/2) \times (N(N+1)/2)$ matrices. This general formulation rapidly produces huge numbers of parameters as N rises (for just 1 lag in A and B and a five variable system we generate 465 parameters to be estimated) so for anything beyond the simplest system this will almost certainly be intractable. A second problem with this model is that without fairly complex restrictions on the system the conditional covariance matrix cannot be guaranteed to be positive semi definite. So much of the literature in this area has focused on trying to find a parameterization which is both flexible enough to be useful and yet is also reasonably tractable.

One of the most popular formulations was first proposed by Baba, Engle, Kraft and Kroner, sometimes referred to as the BEKK (Engle and Kroner, 1993) representation, this takes the following form

$$\Omega_t = C'C + \sum_{i=1}^{q} A_i' e_{t-i} e_{t-i}' A_i + \sum_{j=1}^{p} B_j' \Omega_{t-j} B_{t-j} \qquad (1.3)$$

This formulation guarantees positive semi definiteness of the covariance matrix almost surely and reduces the number of parameters considerably. However, even this model can give rise to a very large number of parameters and further simplifications are often applied in terms of making A and B symmetric or diagonal.

1.2.1. *Orthogonal GARCH*

Any of the multivariate GARCH models listed above is severely limited in the size of model, which is tractable. Even a restricted BEKK model becomes largely unmanageable for a system above four or five variables. An alternative approach, however which can be applied, potentially to a system of any size rests on the use of principal components and is sometimes referred to as orthogonal GARCH. This technique seems to be first referred to by Ding (1994) in his PhD thesis and he ascribes it to Ron Kahn who suggested it to him in a conversation. Consider a set of n stochastic variables X, which have a covariance structure V. Principal components then produces a set of n variables (P), which contain all the variation of X but are also orthogonal to each other. The standard principal component representation can be written as follows:

$$X_i = \mu_i + \sum_{j=1}^{n} \omega_{ij} p_j \qquad i = 1, \dots, n \qquad (1.4)$$

so if all n principal components are used each X_i can be exactly reproduced by weighting the principal components together with the correct loading weights. Now by simply taking the variance of both sides of this equation we can see that

$$\text{VAR}(X) = V = W(\text{VAR}(P))W' = W \Psi W' \qquad (1.5)$$

The advantage of this is of course that as the principal components are orthogonal Ψ will be a diagonal matrix with zeros on all non-diagonal elements. From applying principal components we know W; we then simply have to derive a set of univariate GARCH models to each principal component to derive estimates of the conditional variance at each point in time and apply the above formulae to derive an estimate of the complete covariance matrix V. The conditional variance may be obtained from any chosen procedure (GARCH, EGARCH or even an EWMA model of the squared errors).

There are, however, two further issues here:

(i) As the principal components are ordered by their explanatory power we often find that a subset of them produces a very high degree of explanatory power. It may then only be deemed necessary to use the first k principal components. It is even suggested that this helps to remove noise from the system as the minor principal components may be reflecting pure random movements. This can easily be done but it introduces an error term into the principal components representation above and the resulting covariance matrix may no longer be positive definite.

(ii) Equation (1.5) above is true exactly for the whole period the principal components are calculated for but it does not necessarily hold at each point in the sample. So this is really only delivering an approximation. It may then be useful to apply the procedure to a moving window of observations so that the W matrix also effectively becomes time varying.

Yhap (2003) has conducted an extensive Monte Carlo study of the properties of the orthogonal GARCH model and one of his findings is that the model performs well for samples of less than 500 observations but that its ability to accurately track conditional covariance's deteriorates substantially as the sample increases beyond this number of observation.

1.3. A conditional covariance matrix for the shocks between the UK and Europe

This section summarizes the results in the work of Hall and Yap (2003). Recent years have seen considerable interest in the optimal currency area literature for obvious reasons, given developments in Europe with Monetary Union. Following the seminal early works of Mundell (1961) and McKinnon (1963), a small selection of the vast recent literature would include McKinnon (1994), Frankel and Rose (1997), Buiter (1999), McCallum (1999), Rogoff (2001), Alesina and Barro (2002) and Artis (2002). One theme common to this literature is that a key criterion for the success of a monetary union is that the shocks which hit the economies should be reasonably common and well correlated. Artis (2002), for example, in his Table 2 assesses the appropriateness of a number of countries joining a monetary union based on a number of criteria including the symmetry of shocks and concludes that on these criteria the UK should not join EMU. Hall and Yap, therefore, examine the issue of the correlation of inflation and output shocks among the four large European countries (UK, Germany, France and Italy). They undertake two experiments to calculate the complete conditional correlation matrix first for CPI inflation and then for real GDP.

The full set of six conditional correlations for inflation are presented in Figures 1.1 and 1.2. Figure 1.1 focuses on the correlations with the UK while Figure 1.2 focuses on the correlations among France, Germany and Italy. The first thing to be said is that there is clearly considerable and systematic variation in the correlation. This emphasizes the need to calculate a true conditional correlation rather than a sample average. Many of the individual spikes are also quite easily interpreted. For example there is a spike increase after the 1973 oil price rise in all series. Apart from this,

**Figure 1.1.   Conditional correlation of the inflation shocks between the
UK and Germany, France and Italy**

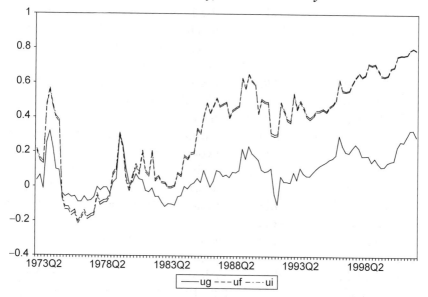

**Figure 1.2.   Conditional correlation for inflation shocks among
Germany, France and Italy**

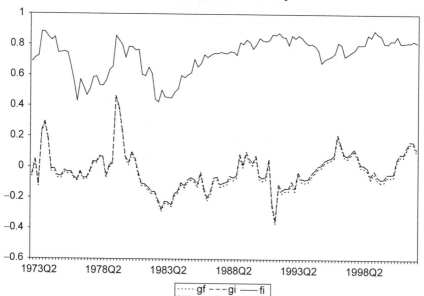

however, there was clearly almost no correlation between the UK and the rest of Europe in inflationary shocks in the 1970s. But since the early 1980s there has been a very steady trend rise in the correlation, especially with respect to France and Italy although much less so with respect to Germany. In Figure 1.2, we see that the correlation between France and Italy is very high and stable, close to 0.9 while the correlation of both countries with Germany is almost zero. Only at the very end of the sample is there any sign of inflation correlation and this is still very small.

So by the end of the sample the UK, France and Italy all exhibit conditional correlations around 0.8 with respect to inflationary shocks. Germany has a very low conditional correlation with each of them. While this picture is much richer than the simple correlation matrix above, it certainly confirms the basic picture presented there. In terms of inflationary shocks the UK is now highly correlated with France and Italy, only Germany seems to be an outlier.

The results for GDP correlations are shown in Figures 1.3 and 1.4. Figure 1.3 again shows the correlations with the UK. During the 1970s, France and Italy were almost completely uncorrelated with the UK in terms of GDP shocks after the middle 1980s however this changed and a gradual increase in symmetry emerged until by the end of the sample the conditional correlation between the UK and France and Italy was close to

Figure 1.3.   Condition correlation of GDP shocks between the UK and Germany, France and Italy

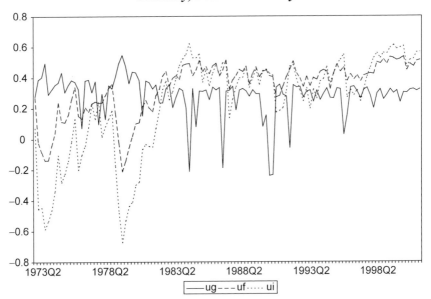

Figure 1.4. Conditional correlation of GDP shocks among Germany, France and Italy

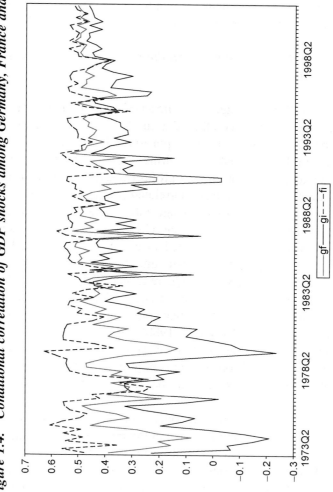

0.5 and quite stable. The correlation between the UK and Germany has again behaved quite differently with an almost constant average conditional correlation around 0.2 with no sign of any trend. The correlation between France and Italy has been fairly stable around 0.5 with a small rise in their correlation with Germany towards the end of the period.

Again by the end of the period the UK seems to be very similar to France and Italy. It is Germany, which has a lower conditional correlation in its shocks with the rest of Europe.

1.4. Foreign direct investment and the conditional correlation of exchange rates

Barrel *et al.* (2004) investigate the impact of exchange rate uncertainty and exchange rate correlation on the location of US FDI in price-making firms in Europe. They apply standard portfolio theory to the q theory of investment to show that risk-averse firms can reduce the negative impact of exchange rate fluctuations on their profits by diversifying their investment across locations with negatively correlated exchange rates. Few empirical papers analyse the role of exchange rate correlation on foreign direct investment, among them Cushman (1988) and Bénassy-Quéré *et al.* (2001). Both construct a two-period mean-variance framework, to show that an increase in exchange rate uncertainty reduces foreign direct investment. In addition, Bénassy-Quéré *et al.* (2001) present evidence that, given a negative exchange rate correlation, an increase in one country's competitiveness increases FDI to that country at the expense of investment in alternative locations. Cushman (1988) and Bénassy-Quéré *et al.* (2001) assume firms are perfectly competitive. This paper extends the earlier work by considering the location strategies of price-making firms, since, as was seen above, these firms tend to be less sensitive to exchange rate uncertainty.

The basic idea of the formal model developed is that if a firm wants to maximize its expected return from a number of foreign investments but to also minimize the variance of that return, it should diversify across a number of different countries to exploit the less than full correlation which exists between country exchange rates. The importance of this in the context of Europe is simply that if two countries form a monetary union then the one certain consequence is that the correlation between the exchange rates becomes one. There is no longer any incentive to diversify investment across both countries and the investment will tend to flow into whichever country has the higher expected return. So if the UK joins the EMU the correlation between the Sterling and Euro will go to one, FDI into the UK may then either decrease or increase depending on the relative return expected from the two regions, but certainly the diversification of exchange rate risk effect will disappear.

The first stage in investigating this hypothesis was to estimate a GARCH model (as above) for the Sterling and Euro exchange rates so that a conditional correlation could be estimated. This is shown in Figure 1.5.

This measure of correlation was then incorporated into a panel data investigation of FDI flows into the UK and Europe. Annual data from the US Bureau of Economic Analysis (BEA) survey of US direct investment abroad were used in the empirical analysis. We used FDIs by non-bank US firms in Europe. The countries covered are the UK and Austria, Belgium, France, Germany and the Netherlands. This group of members of the single currency had effectively fixed exchange rates over the period. They can, therefore, be treated as the same location and aggregated together. Seven two-digit manufacturing industries were considered: Food, Chemicals, Primary and fabricated metals, Machinery, Electrical equipments, appliances and components, Transportation equipment and Other manu-facturing. Data on direct investment include all foreign affiliates where US firms have direct or indirect ownership or control of more than 10% of voting securities. Year-to-year changes in the stock of FDI include net capital outflows between the US parent and its affiliate, inter-company debt and reinvested earnings. Valuation adjustments, e.g. exchange rate adjustments, price changes and other capital gains and losses, are also included in year-to-year changes.

Figure 1.5.   *Conditional correlation of the nominal exchange rate between the Sterling and Euro*

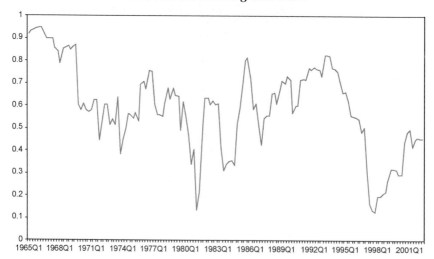

The following equation for location $l \neq m$ then formed the basis of the panel data study:

$$\Delta \text{FDI}_{l,i,t} = \phi \text{FDI}_{l,i,t-2} + a_1 \text{RR}_{l,i,t-2} + a_2 \text{USLR}_{t-2} + a_3 \sigma^2_{l,t-1} + a_4 \rho_{l,m,t-1}$$
$$+ a_5 S_{l,i,t-2} + \sum_k b_{1k} \Delta \text{FDI}_{l,i,t-k} + \sum_k b_{2k} \Delta \text{RR}_{l,i,t-k}$$
$$+ \sum_k b_{3k} \Delta \text{USLR}_{t-k} + \sum_k b_{4k} \Delta \rho_{l,m,t-k} + \sum_k b_{5k} \Delta \sigma^2_{l,t-k}$$
$$+ \sum_k b_{6k} \Delta S_{l,i,t-k} + \gamma_{l,i} + u_{l,i,t}$$

where $\text{FDI}_{l,i,t}$ is the log of real US FDI in industry i in location l, $\text{RR}_{l,i,t}$ is the rate of return reported by affiliates in industry i in location l. $S_{l,i,t}$ represents real sales of industry i in location l. $S_{l,i,t}$ includes local sales and exports to the rest of the world, and are in millions of dollars. Sales have been deflated by the CPI. $\sigma^2_{l,t-1} \equiv \text{Var}[e_{l,t-1}]$ is the GARCH estimate of the variance. $\rho_{l,m,t-1} \equiv \text{Corr}[e_{l,t-1}, e_{m,t-1}]$ is the GARCH estimate of the correlation between the Euro dollar exchange rate and the Sterling dollar exchange rate. $u_{l,i,t}$ is the error term and $\gamma_{l,i,t}$ individual effects. An error-correction form was chosen to highlight both the importance of adjustment and the differences in the speed of adjustment between locations to changes in investment.

The results of GMM estimation on this panel are reported in Table 1.1, the main point of interest here is that the coefficients on the variance of Sterling and the Euro are negative and positive as expected and are

Table 1.1. FDI equation into the UK

Variable	Coefficient	t-value
USLR($t - 2$)	−0.327862**	−2.19
RRX($t - 2$)	0.0443337*	1.77
σuk($t - 2$)	−0.367782**	−2.17
σeu($t - 2$)	0.696059**	2.16
$\rho(t - 2)$	0.213677**	2.11
RFDI(−2)	−0.378010**	−2.05
RRR(−2)	0.349345**	2.26
ΔRRuk(t)	0.001941**	2.15
ΔRRuk($t - 1$)	−0.000454**	−2.02
ΔRRuk($t - 2$)	0.000068**	1.71
$\sigma\Delta$uk(t)	−0.078842**	−1.97
$\sigma\Delta$uk($t - 1$)	−0.203332**	−2.23

* Significant at 10% level; ** Significant at 5% level.

both significant. So when the variance of Sterling increases FDI into the UK is reduced but if the variance of the Euro increases this offsets the effect. Also the coefficient on the correlation is positive and significant. This suggests that when the correlation rises, as it must on entry into EMU more FDI would flow into the UK suggesting that the expected return in the UK is actually higher than in Europe.

1.5. A VAR analysis of GDP spillovers when the correlation structure is changing

The final paper to be considered here is Hall (2003) which investigates the impact on standard VAR analysis when the covariance structure of the structural errors is changing over time.

VAR analysis and the use of impulse responses have become the main ways to analyse reasonable size data sets following the key paper of Sims (1980). It has a number of attractions and also some disadvantages; the lack of a need for conventional theoretical restrictions is one obvious attraction although the need to impose identification to calculate the impulse responses partly offsets this. The widely used orthogonalized impulse responses have the disadvantage that the ordering of the variables changes the results. More recently the proposal of Pesaran and Shin (1998) to use generalised impulse responses has overcome this disadvantage although at the cost of making the interpretation of the results a little less clear-cut.

This paper raises a question, which has not so far been addressed. What is the impact on VAR analysis if the structural errors have a changing correlation structure? The issue to be addressed here then is what should be the consequence of a changing correlation structure for VAR analysis and how might we approach the modelling problems in a tractable way.

Consider the structural VAR model

$$A_0 x_t = \sum_{i=1}^{p} A_i x_{t-i} + B w_t + e_t, \qquad t = 1, 2, \dots, T \qquad (1.6)$$

where $x_t = (x_{1t}, x_{2t}, \dots, x_{mt})'$ is an $m \times 1$ vector of jointly determined variables, w_t is a $q \times 1$ vector of exogenous or deterministic components and A_i and B are $m \times m$ and $m \times q$ coefficient matrices. Also, as usual, assume that $E(e_t) = 0$, but in addition that $E(e_t e_t') = \Psi_t$, that is the covariance matrix of the structural shocks is time varying. For simplicity, I also assume that x_t are weakly stationary, although the analysis carries over to a cointegrated VAR quite easily.

The standard reduced form VAR representation of this model is

$$x_t = \sum_{i=1}^{p} \Phi_i x_{t-i} + \Psi w_t + \varepsilon_t, \qquad t = 1, 2, ..., T \tag{1.7}$$

where of course $\Phi_i = A_0^{-1} A_i$, $\Psi = A_0^{-1} B$ and $\varepsilon_t = A_0^{-1} e_t$ the covariance structure of the reduced form errors will then be given by $E(\varepsilon_t \varepsilon_t') = \Sigma_t = A_0^{-1} \Psi A_0^{-1'}$, which is of course time varying.

This model now raises two questions: How should we estimate such a system? How should we calculate impulse responses?

In principal, the specification of the likelihood function for Equation (1.7) is quite straightforward once we have specified a parametric form for the evolution of Σ_t. A natural choice would be to specify a multivariate GARCH process as discussed in Section 1.2. For example if we used Equation (1.2) then estimation of such a model would be, in principle, quite straightforward as the log likelihood is proportional to the following expression:

$$l = \sum_{t=1}^{T} \ln|\Sigma_t| + \varepsilon_t' \Sigma_t^{-1} \varepsilon_t \tag{1.8}$$

However, as pointed out in Section 1.2, this model will quickly become intractable so Hall proposes estimating the model in two stages: first, standard VAR estimation techniques will still give consistent parameter estimates. Second, the orthogonal GARCH model may be used to calculate the time varying covariance matrix for use in the impulse response analysis.

1.5.1. The impulse response function

In general the impulse response function may be simply described following Koop *et al.* (1996) as,

$$I(n, \delta, \Omega_{t-1}) = E(x_{t+n}|\varepsilon_t = \delta, \Omega_{t-1}) - E(x_{t+n}|\Omega_{t-1}) \tag{1.9}$$

where Ω_t is the information set at time t and δ is a vector of shocks applied at time t. Different choices of the structure of δ characterize different schemes of identification. The dominant procedure is the orthogonalized residuals originally proposed by Sims, here we simply define

$$P_t P_t' = \Sigma_t \tag{1.10}$$

Using a Cholesky decomposition where P is a lower triangular matrix then, defining p_{it} as the ith row of P_t we may define the orthoganalized impulse response for the ith variable by setting

$$\delta = p'_{it}\sigma \qquad (1.11)$$

where σ is a suitable scaling factor, normally one standard deviation. Equation (1.11) will of course be dependent on the ordering of the variables in the decomposition, Equation (1.10), as is well known.

An alternative method is the generalized impulse response of Koop *et al.* (1996) or Pesaran *et al.* (1998), here rather than using an identifying assumption such as orthogonality they simply take the estimated structure of the covariance matrix so that if we take s_{it} to be the ith row of Σ_t then the generalized impulse response is generated by setting

$$\delta = s'_{it}\sigma \qquad (1.12)$$

The issue being considered here is not which alternative is preferable but that whichever method is used the results will vary over time if Σ is time varying. Also it is obvious that once an estimate of Σ_t is available the application of any of these identification schemes is entirely straightforward, even on a time varying basis.

To illustrate the empirical relevance of this analysis, a standard VAR model of GDP for the UK, France, Italy and Germany is first estimated in the usual way and then the conditional correlation structure of the errors is assessed using the orthogonal GARCH technique above. The potential change, which can occur in the impulse responses if they are calculated based on the conditional covariance matrix at different points in time, is then investigated. This is an interesting application given the importance of the question of the correlation of economic shocks to the formation of a currency union within the standard optimal currency area literature and hence the issue of the UK's membership of the European Monetary Union. Clearly we should be making the judgement over entry based on an estimate of the current conditional correlation of errors not some average over the past. And if convergence has been taking place we might expect this to show up in the conditional correlation structure of the residuals.

The starting place is therefore to estimate a standard VAR for the log of the four GDP series, quarterly data is used for the period 1973Q3–2002Q2. A VAR(2) is chosen based on the Schwarts criteria and a series of joint F tests of excluding each lag (the probability level of these tests were lag $1 = 0.0000$, lag $2 = 0.0069$, lag $3 = 0.78$ and lag $4 = 0.15$). The following diagnostics confirm that this VAR seems to be reasonably well specified.

	Germany	France	UK	Italy
Serial corr	0.12	0.47	0.07	0.1
ARCH	0.59	0.86	0.008	0.34
Hetero	0.74	0.41	0.02	0.14
Hetero-X	0.69	0.59	0.25	0.14

Figures in each cell denote probability levels, hence a figure less than 0.05 denotes rejection at the 5% critical value. Serial corr is a test of up to fifth order serial correlation, ARCH is a test of up to a fourth order ARCH process, Hetero tests for heteroskedasticity related to any of the lagged variables, Hetero-X allows for cross products of all the variables.

Given the analysis later it is particularly interesting to note that this VAR has very little signs of ARCH or heteroskedasticity. In addition it appears to be quite stable as recursive estimation shows very little sign of instability (A recursive one period ahead chow test finds only one period out of 320 tests which exceed the 1% critical value.).

The paper then applies the orthogonal GARCH model to the residuals of this VAR. The details of the orthogonal GARCH estimation will not be given as there is no particular intuition to attach to the GARCH models for the principal components. Given the lack of serial correlation in the residuals the mean equation for each principal component is specified as a simple constant and a GARCH(1,1) model was specified for the conditional variance. This seemed to be adequate in all four estimated equations.

The results of the orthogonal GARCH process are given in Figures 1.6 and 1.7. Figure 1.6 shows the conditional correlations for the UK with Germany, France and Italy while Figure 1.2 shows the correlation among Germany, France and Italy. The broad picture is fairly simple; the correlation between Germany, France and Italy seems to be quite stable with little sign of any trend. The correlation with the UK however shows quite strong trends especially with France and Italy, the 1970s and early 1980s exhibit quite strong variations in the correlation with average values below 0.2 and some values actually being negative, by the last half of the 1990s the correlation was much more stable and averages over 0.4. There has, however, been little trend change in the correlation with Germany.

Clearly the change which has taken place in the correlation structure could profoundly affect the impulse responses of this system no matter what form of identification structure we use to identify them. To illustrate this point, we present the generalized impulse response to a shock to Italy calculated first on the basis of the covariance matrix calculated for 1979Q3 (which exhibits the most extreme negative correlation for the UK) and for 2002Q1 which is fairly representative of the final years of the period

Figure 1.6. ***Conditional correlation between the shocks to the UK and Germany, France and Italy***

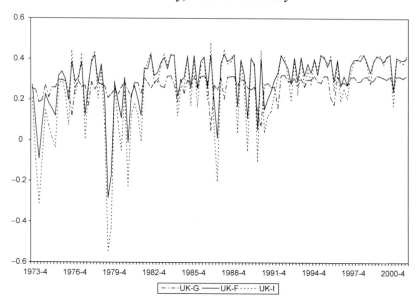

Figure 1.7. ***Conditional correlation among Germany, France and Italy***

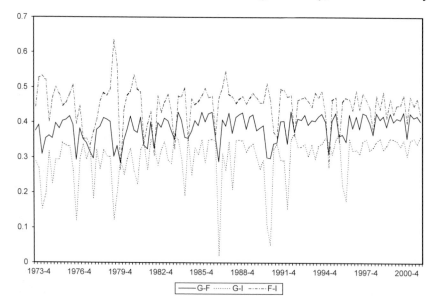

Figure 1.8. ***Generalized impulse response based on the covariance matrix in 1979Q3***

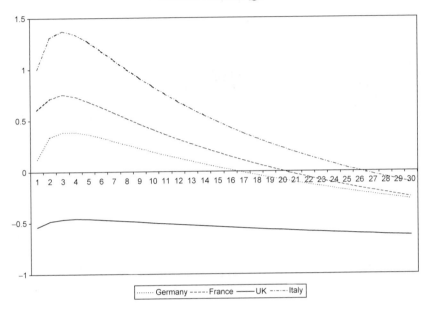

Figure 1.9. ***Generalized impulse response based on the covariance matrix in 2002Q1***

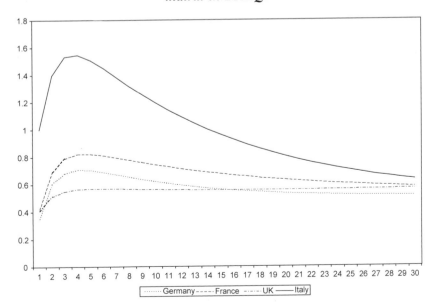

(Figure 1.8). The conclusions of these two pictures are very clear; in the first chart the UK is an obvious outlier and responds very differently to the other European countries. In Figure 1.9, the UK is responding in a way which is almost identical to the other countries.

1.6. Conclusion

This paper has considered three applications of the use of fairly large conditional covariance structures. Each one has offered a new insight into the issue of European Integration and the basis of these insights is that the structure of the European economy is changing. To understand where we are now and where we are likely to be in the immediate future we must use techniques which allow for this change rather than simply averaging the past.

Acknowledgements

I gratefully acknowledge the support of the ESRC under Grant No. L138250122. Final responsibility for the contents of this paper rest solely with the author.

References

Alesina, A. and R.J. Barro (2002), "Curency unions", *Quarterly Journal of Economics*, Vol. 117, pp. 409–436.

Artis, M.J. (2002), "Reflections on the optimal currency area (OCA) criteria in the light of EMU", Osterreichische Nationalbank Working Paper No. 69.

Barrel, S. Gottschalk and S.G. Hall (2004), "Foreign direct investment and exchange rate uncertainty in imperfectly competitive industries", mimeo, NIESR, London.

Bénassy-Quéré, A., L. Fontagné and A. Lahrèche-Revil (2001), "Exchange-rate strategies in the competition for attracting foreign direct investment", *Journal of the Japanese and International Economies*, Vol. 15(2), pp. 178–198.

Bollerslev, T., R.F. Engle and J.M. Wooldridge (1988), "A capital asset pricing model with time varying covariances", *Journal of Political Economy*, Vol. 96, pp. 116–131.

Buiter, W. (1999), "Optimal curency areas: Why does the exchange rate regime matter? (with an application to UK membership of EMU)", Sixth Royal Bank of Scotland Lecture at the Scottish Economic Society Annual Conference.

Cushman, D.O. (1988), "Exchange rate uncertainty and foreign direct investment in the United States", *Weltwirtschaftliches Archiv*, Vol. 124, pp. 322–336.

Ding, Z. (1994), Time Series Analysis of Speculative Returns, PhD thesis, UCSD.

Engle, R.F. and K.F. Kroner (1993), "Multivariate, simultaneous, generalised ARCH", University of California at San Diego Discussion Paper No. 89-57.

Engle, R.F. and K.F. Kroner (1995), "Multivariate simultaneous generalized ARCH", *Econometric Theory*, Vol. 11(1), pp. 122–150.

Frankel, J. and A. Rose (1997), "Is EMU more justifiable ex-post than ex-anti?", *European Economic Review*, Vol. 41, pp. 753–760.

Hall, S.G. (2003), "VAR analysis in the presence of a changing correlation in the structural errors", mimeo, NIESR, London.

Hall, S.G. and D.K. Miles (1992), "An empirical study of recent trends in world bond markets", *Oxford Economic Papers*, Vol. 44, pp. 599–625.

Hall, S.G. and B. Yap (2003), "Measuring the correlation of shocks between the UK and the core of Europe", mimeo, NIESR, London.

Hall, S.G., D.K. Miles and M.P. Taylor (1990), "A multivariate GARCH in mean estimation of the capital asset pricing model", in: K. Patterson and S.G.B. Henry, editors, *Economic Modelling at the Bank of England*, London: Chapman and Hall.

Koop, G., M.H. Pesaran and S.M. Potter (1996), "Impulse response analysis in non-linear multivariate models", *Journal of Econometrics*, Vol. 74, pp. 119–147.

Kraft, D.F. and R.F. Engle (1982), "Autoregressive conditional heteroskedasticity in multiple time series", UCSD Manuscript.

McCallum, B.T. (1999), "Theoretical issues pertaining to monetary unions" NBER Working Paper No. 7393.

McKinnon, R.I. (1963), "Optimum currency areas", *American Economic Review*, Vol. 53, pp. 717–725.

McKinnon, R.I. (1994), "A common monetary standard or a common currency for Europe? Fiscal lessons from the United States", *Scottish Journal of Political Economy*, Vol. 41, pp. 337–357.

Mundell, R.A. (1961), "A theory of optimal currency areas", *American Economic Review*, Vol. 51, pp. 657–665.

Pesaran, M.H. and Y. Shin (1998), "Generalised impulse response analysis in linear multivariate models", *Economics Letters*, Vol. 58, pp. 17–29.

Rogoff, K. (2001), "On why not a global currency", *American Economic Review*, Vol. 91, pp. 243–247.

Sims, C. (1980), "Macroeconomics and reality", *Econometrica*, Vol. 48, pp. 1–48.

Yhap, B. (2003), The Analysis of Principal Component GARCH Models in Value-at-Risk Calculations, PhD thesis, London University.

New Directions in Macromodelling
A. Welfe (Editor)
© 2004 Published by Elsevier B.V.
DOI: 10.1016/S0573-8555(04)69002-X

CHAPTER 2

Causality and Exogeneity in Non-stationary Economic Time Series

David F. Hendry

Economics Department, University of Oxford, Manor Road, Oxford OX1 3UQ, UK

Abstract

We review the roles of causality and exogeneity in macro-econometric time-series modelling, forecasting and policy; their inter-relationships; problems in establishing them empirically; the importance played by non-stationarity in the data generation process (DGP), and the relation of causality to Granger causality. Although, causality and exogeneity need not be invariant features of the DGP, they remain relevant in non-stationary processes, and inferences about them become easier in some ways, though more difficult in others.

Keywords: causality, exogeneity, non-stationarity, granger causality, forecasting, policy analysis

JEL classifications: E41, C52

2.1. Introduction

Scientific knowledge is always and everywhere fallible. The history of Newtonian gravitational theory is the classic example – once deemed unassailable truth and repeatedly confirmed by experiment, it is now seen as an approximate model. Interestingly, that view was in fact first proposed by Smith (1795). 'Causal knowledge' is simply a special case of this general problem, exacerbated by disputable formulations of the concept, doubts about inference procedures, and in economics, by the complexities of data processes. This chapter considers causality in non-stationary macro-economic time-series, where causality is viewed as 'actually determining an aspect of behaviour': exogeneity – the property of being 'determined outside the system under analysis' – is also considered, but primarily in relation to causality.

The literature on both concepts is vast, and thoroughly discussing them is well beyond the scope of this chapter. However, many of the implications of causality and exogeneity were developed in weakly stationary systems, where it can be difficult to test for their presence or absence. All modern macro-economies are non-stationary from both stochastic and deterministic changes, often modelled as integrated–cointegrated systems prone to intermittent structural breaks – sudden large changes, invariably unanticipated. In such non-stationary data generation processes (DGPs), many results concerning modelling, forecasting, and policy change substantially relative to the stationary case. The primary difficulty becomes that of establishing time invariant relationships, but once that is achieved, the roles of causality and exogeneity are often more easily ascertained.

The precursor to the approach here lies in the theory of forecasting developed by Clements and Hendry (1999, 2002) and reviewed by Hendry and Clements (2003). Those authors are concerned with the historical prevalence of forecast failure, defined as a significant deterioration in forecast performance relative to the anticipated outcome (usually based on the historical performance of a model); for documentation see, e.g. Stock and Watson (1996) and Clements and Hendry (2001b). The forecast-error taxonomies established by the latter authors show that the main sources of such forecast failures are changes in coefficients of deterministic terms, or location shifts. Structural breaks affecting mean-zero variables pose fewer difficulties (see, e.g. Hendry, 2000b), as do mis-specification and mis-estimation when breaks do not occur. Such results entail reconsidering how causality and exogeneity apply when empirical models are mis-specified for complicated, evolving and non-stationary DGPs. For example, since one cannot prove that causal models need dominate in forecasting, neither forecast success nor failure is informative about causal links. Nevertheless, in other settings, non-constancy can help determine causal direction.

The structure of the chapter is as follows. Section 2.2 describes the econometric background, noting some of the many salient contributions to the literature. Then Section 2.3 reviews the three well-known forms of weak, strong and super exogeneity in relation to inference, forecasting, and policy, and notes their role in non-stationary systems. Analyzing exogeneity first is convenient for Section 2.4, which then provides a similar approach for causality, before briefly discussing Granger causality, following the overview in Hendry and Mizon (1999). Section 2.5 notes some links between exogeneity and causality. Section 2.6 examines their role in forecasting, and Section 2.7 discusses the roles of exogeneity and causality in policy analyses. Section 2.8 concludes.

2.2. Background

Let $(\Omega, \mathcal{F}, P(\cdot))$ denote the probability space supporting a vector of m discrete-time, real random variables $\mathbf{w}_t$, with sample space Ω and event space $\mathcal{F}_{t-1}$ at each time $t \in \mathcal{T}$. The joint density $D_{w_t}(\mathbf{w}_t|\mathcal{F}_{t-1}, \boldsymbol{\lambda})$ for $\boldsymbol{\lambda} \in \Lambda \subseteq \mathbb{R}^q$ is the DGP of the economy under analysis. The q-dimensional parameter (or 'index') $\boldsymbol{\lambda}$ does not depend on $\mathcal{F}_{t-1}$ at any t, but need not be constant over time since $\boldsymbol{\lambda}$ is determined by economic agents' decisions. The history of the stochastic process $\{\mathbf{w}_t\}$ up to time $(t-1)$ is denoted by $\mathbf{W}_{t-1} = (\mathbf{W}_0, \mathbf{w}_1, ..., \mathbf{w}_{t-1}) = (\mathbf{W}_0, \mathbf{W}_{t-1}^1)$, where $\mathbf{W}_0$ is the set of initial conditions. For a sample period $t = 1, ..., T$, the DGP becomes $D_W(\mathbf{W}_T^1|\mathbf{W}_0, \boldsymbol{\lambda})$, and is sequentially factorized as:

$$D_W(\mathbf{W}_T^1|\mathbf{W}_0, \boldsymbol{\lambda}) = \prod_{t=1}^{T} D_{w_t}(\mathbf{w}_t|\mathbf{W}_{t-1}, \boldsymbol{\delta}_t) \qquad (2.1)$$

where $\mathbf{g}_\delta(\boldsymbol{\lambda}) = (\boldsymbol{\delta}_1...\boldsymbol{\delta}_T)$ for a 1–1 function $\mathbf{g}_\delta(\cdot)$. While the notation potentially allows the parameters of Equation (2.1) to shift every period, we assume that such changes are in practice intermittent. Historical sources of non-constancy are regime shifts (changes in policy), and technological, legislative, behavioural and institutional structural breaks (shifts in the parameters of the system). Since economic processes also evolve for many reasons, the $\{\mathbf{w}_t\}$ are likely to be integrated of at least first order (denoted I(1)). Thus, a key feature of Equation (2.1) is the non-stationarity of $\{\Delta\mathbf{w}_t\}$ (or of $\{\Delta^2\mathbf{w}_t\}$ if the level is I(2)), with changing first and second data moments. Because $D_{w_t}(\cdot)$ alters over time, all expectations operators have to be time dated, as in $E_t[\mathbf{w}_t]$ and $V_t[\mathbf{w}_t\mathbf{w}_t']$ for unconditional expectations and variances, respectively. Such dating is separate from the timing of any conditioning information, such as $\mathbf{W}_{t-1}$. While $D_{w_t}(\mathbf{w}_t|\mathbf{W}_{t-1}, \boldsymbol{\delta}_t)$ characterizes the generation of the outcomes, measurement errors are bound to add a further layer of complexity to empirical analyses (especially of causality), but as they are not germane to the concepts per se, the $\{\mathbf{w}_t\}$ are assumed to be observed.

2.2.1. Local DGP

Reductions from the DGP for $\{\mathbf{w}_t\}$ to that of the transformed subset of $n < m$ variables $\{\mathbf{x}_t\}$ to be analyzed can radically alter the causality and exogeneity status of variables. In general (see, inter alia, Hendry, 1995a; Mizon, 1995), there exists a 'local DGP' $D_{x_t}(\mathbf{x}_t|\mathbf{X}_{t-1},\boldsymbol{\gamma}_t)$ with $\boldsymbol{\gamma}_t \in \Gamma \subseteq \mathbb{R}^\ell$ derived from $D_{w_t}(\mathbf{w}_t|\cdot)$ by aggregation, transformation, and marginalization with respect to all excluded current-dated and lagged variables. Map from $\mathbf{w}_t$ by an information-preserving transform $\mathbf{h}(\cdot)$ such that $\mathbf{h}(\mathbf{w}_t) = (\mathbf{x}_t', \boldsymbol{\eta}_t')'$. Then $\boldsymbol{\delta}_t$ is transformed to $(\boldsymbol{\rho}_t', \boldsymbol{\gamma}_t')$, such that:

$$D_{w_t}(\mathbf{w}_t|\mathbf{W}_{t-1},\boldsymbol{\delta}_t) = D_{\eta_t|x_t}(\boldsymbol{\eta}_t|\mathbf{x}_t,\mathbf{W}_{t-1},\boldsymbol{\rho}_t)D_{x_t}(\mathbf{x}_t|\mathbf{W}_{t-1},\boldsymbol{\gamma}_t). \qquad (2.2)$$

To restrict attention to the marginal model, $D_{x_t}(\cdot)$, without loss of information requires that:[1]

$$D_{x_t}(\mathbf{x}_t|\mathbf{W}_{t-1},\boldsymbol{\gamma}_t) = D_{x_t}(\mathbf{x}_t|\mathbf{X}_{t-1},\boldsymbol{\gamma}_t), \qquad (2.3)$$

so that lagged $\boldsymbol{\eta}$ must be irrelevant. Finally, the $r \leq \ell$ parameters of interest, $\boldsymbol{\mu}$, must be a function of $\boldsymbol{\gamma}_t$ alone, so $\boldsymbol{\rho}_t$ does not provide information about $\boldsymbol{\gamma}_t$. For example, if important explanatory variables are omitted from Equation (2.3), and $\boldsymbol{\rho}_t$ is non-constant, so will be the coefficients in Equation (2.3) even when $\boldsymbol{\gamma}$ in Equation (2.2) is constant (see, e.g. Hendry and Doornik, 1997). Such parametric links are intrinsic to Equation (2.2), and the usual assumption that the parameters in models thereof are variation free, so $(\boldsymbol{\gamma}_t, \boldsymbol{\rho}_t) \in \Gamma \times \mathcal{R}$, is insufficient. When Equation (2.3) holds, it is fully informative about the roles of the variables; but in general, there will be a loss of information from the elimination of $\{\boldsymbol{\eta}_t\}$, with a consequential (unintended) transformation of the parameters.

2.2.2. The econometric model

The econometric model $f_x(\cdot)$ for $\mathbf{x}_t$ is denoted by:

$$f_X(\mathbf{X}_T^1|\mathbf{X}_0,\boldsymbol{\theta}) = \prod_{t=1}^{T} f_x(\mathbf{x}_t|\mathbf{X}_{t-1},\boldsymbol{\theta}) \qquad \text{where } \boldsymbol{\theta} \in \Theta \subseteq \mathbb{R}^k \qquad (2.4)$$

---

[1] We ignore any complications related to the role of the initial conditions, $\mathbf{W}_0$.

when $f_x(\mathbf{x}_t|\mathbf{X}_{t-1}, \boldsymbol{\theta})$ is the postulated sequential joint density at time t. We assume that $k < \ell$ and that $\boldsymbol{\theta}$ represents the constant (meta)parameters postulated by the model builder. Inevitably, $f_x(\cdot) \neq D_{x_t}(\cdot)$, which may affect inferences about exogeneity or causality. An econometric model is congruent if it matches the data evidence in all relevant directions, and Bontemps and Mizon (2003) show that such a model would encompass the local DGP (denoted LDGP). Further, a successful analysis requires that $\boldsymbol{\mu} = \mathbf{g}_\mu(\boldsymbol{\theta})$, and while achieving that goal is difficult, progressive research can glean important insights even in processes that are not time invariant.

2.3. Exogeneity

The notion of exogeneity, or synonyms thereof, in relation to econometric modelling dates back to the origins of the discipline (see, e.g. Morgan, 1990; Hendry and Morgan, 1995), including important contributions by Koopmans (1950) and Phillips (1957). Here we follow the approach in Richard (1980), formalized by Engle *et al.* (1983); Ericsson (1992) provides an exposition.

We assume that $f_x(\mathbf{x}_t|\mathbf{X}_{t-1}, \boldsymbol{\theta})$ in Equation (2.4) is a valid reduction to a congruent model of the LDGP, and partition $\mathbf{x}_t' = (\mathbf{y}_t' : \mathbf{z}_t')$ where $\mathbf{y}_t$ is $n_1 \times 1$ and $\mathbf{z}_t$ is $n_2 \times 1$ with $n = n_1 + n_2$, with $\mathbf{X}_{t-1}$ partitioned accordingly as $(\mathbf{Y}_{t-1}, \mathbf{Z}_{t-1})$. To model $\mathbf{y}_t$ conditional on $\mathbf{z}_t$, factorize $f_x(\mathbf{x}_t|\mathbf{X}_{t-1}, \boldsymbol{\theta})$ into a conditional and a marginal density, transforming $\boldsymbol{\theta} \in \Theta$ to $\boldsymbol{\psi} \in \Psi$:

$$\boldsymbol{\psi} = \mathbf{g}_\psi(\boldsymbol{\theta}) \qquad \text{where } \boldsymbol{\psi} \in \Psi \text{ and } \boldsymbol{\theta} \in \Theta, \tag{2.5}$$

such that $\mathbf{g}_\psi(\cdot)$ is a $1-1$ reparametrization which sustains the partition $\boldsymbol{\psi}' = (\boldsymbol{\psi}_1' : \boldsymbol{\psi}_2')$, when $\boldsymbol{\psi}_i$ has k_i elements ($k_1 + k_2 = k$), and:

$$f_x(\mathbf{x}_t|\mathbf{X}_{t-1}, \boldsymbol{\theta}) = f_{y|z}(\mathbf{y}_t|\mathbf{z}_t, \mathbf{X}_{t-1}, \boldsymbol{\psi}_1) f_z(\mathbf{z}_t|\mathbf{X}_{t-1}, \boldsymbol{\psi}_2). \tag{2.6}$$

As only $f_{y|z}(\mathbf{y}_t|\mathbf{z}_t, \mathbf{X}_{t-1}, \boldsymbol{\psi}_1)$ is to be retained, the analysis of $\boldsymbol{\mu}$ is without loss of information relative to Equation (2.4) when $\mathbf{z}_t$ is weakly exogenous for $\boldsymbol{\mu}$, namely $\boldsymbol{\mu} = \mathbf{h}(\boldsymbol{\psi}_1)$ alone and $(\boldsymbol{\psi}_1, \boldsymbol{\psi}_2) \in \Psi_1 \times \Psi_2$. Thus exogeneity is not a property of a variable: in Equation (2.3), all variables are endogenous. Moreover, weak exogeneity is just as relevant to instrumental variables estimation, as the marginal density of $\mathbf{z}_t$ then relates to the distribution of the putative instruments: merely asserting orthogonality is inadequate, as illustrated by counter examples in Hendry (1995a,c).

Strong exogeneity also requires the absence of feed back from lagged $\mathbf{y}_{t-i}$ onto $\mathbf{z}_t$ so that:

$$\prod_{t=1}^{T} f_z(\mathbf{z}_t|\mathbf{X}_{t-1}, \boldsymbol{\psi}_2) = f_Z(\mathbf{Z}_T^1|\mathbf{X}_0, \boldsymbol{\psi}_2). \tag{2.7}$$

Finally, super exogeneity requires weak exogeneity and the invariance of $\boldsymbol{\mu}$ to changes in $\boldsymbol{\psi}_2$. As is well known, the three concepts respectively sustain conditional inference; conditional multi-step forecasting;[2] and conditional policy analysis (when components of $\mathbf{z}_t$ are policy instruments).

The absence of links between the parameter spaces Ψ_1 and Ψ_2 is not purely a matter of model specification, dependent on the parameters of interest, and at the choice of the investigator. In some settings, as neatly illustrated by Ericsson (1992), changing the parameters of interest can deliver or lose weak exogeneity. But in other settings, the LDGP determines the actual, as opposed to the claimed, exogeneity status. Factorize Equation (2.3) as:

$$D_{x_t}(\mathbf{x}_t|\mathbf{X}_{t-1}, \boldsymbol{\gamma}_t) = D_{y_t|z_t}(\mathbf{y}_t|\mathbf{z}_t, \mathbf{X}_{t-1}, \boldsymbol{\phi}_{1,t})D_{z_t}(\mathbf{z}_t|\mathbf{X}_{t-1}, \boldsymbol{\phi}_{2,t}) \tag{2.8}$$

When $\boldsymbol{\mu}$ enters both $\boldsymbol{\phi}_{1,t}$ and $\boldsymbol{\phi}_{2,t}$ in Equation (2.8), inference can be distorted if Equation (2.6) falsely asserts weak exogeneity, see, e.g. Phillips and Loretan (1991). The consequences of failures of weak exogeneity can vary from a loss of estimation efficiency through to a loss of parameter constancy, depending on the source of the problem, see Hendry (1995a, Chapter 5). We now illustrate both extreme cases.

First, consider an experimental setting where the Gauss–Markov conditions might appear to be satisfied so that:

$$\mathbf{y} = \mathbf{Z}\boldsymbol{\beta} + \boldsymbol{\epsilon} \text{ with } \boldsymbol{\epsilon} \sim N_T[0, \sigma_\epsilon^2 \mathbf{I}], \tag{2.9}$$

when $\mathbf{Z}' = (\mathbf{z}_1...\mathbf{z}_T)$ is a $T \times k$ matrix, rank $(\mathbf{Z}) = k$, and $\boldsymbol{\epsilon}' = (\boldsymbol{\epsilon}_1...\boldsymbol{\epsilon}_T)$, with:

$$E[\mathbf{y}|\mathbf{Z}] = \mathbf{Z}\boldsymbol{\beta},$$

and hence $E[\mathbf{Z}'\boldsymbol{\epsilon}] = 0$. Nevertheless, OLS need not be the most efficient unbiased estimator of $\boldsymbol{\beta}$. An explicit weak exogeneity condition is required when $\mathbf{Z}$ is stochastic, such that $\boldsymbol{\beta}$ cannot be learned from its marginal distribution. Otherwise, an unbiased estimator which is an affine function

---

[2] Projecting $\mathbf{Y}_{T+h}$ onto $\mathbf{X}_{T-i}$ also circumvents any feedback problem, see, e.g. Bhansali (2002).

of **y** can dominate, possibly dramatically, see Hendry (2003). Secondly, if $\mathbf{z}_t$ is simultaneously determined with $\mathbf{y}_t$, yet experiences a location shift, then a conditional model of $\mathbf{y}_t$ given $\mathbf{z}_t$ (incorrectly treating $\mathbf{z}_t$ as weakly exogenous) will have non-constant parameters even though the DGP equation for $\mathbf{y}_t$ is constant.

Although it can be difficult to test exogeneity claims when unconditional second moments are constant over time, as Engle *et al.* (1983) note, despite only one specification corresponding to reality, both main forms of non-stationarity (integrability and breaks) alter the analysis as we now show.

First, cointegrated systems provide a major forum for testing one aspect of exogeneity, see inter alia, Boswijk (1992), Dolado (1992), Hunter (1992a,b), Johansen (1992), Urbain (1992) and Paruolo and Rahbek (1999). Equilibrium-correction mechanisms which cross-link equations violate long-run weak exogeneity, confirming that weak exogeneity cannot necessarily be obtained merely by choosing the 'parameters of interest'. Conversely, the presence of a given disequilibrium term in more than one equation is testable.

Secondly, processes subject to structural breaks sustain tests for super exogeneity and the Lucas (1976) critique, see, e.g. Hendry (1988), Fischer (1989), Favero and Hendry (1992) and Engle and Hendry (1993). When conditional models are constant despite data moments changing considerably, there is prima facie evidence of super exogeneity for that model's parameters; and if the model as formulated does not have constant parameters, resolving that failure ought to take precedence over issues of exogeneity. However, while such tests are powerful for location shifts, changes to 'reaction parameters' of mean-zero stochastic variables are difficult to detect, see, e.g. Hendry (2000b).

Richard (1980) considers changes in causal direction, reconsidered in Section 2.5.1 in relation to determining 'causal direction' through a lack of time invariance.

2.4. Causality

The concept of causality has intrigued philosophers for millennia, so Section 2.4.1 provides a brief incursion into the philosophy of causality. Section 2.4.2 looks at notions of causality in economic discourse, then Sub-section 2.4.3 considers causal inference in observational disciplines. Both statisticians and economists have attempted to test for its existence, as it is particularly important if one is interested in testing theories or conducting policy analysis, see Simon (1952), Zellner (1979), Hoover (1990) and Hendry (1995a) for general discussions of causality and causal inference in econometrics; and, e.g. Holland (1986), Cox (1992) and Lauritzen and Richardson (2002) in statistics. Finally, Sub-section 2.4.4 evaluates the concept of Granger causality, and its empirical implementation. Section 2.5 considers links between causality and exogeneity.

2.4.1. Philosophy of causality

As remarked in Hendry (1995a), 'causality' is a philosophical mine field – even without the complexities introduced by quantum physics, one-off events, anticipations, 'simultaneity', and the issue that, for example, changes may enlarge or restrict the opportunity sets of agents who could choose to do otherwise than just react mechanically. Thus, we will step as lightly as feasible: the increase in the prevalence of footnotes signals the difficulty. Fortunately, Hoover (2001) provides an excellent discussion. In particular, he notes that many analyses conflate the concept with inference about it, which he calls 'the epistemic fallacy', essentially confusing truth with its criterion. We will first consider the concept, briefly comment on what makes something a cause, then turn to how one might ascertain causal relationships.[3]

What makes a cause just that? A cause is a quantitative process that induces changes over time, mediated within a structure. In turn, a structure is an entity that remains invariant to interventions 'and directly characterizes the relationships involved' (i.e. corresponds to reality), see Hendry (1995a, Chapter 2).[4] The relation between cause and effect is asymmetric; the latter does not induce the former. The 'causal field' or structure is central, as changes to that structure can alter what causes what.

This notion of cause is consistent with at least some earlier formulations, such as Simon (1957, Chapters 1 and 3) who formalizes causal order as an asymmetric relation invariant under interventions to the 'basic' parameters of the system; Cartwright (1989) who discusses

---

[3] This organization partially follows Hoover's discussion of Hume, who distinguished between the conceptual, ontological, epistemological, and pragmatic aspects of causality. Hoover cites Hume as complaining that his efforts at clarification 'heated [his] brain', a view with which I sympathize.

[4] The perceptive reader will not miss the problem: it is impossible to define systems that are invariant to all interventions – else nothing would change. While that is a view of the world which Parmenides might have endorsed, Heraclitus would have disagreed, since he regarded flux as so intense one cannot even step into the same river twice (on both views, see Gottlieb, 2000). Neither of theses settings is conducive to causal inference – but then neither seems realistic. However, Nancy Cartwright has correctly noted that my definition is in the nature of a sufficient condition to discern a cause, rather than defining cause per se. For example, a rope can cause an object to which it is attached not to move.

'causal capacities', such that causes out need causes in (i.e. we need to postulate that causal links already exist); Hoover (1990) who argues for invariance under interventions; and Hoover (2001) where cause is an asymmetric relationship with 'unconnected parameters' within a causal structure that is a feature of reality.[5]

Our everyday thinking is replete with causal assertions: the car stopped because the driver braked; the atom disintegrated because it was hit by the proton; the pressure of the gas rose because heat was applied; output rose because interest rates fell;.... At one level, such statements seem unexceptional. Consider the first example: the brakes were first applied; the braking system remained intact; the harder the brakes were applied, the more the car slowed; the brakes stopped the car (not the car slowing 'caused' the brakes to come on). If the brake cable were cut (as in some murder stories), or the brake fluid was too low (as happens in reality) and so on, pressing the brake pedal would achieve little: that system is not invariant to such 'interventions'. More fancifully, the car might be attached to a cable, the tightening of which 'actually causes' it to slow, so the braking is incidental – causal discussion is often based on thought experiments involving counterfactuals. More realistically, it could be argued that the driver caused the car to stop, or even that the trigger for the driver pressing the brakes was the cause.... 'Causal chains' may have many steps, with the 'ultimate causes' possibly hidden from human knowledge.

Consequently, it is difficult to independently specify what makes something a cause. Given the key role of the 'causal structure', causal connections need be neither necessary nor sufficient. The former (necessity) implies that if A is to cause B, then not-A entails not-B; the latter (sufficiency) that not-B entails not-A. Counter examples to necessity arise when there are multiple possible causes, as in medicine–smoking causes lung cancer, but so might environmental pollution. Equally, sufficiency crumbles if (say) whether or not lung cancer occurs in any given smoker may depend on the quality of their 'DNA repair kit': a really good 'kit' may continually repair the incipient damage so the disease never appears. Such examples reinforce that the 'causal field' characterizing the system and its background conditions are central: economists are anyway used to the idea that non-stationarities and non-linearities may mean that a cause sometimes has an effect, and sometimes does not,

---

[5] Conversely, the notion of a 'causal chain', in (say) Strotz and Wold (1960), was shown to be insufficient to characterize exogeneity by Engle *et al.* (1983) precisely because it failed to specify the absence of links between parameters.

depending on thresholds. But these are difficulties for inference about causal links, not about causality as a concept.

It can be of no surprise that ascertaining actual causes is difficult. My countryman, Hume (1758) tends to be the source of much thinking about the topic.[6] Hume asserted that we cannot *know* necessary connections in reality (my italics). The key word is know, for therein lies the difficulty: causal inference is uncertain (although, as Hoover, 2001 notes, this did not stop Hume from arguing in 'causal' terms about economics). Just as we cannot have a criterion for truth, yet science seeks for 'truth', so with causal models, we cannot have a criterion for knowing that the necessary connections have been ascertained. Hoover himself remarks (p. 24) that "our knowledge of reality consists of empirically based conjectures and is necessarily corrigible". Even greater problems arise when inferring anything from probability relations. Scientists – and economists – often formulate theory models with theory causal connections between variables, test those models empirically, and if they are not rejected, use the theory connections as if they held in reality: the 'causes in' come from the theory, and the 'causes out' from the evidence not rejecting that theory – rather a weak basis. Policy changes often provide the backdrop for such testing, and play an important role below, so we turn to economics.

2.4.2. Notions of causality in economics

Economists often conceptualize cause as a well-defined dependence in a theoretical model, such as $y = f(z)$, implying that a change in z will induce a change in y: most recently, see Heckman (2000). That approach suffers from four drawbacks. First, it is essentially circular, since a model would presumably not be 'well defined' if the relation in question did not sustain the conclusion. Secondly, some form of asymmetry needs to be independently added so that, for example, when $f(\cdot)$ is invertible, y does not then cause z. Thirdly, a theory can be well defined but irrelevant to the behaviour of the actual economy, whereas the objective of most economic analyses is doubtless to infer some properties of reality. Finally, a theory-dependent definition is insufficient to characterize all the important examples of causal links, for example, 'aspirin' clearly caused the removal of headaches even before the key ingredient (acetylsalicylic acid) was isolated from willow-tree bark, yet there was no 'well-defined model' of how it worked till very recently (see Weissmann, 1991). In any case, the

---

[6] Bibliographical references to him are also a bit of minefield, as Hume often re-issued essays or parts thereof under different titles and editions.

'superlative' theories of the natural sciences represent the outcome of close interaction between successive theories and accumulating evidence, sometimes reinterpreted retrospectively (see, e.g. Penrose, 1989), not pure a priori postulates as to causal links. Thus, a more general formulation is needed.

The key point is that causality is a property of reality not of a model, either z does or does not cause y, so causality is not usefully defined purely in a theory context. Conversely, commencing from observational evidence alone raises that frightening spectre of 'inferring causes from correlations', which worries so many economists, and is the subject of Section 2.4.3. Rather, in economics, theoretical implications are tested against the observed correlations. Although corroboration is clearly insufficient, and rejection is not definitive, knowledge about possible causal links can accumulate by progressive research, as has happened in other sciences.

An issue that is not necessarily problematic for the conceptualization of causality, but is for practical inference, is that action in anticipation of a change can mask the 'true' effect. For example, if the Bank of England is expected to cut its interest rate, futures markets may adjust in anticipation, so nothing happens when the cut actually occurs. Indeed, some causality tests might infer that the market 'caused' the Bank to react. Care is required here – it is the anticipation which does the causing, not the later outcome that was anticipated. The timing effect is correct but hidden, and in (say) tests of Granger causality (see Section 2.4.4) might incorrectly suggest the reversal of the actual causal direction.

Potentially immense problems and benefits are raised by non-stationarity. At one extreme, causal relations themselves may be transient and render inference completely unreliable. Alternatively, by 'excitation' of the data space, considerable advantages could accrue, by refuting false attributions and providing powerful evidence in favour of valid theories. We resume this line in Sections 2.5.1 and 2.7.1.

2.4.3. *Causal inference in observational sciences*

It may be thought that non-experimental research is at a severe disadvantage for causal inference compared to experimental (see Blalock, 1961; Wold, 1969 on causal inference in non-experimental research). While it is undoubtedly true in many cases that an efficacious, well-designed and carefully controlled experiment can deliver important insights, experimental evidence may also mislead (see Cartwright, 1983, for a general critical appraisal of physical 'laws' mainly derived from experiments). Doll (2001) recounts the fascinating tale of how cigarette smoking was implicated in lung cancer. Initial suggestions in the 1920s of a possible connection (based on the steady rise in both) prompted a series of laboratory 'tests' on animals, which failed to find any link. When Doll commenced his own observational study, he suspected that the widespread use of 'tar' as a road surfacing material might be to blame, and focused on testing that idea. Fortunately, he also collected data on other aspects of the sample of hospital patients investigated. Tabulating their smoking prevalence against lung cancer incidence revealed a dramatically strong connection. Later experiments confirmed his finding. In retrospect, we can understand why the early experiments had not found the link: there is a long latency between smoking and contracting the disease, and the first experiments had not persevered for sufficiently long, whereas later investigators were more persistent. Doll provides several other examples where theoretical or experimental analyses failed to suggest links whereas careful study of the observational data revealed the causal connections.[7]

Economists, of course, have long been aware of both spurious (see Yule, 1897) and nonsense (see Yule, 1926) correlations. Indeed, the claim that causal inference is hazardous from observational data alone is buttressed by issues of observational equivalence (see, e.g. Basmann, 1988), lack of identification, and model mis-specification (see, e.g. Lutkepohl, 1982). However, the potential dangers for empirical research from these sources may have been over-emphasized: it is here that non-stationarities due to DGPs suffering structural breaks begin to offer dividends, and not just complications. In a world subject to intermittent large shifts, observational equivalence and lack of unique identification seem most unlikely; the problem is finding any autonomous relations, not a plethora of them. Model mis-specification is manifestly ubiquitous, and poses problems for all aspects of inference, not just about causality. However, enhanced data variation can help to diagnose mis-specification in a progressive research strategy, namely an approach in which knowledge is gradually accumulated as codified, reproducible, information about the world without needing complete prior information as to its nature (see, e.g. Hendry, 1995a, Chapter 8; Hendry, 2000a, Chapter 8). For example, location shifts in policy variables that do not induce forecast failure in relationships linking them to targets provide strong evidence of a causal link; see Section 2.7.

---

[7] Doll also highlights the possible dangers in such inferences, citing the close observational link between cirrhosis of the liver and smoking, which we now know is intermediated by alcohol (a higher proportion of smokers drink heavily than non-smokers).

2.4.4. Granger causality

Most economic relations are inexact, so stochastic formulations are inevitable, leading to both statistical testing and, more fundamentally, to the idea of evaluating causality in terms of changes to the joint distributions of the observables. Granger (1969, 1980, 1988b) has been the most forceful advocate of such an approach; also see Chamberlain (1982), Newbold (1982), Geweke (1984), Phillips (1988), Florens and Mouchart (1982, 1985), Mosconi and Giannini (1992), and Toda and Phillips (1993, 1994). Granger (1969) provided a precise definition of his concept, although most later investigators followed a different route. The fundamental basis for such tests is that causes contain 'special information' about effects not contained elsewhere in the information set; and that 'time's arrow' is unidirectional – only the past can cause the present, the future cannot. Anticipations of future events can influence present outcomes, but absent a crystal ball, those must be functions of available information. Thus, "We inhabit a world in which the future promises endless possibilities and the past lies irretrievably behind us." (Coveney and Highfield, 1990, p. 297, who base the direction of time on increasing entropy).

Specifically, Granger (1969) proposed that if in the universe of information, deleting the history of one set of variables does not alter the joint distribution of any other variables, then the omitted variables do not to cause the others; we refer to this property as Granger non-causality (denoted GNC). Conversely, knowing the cause should help forecast the future.

Equation (2.3) above required that $\boldsymbol{\eta}$ did not Granger cause $\mathbf{x}$. There, $D_{x_t}(\mathbf{x}_t | \mathbf{W}_{t-1}, \boldsymbol{\gamma}_t)$ defined the causal structure which directly characterizes the relationships (i.e. it is the DGP of $\mathbf{x}_t$); the causality takes place in time, and is asymmetric (without precluding that the opposite direction may also hold); and the past induces changes in other variables. Granger causality, therefore, has many attributes in common with the earlier characterization of cause. However, the issue of invariance is not resolved, Granger's definition of causality does not explicitly involve parameters (see, e.g. Engle *et al.*, 1983; Buiter, 1984; Hoover, 2001), and contemporaneous links are eschewed. Consequently, Granger causality does not seem to completely characterize the notion of 'cause'. The 'anticipations' example in Section 2.4.2 is sometimes cited as a counter example, but does not in fact violate the concept, and would anyway confuse inference procedures for most definitions of causality unless the entire mechanism was known.

2.4.4.1. Empirical Granger non-causality

Perhaps most importantly, the definition of GNC is non-operational as it relates to the *universe* of information. Empirical tests for Granger causality are usually based on reductions within $f_x(\mathbf{x}_t|\mathbf{X}_{t-1}, \cdot)$, often without testing its congruence. Hendry and Mizon (1999) defined empirical Granger non-causality (EGNC) with respect to the information set generated by $\{\mathbf{X}_t\}$ as follows. If the density $f_z(\cdot)$ does not depend on $\mathbf{Y}_{t-1}$, so that:

$$f_z(\mathbf{z}_t|\mathbf{X}_{t-1}, \cdot) = f_z(\mathbf{z}_t|\mathbf{Z}_{t-1}, \mathbf{X}_0, \cdot), \qquad (2.10)$$

then $\mathbf{y}$ does not empirically Granger-cause $\mathbf{z}$. Since causality in the LDGP need not entail that in the DGP, and vice versa, it cannot be a surprise that the same is true of EGNC. Among the drawbacks of EGNC, Hendry and Mizon (1999) list:

- the presence of EGNC in a model does not entail the existence of GNC in the DGP;
- the existence of GNC in the DGP need not entail the presence of EGNC in a model (see, e.g. Hendry, 1997);
- the existence of GNC is specific to each point in time, but detecting EGNC requires extended sample periods.

Any or all of these drawbacks can seriously confound empirical tests. The first two are important results for interpreting empirical modelling, and are almost certainly difficult to disentangle in stationary processes. However, concerning the third, if parameter change is a feature of reality, that is hardly the fault of Granger's conceptualization. In any case, location shifts in subsets of the variables should help clarify what the genuine links are – bringing Granger causality close to the concept in Section 2.4.1. Hendry and Mizon (1999) also show that EGNC plays a pervasive role in econometrics, irrespective of whether or not there exist 'genuine DGP causes'. They illustrate their claim for 10 areas of econometric modelling, namely marginalizing; conditioning; distributions of estimators and tests; inference via simulation; co-integration; encompassing; forecasting; policy analysis; dynamic simulation; and impulse response analysis. As their paper is recent, we skip the details, although several issues recur below.

2.5. Links of causality and exogeneity

Exogeneity is neither necessary nor sufficient for causality, even in the DGP. A variable can be exogenous for the parameters of interest in a given system, but irrelevant – i.e. have a zero coefficient – so sufficiency fails. Equally, a causal variable can operate through parameters linked such that exogeneity is violated, so necessity fails as well. Engle *et al.* (1983) noted that variables may be absent from the conditional density, yet not be weakly exogenous, and also showed that GNC is neither necessary nor sufficient for weak exogeneity, although some authors have mistakenly viewed GNC as sufficient for variables to be 'exogenous' (see, e.g. Sims, 1972; Geweke, 1984). Empirically, matters are even less clear, since variables may act as proxies, induced by invalid reductions, rather than genuine 'forces'.

None of these results entails that causality and exogeneity are unconnected as shown by their interacting roles in strong and super exogeneity, respectively. The former was discussed above, but we have one aspect of the latter still to explore.

2.5.1. Super exogeneity and causality

Super exogeneity augments weak exogeneity by the requirement that the parameters of interest be invariant to shifts in the parameters of the marginal distribution. Such a condition is far stronger than 'variation freeness', and is more like the condition of 'independent parameters' used in the causality formulation of Hoover (2001). If causality corresponded to a regular response that was invariant under interventions, then super exogeneity would embody several of the key elements of causality. Simon (1952, 1953) used the invariance of a relationship under interventions to an input variable as an operational notion of cause, as did Hoover (1990).

Consider the conditional DGP:

$$D_{y_t|z_t}(\mathbf{y}_t|\mathbf{z}_t, \mathbf{X}_{t-1}, \boldsymbol{\psi}_1) \tag{2.11}$$

when there is a non-zero dependence of $\mathbf{y}_t$ on $\mathbf{z}_t$:

$$\frac{\partial \mathbf{y}_t}{\partial \mathbf{z}_t'} \neq \mathbf{0}, \tag{2.12}$$

and the parameters of interest are $\boldsymbol{\mu} = f_\mu(\boldsymbol{\psi}_1)$. When $\mathbf{z}_t$ is super exogenous for $\boldsymbol{\mu}$, so $\boldsymbol{\psi}_2$ in Equation (2.7) can change without altering the conditional relationship between $\mathbf{y}_t$ and $\mathbf{z}_t$, then many of the ingredients for a cause are satisfied: an asymmetric quantitative process, Equation (2.12) that induces changes over time, mediated within the structure $D_{y_t|z_t}(\cdot)$. Thus, $\mathbf{z}_t$ causes the resultant change in $\mathbf{y}_t$ and the response of $\mathbf{y}_t$ to $\mathbf{z}_t$ remains the same for different sequences $\{\mathbf{z}_t\}$. Our ability to detect changes in $\boldsymbol{\psi}_1$ in response to shifts in $\boldsymbol{\psi}_2$ depends on the magnitude of the changes in the latter: large or frequent changes in $\boldsymbol{\psi}_2$ that left Equation (2.11) invariant would provide strong evidence of a causal link which could sustain policy changes when, e.g. $\mathbf{z}_t$ was under government control.

However, economic policy usually depends on disequilibria in the rest of the economy (such as excess demands), which would appear to interlink private sector and policy parameters, thereby violating weak exogeneity of z_t for ψ_1 as required for super exogeneity. Nevertheless, as Hendry and Mizon (2000) argue, reliable estimates of policy responses can be obtained when z_t is not weakly exogenous provided the parameters to be shifted by the policy agency are not functions of ψ_1: for example, co-integration relations are often the basis of estimated disequilibria, and are usually established at the level of the complete system, whereas their parameters are not generally subject to policy interventions (which might explain the problems arising in cases when they are, as-say-in the transition of economies from controlled to free markets).

A similar argument would seem to hold when nature creates the 'experimental design'. For example, Hume's 'causal' analysis of inflation in response to a major gold discovery assumes invariant relations to propagate the shock.

2.5.1.1. Determining causal direction

The appendix to Engle and Hendry (1993) in Ericsson and Irons (1994) shows that if a given conditional model has both invariant parameters and invariant error variances across regimes, whereas the joint process varies across those regimes, then the reverse regression cannot have invariant parameters. Thus, such a reverse conditioning should fail either or both constancy and invariance tests, precluding its interpretation as a causal link, and leaving at most one possibility. This notion is echoed in the analysis of interventions in relation to interpreting causality in directed acyclic graphs by Lauritzen and Richardson (2002). Importantly, a break in a model for a subset of variables will persist even under extensions of the information set: for example, if an unmodelled jump in CPI inflation is later 'explained' by a jump in oil prices, the latter now reflects the break in the model; see, e.g. Hendry (1988).[8]

2.6. Causality implications in forecasting

Both senses of causality (i.e., from Sections 2.4.1 and 2.4.4) play a role in forecasting, but perhaps not in ways that might be expected.

First, in DGPs subject to location shifts, one cannot prove the dominance of causal variables in forecasting: counter examples are

---

[8] Of course, apparent breaks may be the result of an unmodelled non-linearity: slipping down a gentle bank then over a cliff is a non-linear effect, but the problem is the break at the end…

provided in, e.g. Clements and Hendry (1999). Consequently, models based on variables that do not enter the DGP can outperform in forecasting over models using every variable that was causal in the DGP prior to the forecast period. More generally, the forecasting theory underlying that result has achieved a range of successful explanations of otherwise puzzling features of the empirical forecasting literature, including (see Hendry and Clements, 2003):

- why intercept corrections have value added;
- why extrapolative devices can win forecasting competitions;
- why simplicity does not account for that outcome, but robustness to location shifts does;
- why forecast pooling can dominate the best individual forecasting device; and
- why forecast failure occurs, but is not informative about the presence or absence of causal links.

Fildes and Makridakis (1995) and Makridakis and Hibon (2000) stress the discrepancy between theory and empirical findings in forecasting in general. Clements and Hendry (2001a) show how their theory can help close that gap. Moreover, they also account for the 'principles' based on empirical econometric forecasting performance enunciated by Allen and Fildes (2001), who find that admissible reductions of VARs with relatively generous lag specifications, estimated by least squares, and tested for constant parameters do best on average, even though congruent models need not outperform non-congruent. Such findings stand in marked contrast to what can be established when the economy is representable as a stationary stochastic process (with unconditional moments that are constant over time): well-tested, causally relevant congruent models that embodied valid restrictions would both fit best, and by encompassing, dominate in forecasting on average. Unfortunately, new unpredictable events continue to occur, so any operational theory of economic forecasting must allow for data moments altering, see Stock and Watson (1996) and Clements and Hendry (2001b) on the prominence of structural change in macroeconomic time-series.

Thus, for forecasting per se, correctly established causality in congruent models does not ensure success. However, care is essential in how that result is interpreted. Location shifts (or mimics thereof) are sufficiently common to have left a less than impressive track record of macro-econometric forecasting. No one can forecast the unpredictable, and all devices will fail for events that were ex ante unpredictable. But some devices do not adjust after breaks and so suffer systematic forecast failure: equilibrium-correction mechanisms based on co-integration relationships whose mean has changed – but that is not known – are a potentially disastrous example. Nevertheless, causal-based modelling should not be abandoned as a basis for forecasting, particularly in a policy context (see Section 2.7); rather, the solution lies in formulating variants of models that are robust to such shifts. Intercept corrections and additional differencing are simple possibilities, but hopefully better ones will be developed now that an explanation exists for the historical outcomes (see, e.g. Hendry, 2004).

However, it is the converse implication that is crucial; causal links are not sensibly tested by forecast evaluation, since neither success nor failure entails correct or incorrect attribution of causality. Forecast failure could, but need not, imply inappropriately attributed causal links. Indeed, all four possibilities can occur without logical contradiction: correct causality followed by forecast failure; incorrect causality followed by forecast failure; correct causality followed by forecast 'success'; incorrect causality followed by forecast success. Worse still, 'tricks' exist that can help avoid forecast failure independently of the validity of any causal attributions by the model in use; intercept corrections are a well-known device with such properties.

Despite such a fundamental result, many economists seem to persist in the view that 'forecasting is the ultimate test of a model'. Three comments can be made about such a view, see Clements and Hendry (2003). First, ex post parameter-constancy tests and ex ante forecast evaluations have very different properties, with the latter susceptible to many additional problems such as (increased) data inaccuracy at the forecast-origin and over the forecast horizon. Secondly, non-constancy in coefficients of mean-zero variables has a much smaller impact on forecast accuracy than changes in location components. Thirdly, when the future can differ substantively from the past, 'because of the things we don't know we don't know' (see Singer, 1997), forecast failure is not so much a diagnostic of a model as an indication of an event unrelated to existing information; thus, it potentially provides new knowledge. Consequently, if the basis for their view is that new evidence is needed for 'independent' checking of inferences, when data moments are non-constant, then great care is needed in using such information correctly, and ex ante forecast evaluation is unlikely to be a reliable approach to doing so.

Turning to the role of Granger causality, for multi-step conditional forecasts, EGNC of the conditioning variables is crucial for valid inferences; neglected feedbacks would otherwise violate the conditioning assumptions. On the other hand, EGNC does not matter in closed models, where every variable is jointly forecast, nor for 1-step ahead forecasts even in open models, nor if multi-step estimation is used.

Surprisingly, therefore, in the forecasting arena, neither sense of causality can be accorded an important role.

2.7. *Exogeneity and causality in policy analysis*

Ericsson (1992), Ericsson *et al.* (1998) and Hendry and Mizon (1998) consider the roles of exogeneity, causality, and co-breaking in policy analysis, so again we merely summarize the discussion, but return to co-breaking in Section 2.7.1. Also, Granger (1988a) discusses the role of Granger causality in policy effectiveness (but see Buiter, 1984), and Granger and Deutsch (1992) investigate the evaluation of policy models.

The use of models for economic policy analysis is the arena where causality plays a fundamentally important role. If a variable changed by an economic policy is causal, but omitted from a model, or is not causal but is deemed such in a model, then incorrect predictions of its effects are virtually bound to occur (although luck can never be excluded). Accurate predictions of the effects of a change in a policy variable will only result if that variable can be changed, is causal in a model that treats it as such, when the transmission of the effect is invariant, and has been appropriately estimated. Thus, stringent conditions must be satisfied for successful policy analysis.

Based on the results reviewed in Section 2.6, Hendry and Mizon (2000) show that the 'best' forecasting model may be useless for policy. Conversely, and perhaps surprisingly in view of the Lucas (1976) critique, forecast failure per se is not sufficient to reject a policy model. The rationale for the first step of their analysis is that extrapolative devices need not even involve policy variables; and for the second, that forecast failure primarily derives from unanticipated location shifts which need not (but of course, could) affect policy conclusions. Moreover, since extrapolative devices rarely include the policy instruments, shifts in those instruments then act as post-forecasting breaks to such devices, inducing a failure not present in an econometric model, which is well specified for the policy effects. Consequently, compared to in-sample structural breaks, the situation reverses for these two model types. Hence, pooling of both forms of model will be needed in the face of location structural breaks and policy regime shifts.

Policy outcomes depend on reaction parameters connecting target variables with instruments. As shown in Hendry (2000b), structural breaks which do not alter the unconditional expectations of the I(0) transforms of variables are not easily detected by conventional constancy tests, so rarely induce forecast failure. This has adverse implications for impulse response analyses as discussed in Section 2.7.3 below. However, most policy changes entail location shifts in variables (as against, e.g. mean-preserving spreads), and hence provide a crucial step in a progressive research strategy; if causal attribution is incorrect, then forecast failure should result from the policy, allowing substantive learning of causal connections, providing these do not themselves change too often (which seems unlikely). Thus, research effort into establishing which forecast failures resulted from policy changes, and which from other sources of location shifts, would seem merited.

2.7.1. Co-breaking

Co-breaking is the property that when variables shift, there exist linear combinations of variables which do not shift, and so are independent of the breaks (see Clements and Hendry, 1999, Chapter 9; Massmann, 2001; Krolzig and Toro, 2002). Co-breaking is analogous to co-integration, where a linear combination of variables is stationary even though all the component series are integrated. Whenever there is co-breaking between the instruments of economic policy and the target variables, changes in the former will produce consistent changes in the latter, so constant co-breaking implements a causal relation. The existence of co-breaking between the means of the policy instruments and those of the targets is testable; a policy shift that induced forecast failure would be strong evidence that the causal links were incorrectly specified. As Section 2.7.3 shows, co-breaking is also necessary to justify impulse response analysis.

2.7.2. Control

The status of variables in a system can be altered by deliberate changes in governmental control procedures. For example, a variable (such as an interest rate) that was weakly exogenous for the parameters of (say) an inflation equation, can cease to be so after a control rule is introduced (see, e.g. Johansen and Juselius, 2000), yet the VAR involved need not suffer from forecast failure. Of course, the control rule can be effective only if there is an already existing causal link between the instrument and the target, so the new feedback rule can exploit that link to achieve its objective; control rules cannot create policy-target links by specifying target-instrument links.

2.7.3. *Impulse response analyses*

Although impulse response analyses are widespread (see, e.g. Sims, 1980; Runkle, 1987; Lutkepohl, 1991), they suffer from many drawbacks, see Banerjee *et al.* (1996), Ericsson *et al.* (1998) and Hendry and Mizon (1998).[9] Here, we focus on those problems that are germane to a discussion of exogeneity and causality in non-stationary processes.

First, weak exogeneity is crucial for impulse response analyses since the same size of 'shock' to the error and to the intercept are indistinguishable in a model, but the reaction in the economy will be as anticipated only if the means and variances are linked in the same way – which is (e.g.) the weak exogeneity condition for a conditional equation in a VAR. Specifying a variable to be weakly or strongly exogenous alters the calculated impulse responses, irrespective of whether or not that variable actually is exogenous. Moreover, results are dependent on the ordering of variables – but 'orthogonalized impulses' violate weak exogeneity for most selections, so may lose invariance to the very shocks to be analyzed.

Secondly, in closed systems – where policy variables are 'modelled' – impulse-response analyses assume that the process remains constant under the shock, so actually requires super exogeneity of the appropriate policy conditioning variables. Alternatively expressed, unless there is mean co-breaking between the shocked variable and the target, the actual responses in the economy will not match those derived from the model. Impulse response approaches to evaluating the policy implications of models are also dependent on the absence of 'undetected breaks', so can be misleading in both sign and magnitude when shifts have occurred in zero-mean variables, even when models are rigorously tested (and certainly so when no such testing has occurred), see Hendry and Mizon (2000).

Thirdly, even when a model is rigorously derived from a consistent theory, is congruent and encompasses rival models, and its policy implications are invariant to extensions of the information used – so it embodies structure (see Hendry, 1995b) – that does not imply that its residuals are structural. Residuals can only be invariant to extensions of information over time, regimes and variables if the model coincides with the DGP, and not just the LDGP. Error terms in equations induce changes in the values taken by the dependent variable only by an assumption of

---

[9] The literature on 'structural VARs' (see, e.g. Bernanke, 1986; Blanchard and Quah, 1989), faces similar difficulties.

causality so, for example:

$$y_t = \boldsymbol{\beta}' \mathbf{z}_{t-1} + \boldsymbol{\epsilon}_t, \tag{2.13}$$

is usually written on the assumption that:

$$\frac{\partial y_t}{\partial \epsilon_t} = 1. \tag{2.14}$$

This is far from certain in a non-experimental discipline, where Equation (2.13) could simply be a decomposition, so $\epsilon_t = y_t - \boldsymbol{\beta}' \mathbf{z}_{t-1}$, and not a causal model. Conversely, Equation (2.14) does hold if all errors are due to mis-measurement of y_t, but then is uninformative about causal structure. Further, residuals are inevitably derived representations of our ignorance; indeed, residuals may not even contain all the actual 'DGP shocks', because incorrectly included variables may have 'absorbed' some of those. The confusion of residuals with errors is an egregious mistake, as impulse responses are meaningless in a world of derived models.

Finally, GNC may be sufficient for the equivalence of standard-error based impulse responses from systems and conditional models, but does not ensure efficient or valid inferences unless the conditioning variables are weakly exogenous.

The implication of this analysis is that unless causality has been independently established between an input variable and an output, impulse responses are not a reliable inference procedure.

2.8. Conclusion

Both exogeneity and causality play different roles in modelling, forecasting and policy. This is well known for exogeneity, where different concepts have been explicitly defined in Engle *et al.* (1983), but seems less well established for causality. A cause was viewed as an asymmetrical process inducing change over time in a structure. The perceptive reader will not have missed the close connections to dynamic econometric systems, which are invariant to extensions of information (over time, interventions, and additional variables). When causality is defined within a theory model, the correspondence of the model to reality becomes the key link. Thus, we conclude that causality is important in modelling; and manifestly crucial in policy. However, causality cannot be proved to be a necessary property of variables in dominating forecasting models. When location shifts occur, robust forecasting methods can outperform 'causal models'. Nevertheless, by itself, such a finding – or even forecast failure – is insufficient to preclude the use of the causal model for policy; the reaction parameters of interest to policy could have remained constant, perhaps due to co-breaking.

Both concepts (exogeneity and causality) seem robust to extensions to non-stationary systems, but their implications are sometimes less clear cut, and inferences about them can be more hazardous. In particular, pre-existing exogeneity, or causal direction, can alter over time. Conversely, it can be difficult in weakly stationary systems to correctly ascertain exogeneity or causality since the systems in question do not change enough. Thus, the news is not all bad. For example, it is well known that co-integrated relations that remove unit roots provide a basis for testing long-run weak exogeneity; and policy-induced location shifts can highlight the presence or absence of causal links.

Granger causality shares many of the characteristics of the general definition, together with the resultant inferential difficulties. The require-ment that causality be judged against the universe of available information renders it non-operational; but attempts to infer GNC from empirical models become prone to serious errors unless a congruent, encompassing and invariant system is used.

The strength of evidence about causality depends on the magnitudes of changes in inputs, which nevertheless produce consistent output responses. Co-breaking with causal links is needed to sustain economic policy, since few policy changes are of the 'mean-preserving spread' form, and most involve location shifts. Although, the latter are the main problem for forecasting, in a progressive research strategy, the resultant forecast failure can be of benefit for modelling, and so later policy. Conversely, shifts in mean-zero parameters are difficult to detect in forecasting, but can seriously distort impulse response based policy analyses.

Finally, without mean co-breaking, or causal links, impulse responses need not deliver useful information about reactions in the economy. There seems no alternative to modelling the exogeneity and causality structure of the economy if reliable policy inferences are desired.

Acknowledgements

Financial support from the UK Economic and Social Research Council under grants RES-015-27-0035 and RES-000-23-0539 is gratefully acknowledged. I am indebted for helpful comments on an earlier draft to Nancy Cartwright, Mike Clements, Clive Granger, Michael Massmann, Grayham Mizon, Adrian Pagan, and Franz Palm; to participants at the 2001 EC2 meeting on 'Causality and Exogeneity in Econometrics' at Louvain-La-Neuve; and to four anonymous referees.

References

Allen, P.G. and R.A. Fildes (2001), "Econometric forecasting strategies and techniques", in: J.S. Armstrong, editor, *Principles of Forecasting*, pp. 303–362, Boston: Kluwer Academic Publishers.

Banerjee, A., D.F. Hendry and G.E. Mizon (1996), "The econometric analysis of economic policy", *Oxford Bulletin of Economics and Statistics*, Vol. 58, pp. 573–600.

Basmann, R.L. (1988), "Causality tests and observationally equivalent representations of econometric models", *Journal of Econometrics*, Vol. 39, pp. 69–104.

Bernanke, B.S. (1986), "Alternative explorations of the money–income correlation", in: K. Brunner and A.H. Meltzer, editors, *Real Business Cycles, Real Exchange Rates, and Actual Policies*, Carnegie-Rochester Conferences on Public Policy, Vol. 25, pp. 49–99, Amsterdam: North-Holland Publishing Company.

Bhansali, R.J. (2002), "Multi-step forecasting", in: M.P. Clements and D. Hendry, editors, *A Companion to Economic Forecasting*, pp. 206–221, Oxford: Blackwells.

Blalock, H.M.J. (1961), *Causal Inferences in Nonexperimental Research*, Chapel Hill: University of North Carolina Press.

Blanchard, O. and D. Quah (1989), "The dynamic effects of aggregate demand and supply disturbances", *American Economic Review*, Vol. 79, pp. 655–673.

Bontemps, C. and G.E. Mizon (2003), "Congruence and encompassing", in: B.P. Stigum, editor, *Econo-metrics and the Philosophy of Economics*, pp. 354–378, Princeton: Princeton University Press.

Boswijk, H.P. (1992), *Cointegration, Identification and Exogeneity*, Tinbergen Institute Research Series, Vol. 37, Amsterdam: Thesis Publishers.

Buiter, W.H. (1984), "Granger causality and policy effectiveness", *Economica*, Vol. 51, pp. 151–162.

Cartwright, N. (1983), *How the Laws of Physics Lie*, Oxford: Clarendon Press.

Cartwright, N. (1989), *Nature's Capacities and Their Measurement*, Oxford: Clarendon Press.

Chamberlain, G. (1982), "The general equivalence of Granger and Sims causality", *Econometrica*, Vol. 50, pp. 569–582.

Clements, M.P. and D.F. Hendry (1999), *Forecasting Non-stationary Economic Time Series*, Cambridge, MA: MIT Press.

Clements, M.P. and D.F. Hendry (2001a), "Explaining the results of the M3 forecasting competition", *International Journal of Forecasting*, Vol. 17, pp. 550–554.

Clements, M.P. and D.F. Hendry (2001b), "An historical perspective on forecast errors", *National Institute Economic Review*, Vol. 177, pp. 100–112.

Clements, M.P. and D.F. Hendry (2002), "Explaining forecast failure in macroeconomics", in: M.P. Clements and D. Hendry, editors, *A Companion to Economic Forecasting*, pp. 539–571, Oxford: Blackwells.

Clements, M.P. and D.F. Hendry (2003), "Evaluating a model by forecast performance", Unpublished Paper, Economics Department, University of Warwick.

Coveney, P. and R. Highfield (1990), *The Arrow of Time*, New York: Fawcett Columbine.

Cox, D.R. (1992), "Causality: some statistical aspects", *Journal of the Royal Statistical Society, A*, Vol. 155, pp. 291–301.

Dolado, J.J. (1992), "A note on weak exogeneity in VAR cointegrated systems", *Economics Letters*, Vol. 38, pp. 139–143.

Doll, R. (2001), "Proof of causality: deductions from epidemiological evidence", Fisher Memorial Lecture, University of Oxford, Oxford.

Engle, R.F. and D.F. Hendry (1993), "Testing super exogeneity and invariance in regression models", *Journal of Econometrics*, Vol. 56, pp. 119–139, Reprinted in: N.R. Ericsson and J.S. Irons, editors (1994), *Testing Exogeneity*, Oxford: Oxford University Press.

Engle, R.F., D.F. Hendry and J.-F. Richard (1983), "Exogeneity", *Econometrica*, Vol. 51, pp. 277–304, Reprinted in Hendry, D.F. (1993), *Econometrics: Alchemy or Science?*, Oxford: Blackwell Publishers (1993) and Oxford University Press (2000); in: N.R. Ericsson and J.S. Irons, editors (1994), *Testing Exogeneity*, Oxford: Oxford University Press.

Ericsson, N.R. (1992), "Cointegration, exogeneity and policy analysis: an overview", *Journal of Policy Modeling*, Vol. 14, pp. 251–280.

Ericsson, N.R. and J.S. Irons (1994), *Testing Exogeneity*, Oxford: Oxford University Press.

Ericsson, N.R., D.F. Hendry and G.E. Mizon (1998), "Exogeneity, cointegration and economic policy analysis", *Journal of Business and Economic Statistics*, Vol. 16, pp. 370–387.

Favero, C. and D.F. Hendry (1992), "Testing the Lucas critique: a review", *Econometric Reviews*, Vol. 11, pp. 265–306.

Fildes, R.A. and S. Makridakis (1995), "The impact of empirical accuracy studies on time series analysis and forecasting", *International Statistical Review*, Vol. 63, pp. 289–308.

Fischer, A.M. (1989), "Policy regime changes and monetary expectations: testing for super exogeneity", *Journal of Monetary Economics*, Vol. 24, pp. 423–436.

Florens, J.-P. and M. Mouchart (1982), "A note on non-causality", *Econometrica*, Vol. 50, pp. 583–592.

Florens, J.-P. and M. Mouchart (1985), "A linear theory for noncausality", *Econometrica*, Vol. 53, pp. 157–175.

Geweke, J.B. (1984), "Inference and causality in economic time series models", in: Z. Griliches and M.D. Intriligator, editors, *Handbook of Econometrics*, Vol. 2, Chapter 19, Amsterdam: North-Holland.

Gottlieb, A. (2000), *The Dream of Reason*, London: The Penguin Press.

Granger, C.W.J. (1969), "Investigating causal relations by econometric models and cross-spectral methods", *Econometrica*, Vol. 37, pp. 424–438.

Granger, C.W.J. (1980), "Testing for causality – a personal viewpoint", *Journal of Economic Dynamics and Control*, Vol. 2, pp. 329–352.

Granger, C.W.J. (1988a), "Causality, cointegration, and control", *Journal of Economic Dynamics and Control*, Vol. 12, pp. 551–559.

Granger, C.W.J. (1988b), "Some recent developments in the concept of causality", *Journal of Econometrics*, Vol. 39, pp. 199–211.

Granger, C.W.J. and M. Deutsch (1992), "Comments on the evaluation of policy models", *Journal of Policy Modeling*, Vol. 14, pp. 497–516.

Heckman, J.J. (2000), "Causal parameters and policy analysis in economics: a twentieth century retrospective", *Quarterly Journal of Economics*, Vol. 115, pp. 45–97.

Hendry, D.F. (1988), "The encompassing implications of feedback versus feedforward mechanisms in econometrics", *Oxford Economic Papers*, Vol. 40, pp. 132–149, Reprinted in N.R. Ericsson and J.S. Irons, editors (1994), *Testing Exogeneity*, Oxford: Oxford University Press.

Hendry, D.F. (1995a), *Dynamic Econometrics*, New edition, Oxford: Oxford University Press.

Hendry, D.F. (1995b), "Econometrics and business cycle empirics", *Economic Journal*, Vol. 105, pp. 1622–1636.

Hendry, D.F. (1995c), "On the interactions of unit roots and exogeneity", *Econometric Reviews*, Vol. 14, pp. 383–419.

Hendry, D.F. (1997), "The econometrics of macroeconomic forecasting", *Economic Journal*, Vol. 107, pp. 1330–1357, Reprinted in: T.C. Mills, editor (1999), *Economic Forecasting*, Edward Elgar.

Hendry, D.F. (2000a), *Econometrics: Alchemy or Science?*, New edition, Oxford: Oxford University Press.

Hendry, D.F. (2000b), "On detectable and non-detectable structural change", *Structural Change and Economic Dynamics*, Vol. 11, pp. 45–65, Reprinted in: H. Hagemann, M. Landesman and Scazzieri, editors (2002) *The Economics of Structural Change*, Cheltenham: Edward Elgar.

Hendry, D.F. (2003), "A modified Gauss–Markov theorem for stochastic regressors", Unpublished paper, Economics Department, Oxford University.

Hendry, D.F. (2004), "Robustifying forecasts from equilibrium-correction models", Unpublished paper, Economics Department, University of Oxford.

Hendry, D.F. and M.P. Clements (2003), "Economic forecasting: some lessons from recent research", *Economic Modelling*, Vol. 20, pp. 301–329, Working Paper 82, European Central Bank.

Hendry, D.F. and J.A. Doornik (1997), "The implications for econometric modelling of forecast failure", *Scottish Journal of Political Economy*, Vol. 44, pp. 437–461, (Special Issue).

Hendry, D.F. and G.E. Mizon (1998), "Exogeneity, causality, and co-breaking in economic policy analysis of a small econometric model of money in the UK", *Empirical Economics*, Vol. 23, pp. 267–294.

Hendry, D.F. and G.E. Mizon (1999), "The pervasiveness of Granger causality in econometrics", in: R.F. Engle and H. White, editors, *Cointegration, Causality and Forecasting*, Oxford: Oxford University Press.

Hendry, D.F. and G.E. Mizon (2000), "Reformulating empirical macro-econometric modelling", *Oxford Review of Economic Policy*, Vol. 16, pp. 138–159.

Hendry, D.F. and M.S. Morgan (1995), *The Foundations of Econometric Analysis*, Cambridge: Cambridge University Press.

Holland, P.W. (1986), "Statistics and causal inference", *Journal of the American Statistical Association*, Vol. 81, pp. 945–960 and 968–970.

Hoover, K.D. (1990), "The logic of causal inference: econometrics and the conditional analysis of causation", *Economics and Philosophy*, Vol. 6, pp. 207–234.

Hoover, K.D. (2001), *Causality in Macroeconomics*, Cambridge: Cambridge University Press.

Hume, D. (1758), *An Enquiry Concerning Human Understanding* (1927 ed.), Chicago: Open Court Publishing Co.

Hunter, J. (1992a), "Cointegrating exogeneity", *Economics Letters*, Vol. 34, pp. 33–35.

Hunter, J. (1992b), "Tests of cointegrating exogeneity for PPP and uncovered interest rate parity in the United Kingdom", *Journal of Policy Modeling*, Vol. 14, pp. 453–463.

Johansen, S. (1992), "Testing weak exogeneity and the order of cointegration in UK money demand", *Journal of Policy Modeling*, Vol. 14, pp. 313–334.

Johansen, S. and K. Juselius (2000), "How to control a target variable in the VAR model", Mimeo, European University of Institute, Florence.

Koopmans, T.C. (1950), "When is an equation system complete for statistical purposes?", in: T.C. Koopmans, editor, *Statistical Inference in Dynamic Economic Models*, Cowles Commission Monograph, Vol. 10, Chapter 17, New York: Wiley.

Krolzig, H.-M. and J. Toro (2002), "Testing for super-exogeneity in the presence of common deterministic shifts", *Annales d' Économie et de Statistique*, Vol. 67/68, pp. 41–71.

Lauritzen, S.L. and T.S. Richardson (2002), "Chain graph models and their causal interpretations", *Journal of the Royal Statistical Society, B*, Vol. 64, pp. 1–28.

Lucas, R.E. (1976), "Econometric policy evaluation: a critique", in: K. Brunner and A. Meltzer, editors, *The Phillips Curve and Labor Markets, Carnegie–Rochester Conferences on Public Policy*, Vol. 1, pp. 19–46, Amsterdam: North-Holland Publishing Company.

Lütkepohl, H. (1982), "Non-causality due to omitted variables", *Journal of Econometrics*, Vol. 19, pp. 367–378.

Lütkepohl, H. (1991), *Introduction to Multiple Time Series Analysis*, New York: Springer-Verlag.

Makridakis, S. and M. Hibon (2000), "The M3-competition: results, conclusions and implications", *International Journal of Forecasting*, Vol. 16, pp. 451–476.

Massmann, M. (2001), "Co-breaking in macroeconomic time series", Unpublished paper, Economics Department, Oxford University.

Mizon, G.E. (1995), "Progressive modelling of macroeconomic time series: the LSE methodology", in: K.D. Hoover, editor, *Macroeconometrics: Developments, Tensions and Prospects*, pp. 107–169, Dordrecht: Kluwer Academic Press.

Morgan, M.S. (1990), *The History of Econometric Ideas*, Cambridge: Cambridge University Press.

Mosconi, R. and C. Giannini (1992), "Non-causality in cointegrated systems: representation, estimation and testing", *Oxford Bulletin of Economics and Statistics*, Vol. 54, pp. 399–417.

Newbold, P. (1982), "Causality testing in economics", in: O. Anderson, editor, *Time Series Analysis: Theory and Practice 1*, pp. 701–716, Amsterdam, The Netherlands: North Holland.

Paruolo, P. and A. Rahbek (1999), "Weak exogeneity in I(2) systems", *Journal of Econometrics*, Vol. 93, pp. 281–308.

Penrose, R. (1989), *The Emperor's New Mind*, Oxford: Oxford University Press.

Phillips, A.W.H. (1957), "Stabilization policy and the time form of lagged response", *Economic Journal*, Vol. 67, pp. 265–277, Reprinted in: R. Leeson, editor (2000), *A. W. H. Phillips: Collected Works in Contemporary Perspective*, Cambridge: Cambridge University Press.

Phillips, P.C.B. (1988), "Reflections on econometric methodology", *Economic Record*, Vol. 64, pp. 344–359.

Phillips, P.C.B. and M. Loretan (1991), "Estimating long-run economic equilibria", *Review of Economic Studies*, Vol. 58, pp. 407–436.

Richard, J.-F. (1980), "Models with several regimes and changes in exogeneity", *Review of Economic Studies*, Vol. 47, pp. 1–20.

Runkle, D.E. (1987), "Vector autoregressions and reality", *Journal of Business and Economic Statistics*, Vol. 5, pp. 437–442.

Simon, H.A. (1952), "On the definition of causal relations", *Journal of Philosophy*, Vol. 49, pp. 517–527.

Simon, H.A. (1953), "Causal ordering and identifiability", in: W.C. Hood and T.C. Koopmans, editors, *Studies in Econometric Method, Cowles Commission Monograph*, Vol. 14, Chapter 3, New York: Wiley.

Simon, H.A. (1957), *Models of Man*, New York: Wiley.

Sims, C.A. (1972), "Money, income and causality", *American Economic Review*, Vol. 62, pp. 540–552.

Sims, C.A. (1980), "Macroeconomics and reality", *Econometrica*, Vol. 48, pp. 1–48, Reprinted in: C.W.J. Granger, editor (1990), *Modelling Economic Series*, Oxford: Clarendon Press.

Singer, M. (1997), "Thoughts of a nonmillenarian", *Bulletin of the American Academy of Arts and Sciences*, Vol. 51(2), pp. 36–51.

Smith, A. (1795), *The History of Astronomy*, pp. 33–105, Edinburgh: W. Creech. in: I.S. Ross, editor (1982) Liberty Classics edition.

Stock, J.H. and M.W. Watson (1996), "Evidence on structural instability in macroeconomic time series relations", *Journal of Business and Economic Statistics*, Vol. 14, pp. 11–30.

Strotz, R.H. and H.O.A. Wold (1960), "Recursive versus non-recursive systems: an attempt at a synthesis", *Econometrica*, Vol. 28, pp. 417–421.

Toda, H.Y. and P.C.B. Phillips (1993), "Vector autoregressions and causality", *Econometrica*, Vol. 61, pp. 1367–1393.

Toda, H.Y. and P.C.B. Phillips (1994), "Vector autoregressions and causality: a theoretical overview and simulation study", *Econometric Reviews*, Vol. 13, pp. 259–285.

Urbain, J.-P. (1992), "On weak exogeneity in error correction models", *Oxford Bulletin of Economics and Statistics*, Vol. 54, pp. 187–207.

Weissmann, G. (1991), "Asprin", *Scientific American*, pp. 58–64.

Wold, H.O.A. (1969), "Econometrics as pioneering in non-experimental model building", *Econometrica*, Vol. 37, pp. 369–381.

Yule, G.U. (1897), "On the theory of correlation", *Journal of the Royal Statistical Society*, Vol. 60, pp. 812–838.

Yule, G.U. (1926), "Why do we sometimes get nonsense-correlations between time-series? A study in sampling and the nature of time series (with discussion)", *Journal of the Royal Statistical Society*, Vol. 89, pp. 1–64, Reprinted in: D.F. Hendry and M.S. Morgan (1995), *The Foundations of Econometric Analysis*, Cambridge: Cambridge University Press.

Zellner, A. (1979), "Causality and econometrics", in: K. Brunner and A. Meltzer, editors, *The Phillips Curve and Labor Markets*, pp. 9–54, Amsterdam: North-Holland Publishing Company.

New Directions in Macromodelling
A. Welfe (Editor)
DOI: 10.1016/S0573-8555(04)69003-1

CHAPTER 3

A Small Sample Correction of the Dickey–Fuller Test

Søren Johansen

Department of Applied Mathematics and Statistics, University of Copenhagen,
Universitetsparken 5, 2100 Copenhagen O, Denmark

Abstract

The purpose of this chapter is to investigate the small sample correction derived in Johansen (Econometrica (2002) Vol. 70, pp. 1929–1961) for the test for cointegrating rank in the special case of the Dickey–Fuller test. We find an explicit form for the correction and investigate the relevance by simulations. It is seen that for small samples, the Dickey Fuller test has size distortions, and that the correction factor helps conducting reliable inference. For parameters close to the I(2) boundary the size distortion can be serious. The simulation experiments indicate that when the correction factor is less than 1.14 the corrected test gives a rejection probability close to 5%.

Keywords: small sample correction, likelihood ratio test, test for unit root, Dickey–Fuller test

JEL classifications: C32

3.1. Introduction and main result

We consider the likelihood ratio test for the hypothesis $\mathcal{M}_k^0 : \pi = \beta = 0$, in the autoregressive model with k lags for x_t

$$\mathcal{M}_k : \Delta x_t = \pi x_{t-1} + \beta t^d + \sum_{i=1}^{k-1} \gamma_i \Delta x_{t-i} + \sum_{i=0}^{d-1} \beta_i t^i + \varepsilon_t, \tag{3.1}$$

where ε_t are i.i.d. $N(0, \sigma^2)$, see Dickey and Fuller (1981). Note that under the null hypothesis x_t becomes non-stationary, and that it has a trend of order d, both under the null hypothesis and the alternative hypothesis of non-stationarity. We choose this version of the unit root test because the distribution of the test statistic under the null hypothesis does not depend on the parameters of the deterministic terms.

If $\mathcal{M}_k^0$ holds, so that $\pi = \beta = 0$ and the process Δx_t is stationary, the asymptotic distribution of $-2 \log \text{LR}$, under the assumption of i.i.d. errors with mean zero and finite variance, is given by

$$-2 \log \text{LR}(\pi = \beta = 0) \xrightarrow{w} \int_0^1 (dB)F' \left(\int_0^1 FF'du \right)^{-1} \int_0^1 F(dB),$$

where B is a standard Brownian motion on $[0,1]$ and

$$F(u) = \left(\begin{array}{c} B(u) \\ u^d \end{array} \bigg| 1, ..., u^{d-1} \right),$$

that is, the Brownian motion $B(u)$ and the trend u^d corrected for $(1, ..., u^{d-1})$ on the unit interval.

The asymptotic distribution is tabulated by simulation since it contains no parameters, but the finite sample distribution depends on T and the parameters $\gamma = (\gamma_1, ..., \gamma_{k-1})$ under the null hypothesis, but not on $\beta_0, ..., \beta_{d-1}$ and σ^2. For $T \to \infty$ the dependence on γ disappears, but not uniformly in γ. If γ is close to the boundary where Δx_t becomes non-stationary, the approximation can be rather poor, as we shall demonstrate by simulations.

In Johansen (2002) an analytic approximation to the expectation of the likelihood ratio test for cointegrating rank is derived. A special case of that is of course the above Dickey–Fuller test, and the purpose of this chapter is to see what the formulae look like in this univariate case, and by simulations see if the approximation helps making reliable inference. The idea is to use the approximation of the expectation to derive a correction factor to the likelihood ratio test. It turns out that this correction factor depends on the parameters only through the quantity

$$\frac{\sum_{i=1}^{k-1} i\gamma_i}{1 - \sum_{i=1}^{k-1} \gamma_i}, \tag{3.2}$$

see Theorem 1, and the main contribution here is the reduction of the general expression for the correction factor found in Johansen (2002) to an expression involving only Equation (3.2).

Theorem 1. *Under the assumption that x_t is an $I(1)$ process given by model (3.1) with $\pi = \beta = 0$, the correction factor for the likelihood ratio test for $\pi = \beta = 0$ is given by*

$$a_T(d)$$

$$\times \left(1 + \frac{1}{T} \left[\left(k - 1 + 2 \frac{\sum_{i=1}^{k-1} i \gamma_i}{1 - \sum_{i=1}^{k-1} \gamma_i} \right) m(d) + \frac{1}{2}((-1)^{k-1} - 1)g(d) \right] \right).$$

$$(3.3)$$

The functions $g(d), m(d)$, and $a_T(d) = 1 + a_1(d)T^{-1} + a_2(d)T^{-2}$ are given in Table 3.1 for $d = 0, 1, 2$, and for the model without deterministic terms, $d = *$.

We conclude this section by discussing briefly the Bartlett correction and the interpretation of the correction factor. The proofs are given in the Appendix A.

3.1.1. The Bartlett correction

Bartlett (1937) suggested finding the expectation of the likelihood ratio test statistic and use that, or an approximation of it, to correct the likelihood ratio statistic to have (approximately) the same mean as the limit distribution. He proved that in certain cases not only the mean was better approximated but it also held for all higher moments. In order to exploit

Table 3.1.   The values for $g(d), d = *, 0, 1$ are taken from Nielsen (1997a). The coefficients $a_1(d), a_2(d), g(2)$ are found by 2.5 mill. simulations of some moments of random walk. The results for $d = *$ correspond to the model without deterministic terms. The number of simulations for determinations of $m(*), m(0), m(1), m(2)$ is (11, 13.5, 4.7, 4) mill.

	Coefficients for the correction factor				
d	$g(d)$	$m(d)$	$sd\ m(d)$	$a_1(d)$	$a_2(d)$
*	− 0.5601	0.545	0.064	− 0.0233	1.1518
0	− 0.3262	0.748	0.035	0.2123	1.4259
1	− 0.6209	0.860	0.044	0.1212	4.0538
2	− 0.7304	0.932	0.049	0.0788	7.4031

this idea we, therefore, want an approximation to

$$E_{\gamma,T}[-2 \log \text{LR}\{\pi = \beta = 0\}] = E_{\gamma,T}[-2 \log \text{LR}\{\mathcal{M}_k^0 | \mathcal{M}_k\}], \qquad (3.4)$$

which is a function of γ and T under the assumption of Gaussian errors. In Johansen (2002) we derived an analytic approximation of the ratio

$$\frac{E_{\gamma,T}[-2 \log \text{LR}\{\mathcal{M}_k^0 | \mathcal{M}_k\}]}{E_T[-2 \log \text{LR}\{\mathcal{M}_1^0 | \mathcal{M}_1\}]} = 1 + \frac{b(\gamma)}{T} + \cdots,$$

where $\mathcal{M}_1^0$ corresponds to $\pi = \beta = 0$ in the model

$$\mathcal{M}_1 : \Delta x_t = \pi x_{t-1} + \beta t^d + \sum_{i=0}^{d-1} \beta_i t^i + \varepsilon_t. \qquad (3.5)$$

When $\pi = \beta = 0$, the expectation

$$f_T(d) = E_T[-2 \log \text{LR}\{\mathcal{M}_1^0 | \mathcal{M}_1\}]$$

only depends on d and T, and can, therefore, be tabulated by simulation. We define $f(d) = \lim_{T \to \infty} f_T(d)$, and approximate $f_T(d)$ by

$$f(d)(1 + a_1(d)T^{-1} + a_2(d)T^{-2}) = f(d)a_T(d).$$

From Nielsen (1997a) we have the values calculated from analytic expressions

$$f(*) = 1.1416, \ f(0) = 4.0560, \ f(1) = 6.3207, \qquad (3.6)$$

and the remaining coefficients $f(2)$ and $a_i(d)$ are determined by regression of the simulated values of $f_T(d)$ on $(1, T^{-1}, T^{-2})$.

We therefore suggest to use the test statistic

$$\frac{f(d)}{f_T(d)} \frac{-2 \log \text{LR}}{(1 + T^{-1}b(\hat{\gamma}))} = \frac{-2 \log \text{LR}}{a_T(d)(1 + T^{-1}b(\hat{\gamma}))},$$

or equivalently use the usual likelihood ratio test statistic and correct the asymptotic quantiles by the factor $a_T(d)(1 + T^{-1}b(\hat{\gamma}))$.

For the Dickey–Fuller test we cannot expect that the correction factor improves the approximation by an order of magnitude in an expansion, because, as Jensen and Wood (1997) show for the model without deterministics and one lag, this does not hold for the Dickey–Fuller test. However, the correction idea seems to work in practice as investigated by Johansen (2002) and Nielsen (1997b, 2004).

3.1.2. The correction factor

We next want to give an interpretation of the factor (3.2), which depends on the parameters, and, therefore, study the univariate autoregressive process x_t under the null hypothesis by means of the stacked process

$$y_t = (\Delta x_t, \Delta x_{t-1}, \dots, \Delta x_{t-k+2})'$$

corrected for its mean. The process y_t is a stationary AR(1) process of dimension $k - 1$, which satisfies the equations

$$y_t = P y_{t-1} + Q \varepsilon_t,$$

where

$$P = \begin{pmatrix} \gamma_1 & \cdots & \gamma_{k-2} & \gamma_{k-1} \\ 1 & \cdots & 0 & 0 \\ \vdots & & \vdots & \vdots \\ 0 & \cdots & 1 & 0 \end{pmatrix}, \quad Q = \begin{pmatrix} 1 \\ 0 \\ \vdots \\ 0 \end{pmatrix}. \tag{3.7}$$

The process is given by

$$y_t = \sum_{m=0}^{\infty} P^m Q \varepsilon_{t-m},$$

with variance $\Sigma = \mathrm{Var}(y_t)$ and autocovariance function

$$\Sigma = \sigma^2 \sum_{m=0}^{\infty} P^m QQ' P^{m'}, \quad \gamma(h) = \mathrm{Cov}(y_t, y_{t+h}) = \Sigma P^{h'}. \tag{3.8}$$

We define the long-run coefficient

$$\psi = \sum_{m=0}^{\infty} P^m Q = (I_{k-1} - P)^{-1} Q, \tag{3.9}$$

and the long-run variance

$$\Sigma_{\text{long}} = \lim_{T \to \infty} T^{-1} \mathrm{Var}\left(\sum_{t=1}^{T} y_t\right) = \sigma^2 (I_{k-1} - P)^{-1} QQ'(I_{k-1} - P')^{-1}$$

$$= \frac{\sigma^2}{\phi(1)^2} \iota \iota',$$

where $\iota = (1,\dots,1)'$, and $\phi(z) = 1 - \sum_{i=1}^{k-1} \gamma_i z^i$, so that $(I_{k-1} - P)\iota = \phi(1)Q$.

It follows from the general expression for the correction factor, see Appendix A3.2, that the main parameter dependence is through

$$\text{tr}\{\Sigma^{-1}\Sigma_{\text{long}}\} = \frac{\sigma^2 \iota' \Sigma^{-1} \iota}{\phi(1)^2}. \tag{3.10}$$

Another interpretation of this quantity is

$$\text{as.Var}(\log\hat{\phi}(1)) = \frac{\text{as.Var}(\hat{\phi}(1))}{\phi(1)^2} = \frac{\sigma^2 \iota' \Sigma^{-1} \iota}{\phi(1)^2},$$

because the asymptotic variance of $T^{1/2}(\hat{\gamma}_1 - \gamma_1, ..., \hat{\gamma}_{k-1} - \gamma_{k-1})$ is $\sigma^2 \Sigma^{-1}$.

When applying the results we need the process Δx_t to be stationary, that is, $\sum_{i=1}^{k-1} \gamma_i < 1$, and it is seen that

$$\frac{\phi(1)^2}{\sigma^2 \iota' \Sigma^{-1} \iota} = \frac{\left(1 - \sum_{i=1}^{k-1} \gamma_i\right)^2}{\sigma^2 \iota' \Sigma^{-1} \iota}$$

measures the deviation from the unit root using the variance of the estimate.

When the distance is small, we get a large correction factor but then we would probably accept another unit root and the results derived here would not be valid.

We also want to give an interpretation in terms of the eigenvalues $\rho_1, ..., \rho_{k-1}$ of the matrix P, see Equation (3.7). From $\phi(z) = \prod_{i=1}^{k-1}(1 - z\rho_i)$, and $\log\phi(1) = \sum_{i=1}^{k-1} \log(1 - \rho_i)$, we find

$$\text{as.Var}(\log\hat{\phi}(1)) = \sum_{i,j} \frac{1}{1 - \rho_i} \text{as.Var}(\hat{\rho}_i, \hat{\rho}_j) \frac{1}{1 - \rho_j}$$

$$= \left\{\frac{1}{1 - \rho_i}\right\}' \left\{\frac{1}{1 - \rho_i \rho_j}\right\}^{-1} \left\{\frac{1}{1 - \rho_j}\right\},$$

if the eigenvalues are distinct and real, see Johansen (2003). It follows from Equation (3.14) that $\text{tr}\{\Sigma^{-1}\Sigma_{\text{long}}\} = \sigma^2 \iota' \Sigma^{-1} \iota/\phi(1)^2$ and from Equation (3.19) in Corollary 3, that it equals

$$\sum_{i=1}^{k-1} \frac{1 + \rho_i}{1 - \rho_i} = k - 1 - 2\frac{d\log\phi(z)}{dz}\bigg|_{z=1} = k - 1 + 2\frac{\sum_{i=1}^{k-1} i\gamma_i}{1 - \sum_{i=1}^{k-1} \gamma_i}.$$

Thus, the main parameter dependence is summarized in the ratio of the long-run to the short-run variance, or simply in the asymptotic variance of $\log(1 - \sum_{i=1}^{k-1} \hat{\gamma}_i)$, or as the inverse distance to the unit root, and finally as the ratio $(\sum_{i=1}^{k-1} i\gamma_i)/(1 - \sum_{i=1}^{k-1} \gamma_i)$.

It is seen that when the model for Δx_t has a near unit root, $\sum_{i=1}^{k-1} \gamma_i \sim 1$, the correction factor becomes very large and, as will be seen from the simulation experiments, this corresponds to the situation where it is difficult to make reliable inference, because the asymptotic test may have serious size distortions.

3.2. A simulation experiment

In order to illustrate the results we consider the simulation of the rejection probability for the likelihood ratio test for the hypothesis $\pi = \beta = 0$ in the model

$$\Delta x_t = \pi x_{t-1} + \beta t + \sum_{i=1}^{k-1} \gamma_i \Delta X_{t-i} + \beta_0 + \varepsilon_t. \tag{3.11}$$

Under the null hypothesis, the distribution depends on the parameters $\gamma_1, \ldots, \gamma_{k-1}$ and T. We choose $k = 2, 3$, and $T = 10, 15$ and $k = 7$ and $T = 25, 50$. We tabulate the rejection probabilities by simulation for some values of γ_1 and γ_2, and for $k = 7$ we choose $\gamma_3 = \ldots = \gamma_6 = 0$.

In all experiments we assume that the lag length is known, and we give three rejection probabilities. First, the one we get by using the asymptotic tables, p, next the one we get by using the correction factor for the true parameter value, p_{corr}, and finally the one we get by estimating the parameter in every simulation, and then use the estimated correction factor, $p_{\text{corr}}^{\text{est}}$.

For $k = 3, 7$, the parameter values $\gamma_1 + \gamma_2 = 1$ and $0 < \gamma_1 < 2$ correspond to x_t being $I(2)$, and for the point $\gamma_1 = 2$, $\gamma_2 = -1$, the process is $I(3)$. For $k = 2$, we get an $I(2)$ process when $\gamma_1 = 1$. The results, given in Table 3.2, are based on 10,000 simulations.

As an example consider the experiment with $k = 3, T = 10$, and $\gamma_2 = 0$, where the rejection probability of a nominal 5% test ranges from 13 to 23% close to the $I(2)$ boundary given by $\gamma_1 = 0$. Introducing the correction with known parameters inserted, brings these values down to 8–6% for $\gamma_1 \leq 0.3$, but close to the $I(2)$ boundary the correction is too large due to the factor $1/(1 - \gamma_1)$. Strangely enough, by inserting the estimated parameter in the correction for each simulation, we get value

56 S. Johansen

Table 3.2. *For the likelihood ratio test of $\pi = \beta = 0$ in model (3.10) we give the rejection probability of a nominal 5% test based upon 10,000 simulations p. We also give the corrected rejection probabilities with known parameter, p_{corr}, and corrected rejection probabilities with estimated parameters, p_{corr}^{est}. For $k = 7$, we take $\gamma_3 = \cdots = \gamma_6 = 0$. The lag length is assumed known*

		$T = 10$				$T = 15$			
γ_1	γ_2	p	p_{corr}	p_{corr}^{est}	Factor	p	p_{corr}	p_{corr}^{est}	Factor
$k = 2$									
-0.9		0.082	0.050	0.049	1.114	0.066	0.050	0.049	1.066
-0.3		0.097	0.051	0.051	1.158	0.083	0.057	0.056	1.094
0.3		0.135	0.049	0.053	1.277	0.090	0.044	0.047	1.172
0.9		0.178	0.000	0.074	2.829	0.138	0.001	0.054	2.180
$k = 3$									
-0.9	0.0	0.132	0.082	0.080	1.148	0.083	0.059	0.057	1.088
-0.3	0.0	0.129	0.067	0.071	1.192	0.087	0.053	0.055	1.117
0.3	0.0	0.172	0.067	0.089	1.311	0.104	0.046	0.054	1.194
0.9	0.0	0.233	0.001	0.118	2.863	0.178	0.001	0.079	2.203
0.0	-0.9	0.130	0.108	0.107	1.062	0.077	0.068	0.067	1.032
0.0	-0.3	0.130	0.080	0.081	1.150	0.085	0.060	0.060	1.089
0.0	0.3	0.165	0.049	0.075	1.389	0.106	0.039	0.048	1.245
0.0	0.9	0.205	0.000	0.096	4.493	0.159	0.000	0.074	3.262

		$T = 25$				$T = 50$			
γ_1	γ_2	P	p_{corr}	p_{corr}^{est}	Factor	p	p_{corr}	p_{corr}^{est}	Factor
$k = 7$									
-0.9	0.0	0.117	0.059	0.064	1.187	0.087	0.056	0.056	1.109
-0.3	0.0	0.130	0.062	0.070	1.204	0.080	0.050	0.052	1.117
0.3	0.0	0.150	0.060	0.074	1.250	0.093	0.054	0.056	1.140
0.9	0.0	0.238	0.015	0.131	1.846	0.151	0.027	0.068	1.436
0.0	-0.9	0.104	0.057	0.060	1.154	0.069	0.048	0.048	1.075
0.0	-0.3	0.125	0.061	0.067	1.188	0.072	0.049	0.050	1.092
0.0	0.3	0.155	0.057	0.076	1.280	0.089	0.049	0.051	1.137
0.0	0.9	0.225	0.001	0.128	2.473	0.145	0.006	0.056	1.729

from 8–12% for the whole range. This is due to the bias in the estimation of γ_1. Obviously, increasing the sample size to $T = 15$ improves matters, so that the range 8–18% can be reduced to 5–8% for the corrected test.

If one should extract a rule of thumb from these experiments, it would be that when the correction factor is less than 1.14 the corrected test improves the accuracy of the Dickey–Fuller test. Note that the factor $a_T(d)$, for $T = 10$, contributes at most 8% (for $d = 2$) to the correction factor. The rest is due to the parameter dependence.

Acknowledgements

The author would like to thank Henrik Hansen, David Hendry, Bent Nielsen, Peter Boswijk and the participants in the ESF–EMM network for useful reference and discussions. The author is grateful for support from the Danish Social Sciences Research Council.

References

Bartlett, M.S. (1937), "Properties of sufficiency and statistical tests", *Proceedings of the Royal Society of London Series A*, Vol. 160, pp. 268–282.

Dickey, D.A. and W.A. Fuller (1981), "Likelihood ratio statistics for autoregressive time series with a unit root", *Econometrica*, Vol. 49, pp. 1057–1072.

Galbraith, R.F. and J.I. Galbraith (1974), "On the inverses of some patterned matrices arising in the theory of stationary time series", *Journal of Applied Probability*, Vol. 11, pp. 63–71.

Jensen, J.L. and A.T.A. Wood (1997), "On the non-existence of a Bartlett correction for unit root tests", *Statistics and Probability Letters*, Vol. 35, pp. 181–187.

Johansen, S. (2002), "A small sample correction of the test for cointegrating rank in the vector autoregressive model", *Econometrica*, Vol. 70, pp. 1929–1961.

Johansen, S. (2003), "The variance of the estimated roots in a cointegrated vector autoregressive model", *Journal of Time Series Analysis*, Vol. 24(6), pp. 663–678.

Nielsen, B. (1997a), "On the distribution of cointegration tests", Ph.D. thesis, University of Copenhagen.

Nielsen, B. (1997b), "Bartlett correction of the unit root test in autoregressive models", *Biometrika*, Vol. 84, pp. 500–504.

Nielsen, B. (2004), "On the distribution of likelihood ratio test statistics for cointegration rank", *Econometric Reviews*, Vol. 23, pp. 1–23.

Shaman, P. and R.A. Stine (1988), "The bias of autoregressive coefficient estimators", *Journal of the American Statistical Association*, Vol. 83, pp. 842–848.

Wise, J. (1955), "The autocorrelation function and the spectral density function", *Biometrika*, Vol. 42, pp. 151–159.

Appendix A

In this Appendix, we first prove some identities, which we then apply to reduce the general expression in the formula for the correction factor.

A3.1. Some matrix identities

We study the general expression for the correction factor using an eigenvalue decomposition of the matrix P, and we assume in the following that the eigenvalues are all of multiplicity one. This is no loss of generality as the results we prove are continuous functions of P. Let, therefore, ρ be an eigenvalue of P of multiplicity one. The left eigenvector is

$$\tau_\rho' = (1, \rho - \gamma_1, \rho^2 - \rho\gamma_1 - \gamma_2, ..., \rho^{k-2} - \rho^{k-3}\gamma_1 - ... - \gamma_{k-2})$$

and the right eigenvector is

$$\kappa_\rho' = (\rho^{k-2}, \rho^{k-3}, ..., 1)'.$$

We define the vector

$$v_\eta = (1, \eta, ..., \eta^{k-2})',$$

and find the relation

$$(I_{k-1} - \eta P)v_\eta = \phi(\eta)Q. \tag{3.12}$$

Multiplying by τ_ρ' we find

$$\tau_\rho' v_\eta = \frac{\phi(\eta)}{1 - \rho\eta}, \rho\eta \neq 1. \tag{3.13}$$

We collect the left eigenvectors in the matrix

$$\mathcal{T} = (\tau_1, \tau_2, ..., \tau_{k-1}),$$

corresponding to the eigenvalues $\rho, ..., \rho_{k-1}$, and find that the variance can be simplified because

$$\tau_\rho' \Sigma \tau_\eta = \sigma^2 \sum_{m=0}^{\infty} \rho^m \tau_\rho' QQ' \tau_\eta \eta^m = \frac{\sigma^2}{1 - \rho\eta}.$$

We introduce the coefficient

$$c(\eta) = \sigma^2 \frac{v_1' \Sigma^{-1} v_\eta}{\phi(1)\phi(\eta)} = \sigma^2 \frac{v_1' \mathcal{T}(\mathcal{T}' \Sigma \mathcal{T})^{-1} \mathcal{T}' v_\eta}{\phi(1)\phi(\eta)}$$

$$= \left\{\frac{1}{1-\rho_i}\right\}' \left\{\frac{1}{1-\rho_i\rho_j}\right\}^{-1} \left\{\frac{1}{1-\eta\rho_i}\right\}, \tag{3.14}$$

where the last result follows from Equation (3.13). For $\eta = 1$ we get the coefficient in Equation (3.10).

We find the coefficient $c(\eta)$ in Corollary 3 expressed in terms of the eigenvalues of P, but the coefficient $c(1)$ can also be found from a result of Wise (1955), where an explicit expression for Σ^{-1} is given in terms of γ. For $\gamma_0 = -1$ we have

$$\Sigma^{ij} = \sum_{m=0}^{i-1} \gamma_m \gamma_{m+j-i} - \sum_{m=k-j}^{k-1+i-j} \gamma_m \gamma_{m+j-i}, i \le j,$$

see Galbraith and Galbraith (1974, formula (16) p. 70), or Shaman and Stine (1988), where the result $c(1) = k - 1 - 2d \log\phi(z)/dz|_{z=1}$ is given.

We next prove some identities involving the distinct complex numbers $\rho_1, \ldots, \rho_l$.

Lemma 2. *Let the* $\rho \ne 0, \rho_1, \ldots, \rho_l$ *be distinct and less than one in absolute value, then the identities hold*

$$\sum_{i=1}^{l} \frac{1+\rho_i}{1-\rho_i\rho_m} \frac{\prod_{j\ne i}(1-\rho_i\rho_j)}{\prod_{j\ne i}(\rho_i-\rho_j)} = \frac{1}{1-\rho_m}, \tag{3.15}$$

$$\sum_{i=1}^{l} \frac{1+\rho_i}{1-\rho\rho_i} \frac{\prod_{j\ne i}(1-\rho_i\rho_j)}{\prod_{j\ne i}(\rho_i-\rho_j)} = \sum_{i=1}^{l} \frac{1+\rho_i}{\rho-\rho_i} \frac{\prod_{j=1}^{i}(\rho-\rho_j)}{\prod_{j=1}^{i}(1-\rho\rho_j)}. \tag{3.16}$$

Proof. We first prove Equation (3.15). We consider the left hand side as a function of $z = \rho_m$ and find for $z \ne 1, \rho_1, \ldots, \rho_l$

$$f(z) = \frac{1}{1-z} \frac{\prod_{j\ne m}(1-z\rho_j)}{\prod_{j\ne m}(z-\rho_j)} + \sum_{i\ne m} \frac{1+\rho_i}{\rho_i-z} \frac{\prod_{j\ne i,m}(1-\rho_i\rho_j)}{\prod_{j\ne i,m}(\rho_i-\rho_j)}.$$

The rational function $f(z)$ has poles of order one at the points $z = 1$, and $z = \rho_i, i \neq m$, and the value zero at ∞. Hence, it has the expansion

$$f(z) = \frac{b_m}{1-z} + \sum_{i \neq m} \frac{b_i}{z - \rho_i}.$$

We find the coefficients from $b_m = (1-z)f(z)|_{z=1} = 1$, and $b_i = (z - \rho_i)f(z)|_{z=\rho_i}$, which gives

$$b_i = \frac{1 - \rho_i\rho_i}{1 - \rho_i} \frac{\prod_{j \neq m,i}(1 - \rho_i\rho_j)}{\prod_{j \neq m,i}(\rho_i - \rho_j)} - (1 + \rho_i)\frac{\prod_{j \neq i,m}(1 - \rho_i\rho_j)}{\prod_{j \neq i,m}(\rho_i - \rho_j)} = 0,$$

so that $f(z) = 1/(1-z)$, and $f(\rho_m) = 1/(1 - \rho_m)$, which proves Equation (3.15).

The next result, Equation (3.16), is proved by induction in a similar way. We define

$$S_m = \sum_{i=1}^{m} \frac{1 + \rho_i}{1 - \rho\rho_i} \frac{\prod_{j \neq i}(1 - \rho_i\rho_j)}{\prod_{j \neq i}(\rho_i - \rho_j)}, m = 1, \ldots, l,$$

and replace ρ_l by z and define the rational function $f(z)$ for $z \neq \rho^{-1}, \rho_1, \ldots, \rho_{l-1}$

$$f(z) = \frac{1 + z}{1 - \rho z} \frac{\prod_{j=1}^{l-1}(1 - z\rho_j)}{\prod_{j=1}^{l-1}(z - \rho_j)} + \sum_{i=1}^{l-1} \frac{1 + \rho_i}{1 - \rho\rho_i} \frac{1 - \rho_i z}{\rho_i - z} \frac{\prod_{j \neq i,l}(1 - \rho_i\rho_j)}{\prod_{j \neq i,l}(\rho_i - \rho_j)}.$$

The function f has poles at the points $z = \rho^{-1}, \rho_1, \ldots, \rho_{l-1}$, and a value b_0 at infinity. It, therefore, has the representation

$$f(z) = b_0 + \frac{b_l}{1 - \rho z} + \sum_{i=1}^{l-1} \frac{b_i}{\rho_i - z}.$$

We first show that $b_i = (z - \rho_i)f(z)|_{z=\rho_i} = 0$ for $i < l$:

$$b_i = \frac{1 + \rho_i}{1 - \rho\rho_i}(1 - \rho_i^2)\frac{\prod_{j \neq l,i}(1 - \rho_i\rho_j)}{\prod_{j \neq l,i}(\rho_i - \rho_j)} - \frac{1 + \rho_i}{1 - \rho\rho_i}(1 - \rho_i^2)\frac{\prod_{j \neq i,l}(1 - \rho_i\rho_j)}{\prod_{j \neq i,l}(\rho_i - \rho_j)}$$

$$= 0$$

Next we find $b_l = (1 - \rho z)f(z)|_{z=\rho^{-1}}$

$$b_l = (1 + \rho^{-1})\frac{\prod_{j=1}^{l-1}(1 - \rho^{-1}\rho_j)}{\prod_{j=1}^{l-1}(\rho^{-1} - \rho_j)} = \frac{1+\rho}{\rho}\frac{\prod_{j=1}^{l-1}(\rho - \rho_j)}{\prod_{j=1}^{l-1}(1 - \rho\rho_j)}.$$

Finally, we determine b_0 by setting $z = -1$ and find

$$f(-1) = \sum_{i=1}^{l-1}\frac{1+\rho_i}{1 - \rho\rho_i}\frac{\prod_{j\neq i,l}(1 - \rho_i\rho_j)}{\prod_{j\neq i,l}(\rho_i - \rho_j)} = S_{l-1} = b_0 + \frac{1}{\rho}\frac{\prod_{j=1}^{l-1}(\rho - \rho_j)}{\prod_{j=1}^{l-1}(1 - \rho\rho_j)},$$

so that

$$f(z) = b_0 + \frac{b_1}{1 - z\rho} = S_{l-1} + \frac{1+z}{1 - z\rho}\frac{\prod_{j=1}^{l-1}(\rho - \rho_j)}{\prod_{j=1}^{l-1}(1 - \rho\rho_j)}.$$

For $z = \rho_l$ we find

$$f(\rho_l) = S_l = S_{l-1} + \frac{1+\rho_l}{1 - \rho_l\rho}\frac{\prod_{j=1}^{l-1}(\rho - \rho_j)}{\prod_{j=1}^{l-1}(1 - \rho\rho_j)}$$

$$= S_{l-1} + \frac{1+\rho_l}{\rho - \rho_l}\frac{\prod_{j=1}^{l}(\rho - \rho_j)}{\prod_{j=1}^{l}(1 - \rho\rho_j)}.$$

Continuing like this we find

$$f(\rho_l) = \sum_{i=1}^{l}\frac{1+\rho_i}{\rho - \rho_i}\frac{\prod_{j=1}^{i}(\rho - \rho_j)}{\prod_{j=1}^{i}(1 - \rho\rho_j)},$$

and proves Equation (3.16). ∎

Next we apply Lemma 2 for the eigenvalues ρ_i and $l = k - 1$ to calculate the coefficient $c(\eta)$, see Equation (3.14).

Corollary 3. *It follows from Lemma 2 that*

$$c(\eta) = \sum_{i=1}^{k-1}\frac{1+\rho_i}{\eta - \rho_i}\frac{\prod_{j=1}^{i}(\eta - \rho_j)}{\prod_{j=1}^{i}(1 - \eta\rho_j)}, \eta \neq \rho_i^{-1} \tag{3.17}$$

$$c(-1) = \frac{1}{2}(1 - (-1)^{k-1}), \tag{3.18}$$

$$c(1) = \sum_{i=1}^{k-1} \frac{1 + \rho_i}{1 - \rho_i},\tag{3.19}$$

$$c(\rho_m) = \frac{1}{1 - \rho_m}.\tag{3.20}$$

Proof. The identities Equations (3.15) and (3.16) involve the coefficients

$$a_i = (1 + \rho_i)\frac{\prod_{j \neq i}(1 - \rho_i\rho_j)}{\prod_{j \neq i}(\rho_i - \rho_j)}, \quad i = 1, ..., k - 1$$

and Equation (3.15) just states that

$$\left\{\frac{1}{1 - \rho_i\rho_m}\right\}\{a_i\} = \left\{\frac{1}{1 - \rho_m}\right\},$$

and hence that

$$\left\{\frac{1}{1 - \rho_i\rho_m}\right\}^{-1}\left\{\frac{1}{1 - \rho_m}\right\} = \{a_i\}.$$

This proves Equation (3.17):

$$c(\eta) = \left\{\frac{1}{1 - \rho_j}\right\}'\left\{\frac{1}{1 - \rho_i\rho_j}\right\}^{-1}\left\{\frac{1}{1 - \eta\rho_j}\right\} = \sum_{j=1}^{k-1} a_j \frac{1}{1 - \eta\rho_j}$$

$$= \sum_{j=1}^{k-1} \frac{1 + \rho_j}{1 - \eta\rho_j}\frac{\prod_{i \neq j}(1 - \rho_i\rho_j)}{\prod_{i \neq j}(\rho_j - \rho_i)} = \sum_{i=1}^{k-1} \frac{1 + \rho_i}{\eta - \rho_i}\frac{\prod_{j=1}^{i}(\eta - \rho_j)}{\prod_{j=1}^{i}(1 - \eta\rho_j)}.$$

For $\eta = -1$ in this expression, we find Equation (3.18):

$$c(-1) = \sum_{i=1}^{k-1} \frac{1 + \rho_i}{-1 - \rho_i}\frac{\prod_{j=1}^{i}(-1 - \rho_j)}{\prod_{j=1}^{i}(1 + \rho_j)} = -\sum_{i=1}^{k-1}(-1)^i$$

$$= \frac{1}{2}(1 - (-1)^{k-1}).$$

and for $\eta = 1$, we find Equation (3.19):

$$c(1) = \sum_{i=1}^{k-1} \frac{1 + \rho_i}{1 - \rho_i} \frac{\prod_{j=1}^{i}(1 - \rho_j)}{\prod_{j=1}^{i}(1 - \rho_j)} = \sum_{i=1}^{k-1} \frac{1 + \rho_i}{1 - \rho_i}.$$

Finally, in order to prove Equation (3.20), we observe that

$$c(\rho_m) = \left\{\frac{1}{1 - \rho_j}\right\}' \left\{\frac{1}{1 - \rho_i \rho_j}\right\}^{-1} \left\{\frac{1}{1 - \eta \rho_j}\right\}\Bigg|_{\eta = \rho_m} = \frac{1}{1 - \rho_m},$$

because

$$\left\{\frac{1}{1 - \rho_i \rho_j}\right\}^{-1} \left\{\frac{1}{1 - \eta \rho_j}\right\}\Bigg|_{\eta = \rho_m}$$

is the m' th unit vector. ∎

A3.2. Proof of Theorem 1

In Johansen (2002) the correction factor was given for an n-dimensional process with highest order deterministic term t^{n_d} by the expression $a(T, n, n_d)(1 + T^{-1}b(\theta))$, where

$$b(\theta) = c_1(1 + h(n, n_d)) + (nc_2 + 2(c_3 + dc_1))g(n, n_d)/n^2 \qquad (3.21)$$

and

$$\begin{aligned} a(T, n, n_d) = 1 &+ a_1(n_d)(n/T) + a_2(n_d)(n/T)^2 \\ &+ a_3(n_d)(n/T)^3 + b(n_d)/T. \end{aligned}$$

The functions $a(T, n, n_d), h(n, n_d)$ and $g(n, n_d)$ are determined by simulation of expectations of functions of random walk, whereas c_i are analytic functions of the parameters of the model. In the present case $n = 1, n_d = d$, and we decided to perform new simulations to determine the coefficients $f_T(d), a_1(d), a_2(d), h(1, d)$, and $g(1, d)$.

A3.2.1. The coefficients $f_T(d), a_1(d), a_2(d)$

We simulate the model (3.1) with $k = 1$. In this case, $f_T(d) = E_T[-2 \times \log \text{LR}\{\mathcal{M}_1^0 | M_1\}]$ is a function of T and d only and for $T = 10, 25, 50, 100, 300, 500, 700, 1000, 2000, 3000$ we run 2.5 mill. simulations and fit a second order polynomial in T^{-1}, using the intercept

$f(*), f(0), f(1)$ given in Equation (3.6). We thereby find the coefficients $(f(2), a_1(d), a_2(d))$ in the approximation

$$f_T(d) \sim f(d)(1 + a_1(d)T^{-1} + a_2(d)T^{-2}) = f(d)a_T(d).$$

The values for $a_1(d)$ and $a_2(d)$ are given in Table 3.1. The values of $a_1(d)$ for $d = *$ and 0 are also found analytically in Nielsen (1997a), but fitting the two coefficients by regression seems to describe the functions better.

A3.2.2. The coefficients c_i

We find the coefficients c_i from Johansen (2002, p. 1937):

$$c_1 = \text{tr}\{(I_{n_y} - P)^{-1}Q\Omega\alpha_\perp(\alpha'_\perp \Omega\alpha_\perp)^{-1}\alpha'_\perp \Omega Q'(I_{n_y} - P')^{-1}\Sigma^{-1}\},$$

$$c_2 = \text{tr}\{I_{n_y} - (I_{n_y} - P)^{-1}Q\Omega Q'(I_{n_y} - P')^{-1}\Sigma^{-1}\},$$

$$c_3 = \text{tr}\left\{\psi'\Sigma^{-1}\sum_{m=0}^{\infty}\psi_m\right\}\text{tr}\{\Sigma^{-1}\gamma(m+1)$$

$$+ \text{tr}\left\{\psi'\Sigma^{-1}\sum_{m=0}^{\infty}\gamma(m+1)'\Sigma^{-1}\psi_m\right\}.$$

In the present case $\alpha = 0, \alpha_\perp = 1, n_y = k - 1$, and $\Omega = \sigma^2$, so that from Equation (3.12) we get $\psi = (I_{k-1} - P)^{-1}Q = \phi(1)^{-1}v_1$ and find from Equation (3.19)

$$c_1 = \sigma^2\text{tr}\{(I_{k-1} - P)^{-1}QQ'(I_{k-1} - P')^{-1}\Sigma^{-1}\} = \frac{\sigma^2}{\phi(1)^2}v_1'\Sigma^{-1}v_1 = c(1),$$

$$c_2 = k - 1 - c_1.$$

The expression for c_3 depends on the coefficient $\gamma(m+1)' = P^{m+1}\Sigma$ and $\psi_m = P^m Q$. We find, using that $(I_{k-1} - \eta P)^{-1}Q = \phi(\eta)^{-1}v_\eta$, see Equation (3.12),

$$c_3 = \frac{1}{\phi(1)}v_1'\Sigma^{-1}\left[\sum_{m=0}^{\infty}P^m Q\text{tr}\{P^{m+1}\} + \sum_{m=0}^{\infty}P^{2m+1}Q\right]$$

$$= \frac{1}{\phi(1)}v_1'\Sigma^{-1}\left[\sum_{m=0}^{\infty}\sum_{i=1}^{k-1}\rho_i^{m+1}P^m Q + P(I_{k-1} - P^2)^{-1}Q\right]$$

$$= \frac{1}{\phi(1)} v_1' \Sigma^{-1} \left[\sum_{i=1}^{k-1} \rho_i (I_{k-1} - \rho_i P)^{-1} Q \right.$$

$$\left. + \frac{1}{2}((I_{k-1} - P)^{-1} - (I_{k-1} + P)^{-1})Q \right]$$

$$= \frac{1}{\phi(1)} v_1' \Sigma^{-1} \left[\sum_{i=1}^{k-1} \frac{\rho_i}{\phi(\rho_i)} v_i + \frac{1}{2\phi(1)} v_1 - \frac{1}{2\phi(-1)} v_{-1} \right]$$

$$= \sum_{i=1}^{k-1} \rho_i c(\rho_i) + \frac{1}{2}(c(1) - c(-1)).$$

The first term can be expressed in terms of c_2

$$2\sum_{i=1}^{k-1} \rho_i c(\rho_i) = \sum_{i=1}^{k-1} \frac{2\rho_i}{1-\rho_i} = \sum_{i=1}^{k-1} \frac{1+\rho_i}{1-\rho_i} - (k-1)$$

$$= c(1) - (k-1) = -c_2,$$

see Corollary 3, so that the coefficient of $g(d)$ becomes

$$c_2 + 2(c_3 + dc_1) = c_2 - c_2 + c_1 - c(-1) + 2dc_1 = (1+2d)c_1 - c(-1).$$

Therefore, for $n = 1$ we find from Equation (3.21)

$$b(\theta) = c_1(1 + h(1,d)) + (c_2 + 2(c_3 + dc_1))g(d)$$

$$= c_1(1 + h(1,d)) + ((1 + 2d)c_1 - c(-1))g(d)$$

$$= c_1(1 + h(1,d) + (1 + 2d)g(d)) - c(-1)g(d)$$

$$= c_1 m(d) - \frac{1}{2}(1 - (-1)^{k-1})g(d),$$

where we have defined

$$m(d) = 1 + h(1,d) + (1 + 2d)g(d),$$

where $d = *$ is interpreted as 0.

A3.2.3. The coefficients $g(d)$

The bias of the least squares estimator is also found analytically in Nielsen (1997a) for $d = *, 0, 1$. These results can be used to find the function $g(d) = g(1,d)$. In order to see this we need some notation. In the simulations we generate data from

$$\mathcal{M}_1^0 : \Delta x_t = \sum_{i=0}^{d-1} \beta_i t^i + \varepsilon_t$$

with $\sigma^2 = 1$, and we define the notation

$$d_t = (1,...,t^{d-1})', \quad D_t = t^d, \quad S_t = \sum_{i=1}^{t} \varepsilon_i, \quad A_{t-1} = \left(\begin{matrix} S_{t-1} \\ D_t \end{matrix} \middle| d_t \right),$$

that is, S_{t-1} and D_t corrected for d_t. We define the product moments

$$M_{aa} = \sum_{t=1}^{T} A_{t-1} A'_{t-1}, \quad M_{a\varepsilon} = \sum_{t=1}^{T} A_{t-1} \varepsilon_t, \quad M_{a\varepsilon}^+ = \sum_{t=1}^{T} A_{t-1} \varepsilon_{t-1},$$

$$M_{\varepsilon\varepsilon} = \sum_{t=1}^{T} \varepsilon_t^2, \quad M_{ad} = \sum_{t=1}^{T} A_{t-1} d'_t, \quad M_{\varepsilon d} = \sum_{t=1}^{T} \varepsilon_t d'_t, \text{ etc.}$$

We use the notation

$$M_{aa.d} = M_{aa} - M_{ad} M_{dd}^{-1} M_{da}.$$

In terms of these the definition of $g(d)$ is

$$g(d) = \lim_{T\to\infty} E[M_{\varepsilon a.d} M_{aa.d}^{-1} M_{a\varepsilon.d}^+]/E[M_{\varepsilon a.d} M_{aa.d}^{-1} M_{a\varepsilon.d}].$$

We also define $\hat{\pi}_d = M_{\varepsilon S.d,D}/M_{SS.d,D}$, the least squares estimator of π in model $\mathcal{M}_1$.

In Nielsen (1997a) the asymptotic bias for $\hat{\pi}_d, d = *, 0, 1$ when $\pi = \beta = 0$ is found to be

$$\lim_{T\to\infty} E(T\hat{\pi}_*) = -1.7814, \quad \lim_{T\to\infty} E(T\hat{\pi}_0) = -5.3791,$$

$$\lim_{T\to\infty} E(T\hat{\pi}_1) = -10.2455. \tag{3.22}$$

The relation between this bias and the coefficient $g(d)$ is derived from the next Lemma.

Lemma 4. *For all d it holds that*

$$M_{\varepsilon a.d} M_{aa.d}^{-1} M_{a\varepsilon.d}^+ - M_{\varepsilon a.d} M_{aa.d}^{-1} M_{a\varepsilon.d} - T\hat{\pi} \xrightarrow{P} 0$$

Proof. We find from

$$M_{\varepsilon a.d}M_{aa.d}^{-1}M_{a\varepsilon.d}^+ = M_{\varepsilon D.d}M_{DD.d}^{-1}M_{D\varepsilon.d}^+ + M_{\varepsilon S.D,d}M_{SS.D,d}^{-1}M_{S\varepsilon.D,d}^+$$
$$= M_{\varepsilon D.d}M_{DD.d}^{-1}M_{D\varepsilon.d}^+ + \hat{\pi}_d M_{S\varepsilon.D,d}^+,$$

and a similar expression for $M_{\varepsilon a.d}M_{aa.d}^{-1}M_{a\varepsilon.d}$ that

$$M_{\varepsilon a.d}M_{aa.d}^{-1}M_{a\varepsilon.d}^+ - M_{\varepsilon a.d}M_{aa.d}^{-1}M_{a\varepsilon.d} - T\hat{\pi}_d$$

$$= M_{\varepsilon D.d}M_{DD.d}^{-1}(M_{D\varepsilon.d}^+ - M_{D\varepsilon.d}) + T\hat{\pi}_d(T^{-1}(M_{S\varepsilon.D,d}^+ - M_{S\varepsilon.D,d}) - 1).$$

We see that

$$M_{\varepsilon D.d}M_{DD.d}^{-1/2} \in O_P(1),$$

$$M_{DD.d}^{-1/2}(M_{D\varepsilon.d}^+ - M_{D\varepsilon.d}) = M_{DD.d}^{-1/2}\sum_t (D_t|d_t)(\varepsilon_{t-1} - \varepsilon_t) \in o_P(1),$$

so that the first term tends to zero. Next, we use the notation $w_t = (d_t', D_t)'$ and consider

$$T^{-1}(M_{S\varepsilon.w}^+ - M_{S\varepsilon.w}) - 1 = (T^{-1}\sum_{t=1}^T S_{t-1}(\varepsilon_{t-1} - \varepsilon_t) - 1)$$

$$- T^{-1}M_{Sw}M_{ww}^{-1/2}M_{ww}^{-1/2}\sum_{t=1}^T w_t(\varepsilon_{t-1} - \varepsilon_t).$$

The first term is

$$T^{-1}\sum_{t=0}^{T-1} \varepsilon_t^2 - 1 - T^{-1}S_{T-1}\varepsilon_T \in o_P(1)$$

and the second term has the factors

$$T^{-1}M_{Sw}M_{ww}^{-1/2} \in O_P(1),$$

$$M_{ww}^{-1/2}\sum_{t=1}^T w_t(\varepsilon_{t-1} - \varepsilon_t) \in o_P(1),$$

which completes the proof. ■

We have proved convergence in probability, and we shall use that to suggest, as confirmed by the simulations, that we also have

$$E[M_{\varepsilon a.d}M_{aa.d}^{-1}M_{a\varepsilon.d}^+] - E[M_{\varepsilon a.d}M_{aa.d}^{-1}M_{a\varepsilon.d}] - E[T\hat{\pi}_d] \to 0,$$

which together with

$$E[M_{\varepsilon a.d}M_{aa.d}^{-1}M_{a\varepsilon.d}] \to f(d),$$

shows that

$$g(d) = \lim_{T \to \infty} \frac{E[M_{\varepsilon a.d}M_{aa.d}^{-1}M_{a\varepsilon.d}^{+}]}{E[M_{\varepsilon a.d}M_{aa.d}^{-1}M_{a\varepsilon.d}]} = 1 + \lim_{T \to \infty} E[T\hat{\pi}_d]/f(d),$$

so that from Equations (3.6) and (3.22) we find

$$g(*) = -0.5601, \qquad g(0) = -0.3262, \qquad g(1) = -0.6209,$$

as given in Table 3.1.

A3.2.4. The coefficients $m(d)$

The coefficients $m(d) = 1 + h(1,d) + (1 + 2d)g(1,d)$ are more difficult to simulate accurately, as they contain the term

$$\left(\sum_{t=1}^{T} \varepsilon_t \varepsilon_{t-1}\right) M_{\varepsilon a.d}M_{aa.d}^{-1}M_{a\varepsilon.d},$$

which evidently has a variance proportional to T, but many million simulations indicate that the mean is convergent to a non-zero limit. In Table 3.1, the uncertainty of the value of the simulated value $m(d)$ is given as well.

New Directions in Macromodelling
A. Welfe (Editor)
© 2004 Published by Elsevier B.V.
DOI: 10.1016/S0573-8555(04)69004-3

CHAPTER 4

Inflation, Money Growth, and I(2) Analysis

Katarina Juselius

Institute of Economics, University of Copenhagen, Studiestræde 6, 1455 Copenhagen K, Denmark

Abstract

The chapter discusses the dynamics of inflation and money growth in a stochastic framework, allowing for double unit roots in the nominal variables. It gives some examples of typical I(2) 'symptoms' in empirical I(1) models and provides both a non-technical and a technical discussion of the basic differences between the I(1) and the I(2) models. The notion of long-run and medium-run price homogeneity is discussed in terms of testable restrictions on the I(2) model. The Brazilian high inflation period of 1977:1–1985:5 illustrates the applicability of the I(2) model and its usefulness to address questions related to inflation dynamics.

Keywords: co-integrated VAR, price homogeneity, Cagan model, hyper inflation

JEL classifications: C32, E41, E31

4.1. Introduction

The purpose of this chapter is to give an intuitive account of the co-integrated VAR model for $I(2)$ data and to demonstrate that the rich structure of the $I(2)$ model is particularly relevant for the empirical analyses of economic data characterized by highly persistent shocks to the growth rates. Such data are usually found in applications of economic models explaining the determination of nominal magnitudes. For example, the explicit assumption of a non-stationary error term in some models of money demand during periods of high or hyper inflation (Cagan, 1956; Sargent, 1977), implies that nominal money and prices are $I(2)$. Thus, the empirical analysis of such models would only make sense in the $I(2)$ model framework.

However, as argued in Juselius and Vuojosevic (2003), prices in hyper-inflationary episodes should not be modelled as an $I(2)$ but rather as an explosive root process. Though such episodes are (almost by definition) short they are usually preceded by periods of high inflation rates for which the $I(2)$ analysis is more adequate. Even though inflationary shocks in such periods are usually large, it is worth stressing that the (double) unit root property, as such, is not related to the *magnitude* but the *permanence* of shocks. Therefore, we may equally well find double unit roots in prices during periods of low inflation rates, like the nineties, and not just in periods of high inflation rates like the seventies. But, while the persistence of shocks determine whether price inflation is $I(1)$ or $I(0)$, the magnitude of inflationary shocks is probably much more indicative of a risk for hyper inflation. High inflation periods are, therefore, particularly interesting as they are likely to contain valuable information about the mechanisms which subsequently might lead to hyper-inflation.

The empirical application to the Brazilian high-inflation period of 1977–1985 offers a good illustration of the potential advantages of using the $I(2)$ model and demonstrates how it can be used to study important aspects of the inflationary mechanism in periods preceding hyper inflation.

The Cagan hyper inflation model is first translated into a set of testable empirical hypotheses on the pulling and pushing forces described by the co-integrated $I(2)$ model in AR and MA form. The chapter finds strong empirical support for one of the hypothetical pulling forces, the Cagan money demand relation with the opportunity cost of holding money measured by a combination of CPI inflation and currency depreciation in the black market. The Cagan's α coefficient, defining the average inflation rate at which government can gain maximum seignorage, is estimated to be approximately 40–50%, which is usually considered to describe hyper inflation. Thus, it seems likely that the seed to the subsequent Brazilian hyper inflation episode can be found in the present data. This is further supported by the finding that: (1) there is a small explosive root in the VAR model, (2) the condition for long-run price homogeneity was strongly violated, and (3) the CPI price inflation showed lack of equilibrium correction behaviour. The latter is associated with the widespread use of wage and price indexation, which prohibited market forces to adjust back to equilibrium after a price distortion. As a consequence, domestic price inflation gained momentum as a result of increasing inflationary expectations in the foreign exchange market.

The organization of the chapter is as follows: Section 4.2 discusses money growth and inflation in a Cagan type of high/hyper inflation model framework. Section 4.3 reformulates the high inflation problem in a stochastic framework allowing for double unit roots in the nominal variables. It draws heavily on Section 4 in Juselius (1999a). Section 4.4 discusses typical 'symptoms' in the VAR analysis when incorrectly assuming that the data are $I(1)$ instead of $I(2)$ and gives a first intuitive account of the basic difference between the $I(1)$ and the $I(2)$ analysis. Section 4.5 defines formally the $I(2)$ model in the AR and the MA forms, discusses the role of deterministic components in the $I(2)$ model and introduces the two-step procedure for determining the two co-integration rank indices. Section 4.6 gives an interpretation of the various components in the $I(2)$ model and illustrates with the Brazilian data. It draws heavily on Section 2 in Juselius (1999b). Section 4.7 discusses long-run and medium-run price homogeneity and how these can be formulated as testable restrictions on the $I(2)$ model. Section 4.8 presents the empirical model for money growth, currency depreciation and price inflation in Brazil. Section 4.9 concludes.

4.2. Money growth and inflation

It is widely believed that the growth in money supply in excess of real productive growth is the cause of inflation, at least in the long run. The economic intuition behind this is that other factors are limited in scope, whereas money in principle is unlimited in supply (Romer, 1996). Generally, the reasoning is based on equilibrium in the money market so that money supply equals money demand:

$$M/P = L(R, Y^{\mathrm{r}}), \tag{4.1}$$

where M is the money stock, P the price level, Y^{r} real income, R an interest rate, and $L(\cdot)$ the demand for real money balances. In a high (and accelerating) inflation period, the Cagan model for hyper inflation predicts that aggregate money demand is more appropriately described by:

$$M/P = L(\pi^{\mathrm{e}}, Y^{\mathrm{r}}), \qquad L_{\pi^{\mathrm{e}}} < 0, L_{Y^{\mathrm{r}}} > 0 \tag{4.2}$$

where π^{e} is expected inflation.

The latter model (4.2) is chosen as the baseline model in the subsequent empirical analysis of the Brazilian high-inflation experience in the seventies until the mid-eighties. The data consist of money stock measured as M3, the CPI price index, the black market spot exchange rate, and the real industrial production and covers the period 1977:1,...,1985:5.

The graphs of the data in levels and differences (after taking logs) give a first indication of the order of integration. The growth rates of all three

nominal variables in Figure 4.1 exhibit typical $I(1)$ behaviour, implying
that the levels of the variables are $I(2)$. In contrast, the graphs of the log of
the industrial production in levels and differences in Figure 4.2 do not
suggest $I(2)$ behaviour: the smooth behaviour typical of $I(2)$ variables is
not present in the level of industrial production and the differenced process
looks significantly mean-reverting.

The middle part of Figure 4.2 demonstrates how real money stock
(ln M3-ln CPI) and real exchange rates (ln Lexch-ln CPI) have evolved in
a non-stationary manner and increasingly so after 1981. Figure 4.2, lower
panel compares the levels and the differences of the official and black
market exchange rate. While the official rate seems to have stayed below
the black market rate for some periods, the graphs show that the two major
devaluations brought the two series back to the same level. Thus, it seems
likely that the black market exchange rate is a good proxy for the 'true'
value of the Brazilian currency in this period.

When data are non-stationary, the Cagan model can be formulated as a
co-integrating relation, i.e.:

$$(M/P)_t - L(\pi_t^e, Y_t) = v_t \tag{4.3}$$

where v_t is a stationary process measuring the deviation from the steady-
state position at time t.

***Figure 4.1. Nominal M3, CPI, and exchange rates in levels
and differences***

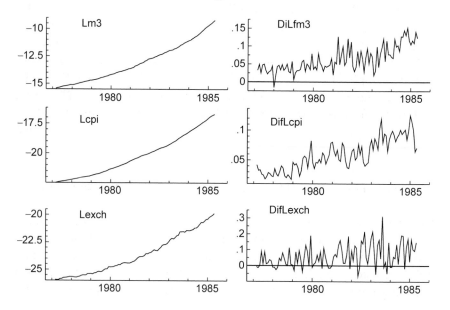

Figure 4.2. The graphs of industrial production in levels and differences (upper part), M3 and exchange rate both deflated with CPI (middle panel), and the black and white market exchange rate in levels and differences (lower panel)

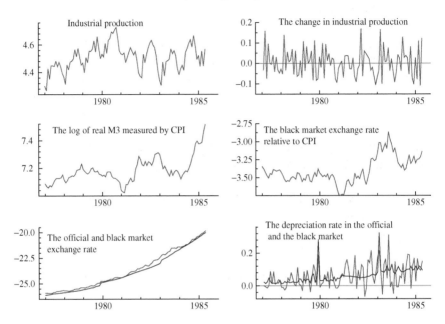

The stationarity of v_t implies that whenever the system has been shocked, it will adjust back to equilibrium and is, therefore, essential for the interpretation of Equation (4.3) as a steady-state relation. If v_t is non-stationary as explicitly assumed by Sargent (1977), money supply has deviated from the steady-state value of money demand. As this case generally implies a double unit root in the data, the choice of the $I(2)$ model for the econometric analysis seems natural. Therefore, when addressing empirical questions related to the mechanisms behind inflation and money growth in a high or hyper inflation regime, we need to understand and interpret the $I(2)$ model.

4.3. Formulating the economic problem in a stochastic framework

Co-integration and stochastic trends are two sides of the same coin: if there are co-integration relations there are also common stochastic trends. Therefore, to be able to address the transmission mechanism of monetary policy in a stochastic framework it is useful first to consider a conventional decomposition into trend, $\mathcal{T}$, cycle, $\mathcal{C}$, and irregular component, $\mathcal{I}$, of a typical macroeconomic variable.

$$X = \mathcal{T} \times C \times I$$

and allow the trend to be both deterministic, $\mathcal{T}_d$, and stochastic, $\mathcal{T}_s$, i.e. $\mathcal{T} = \mathcal{T}_s \times \mathcal{T}_d$, and the cyclical component to be of long duration, say 6–10 years, C_1, and of shorter duration, say 3–5 years, C_s, i.e. $C = C_1 \times C_s$. The reason for distinguishing between short and long cycles is that a long/short cycle can either be treated as non-stationary or stationary depending on the time perspective of the study. For example, the graph of the trend-adjusted industrial production in Figure 4.5, lower panel, illustrates long cycles in the data that were found non-stationary by the statistical analysis.

An additive formulation is obtained by taking logarithms:

$$x = (t_s + t_d) + (c_1 + c_s) + i \tag{4.4}$$

where lower case letters indicate a logarithmic transformation. Even if the stochastic trends are of primary interest for the subsequent analyses, a linear time trend is needed to account for average linear growth rates typical of most economic data.

4.3.1. Stochastic and deterministic trends

As an illustration of a trend-cycle decomposition, we consider the following vector of variables $x_t = [m, p, s^b, y^r]_t$, $t = 1977 : 1, ..., 1985 : 5$, where m is the log of M3, p is the log CPI, s^b is the log of black market exchange rate, and y^r is the log of industrial production. All variables are treated as stochastic and will be modelled, independently of whether they are considered endogenous or exogenous in the economic model.

A stochastic trend describes the cumulated impact of all previous *permanent* shocks on a variable, i.e. it summarizes all the shocks with a long-lasting effect. This is contrary to a *transitory* shock, the effect of which cancels either during the next period or over the next few periods. For example, the income level of a household can be thought of as the cumulation of all previous permanent income changes (shocks), whereas the effect of temporary shocks, like lottery prizes, will not cumulate as it is only a temporary change in income.

If inflation rate is found to be $I(1)$, then the present level of inflation can be thought of as the sum of all previous shocks to inflation, i.e.

$$\pi_t = \sum_{i=1}^{t} \varepsilon_i + \pi_0. \tag{4.5}$$

Because the effect of transitory shocks disappears in the cumulation a stochastic trend, t_s, is defined as the cumulative sum of previous permanent shocks, $t_{s,t} = \sum_{i=1}^{t} \varepsilon_i$. The difference between a linear stochastic and a linear deterministic trend is that the increments of a stochastic trend change randomly, whereas those of a deterministic trend are constant over time. Figure 4.3 illustrates three different stochastic trends measured as the once cumulated residuals from the money, price and exchange rate equations.

A representation of prices is obtained by integrating Equation (4.5) once, i.e.

$$p_t = \sum_{s=1}^{t} \pi_s = \sum_{s=1}^{t} \sum_{i=1}^{s} \varepsilon_i + \pi_0 t + p_0. \tag{4.6}$$

Thus, if inflation is $I(1)$ with a non-zero mean (as most studies find), prices are $I(2)$ with a linear trend. Figure 4.4 illustrates the twice and once cumulated residuals from the CPI price equation of the VAR model defined in the next section.

4.3.2. A trend-cycle scenario

Given the set of variables discussed above, one would expect (at least) two autonomous shocks $u_{1,t}$ and $u_{2,t}$, of which $u_{1,t}$ is a nominal shock and $u_{2,t}$ is a real shock. If there are second-order stochastic trends in

Figure 4.3. The graphs of the cumulated residuals from the money, price, and exchange rate equations of the estimated VAR

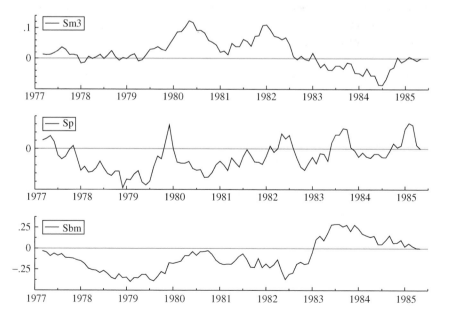

Figure 4.4.   The graphs of the twice and once cumlated residuals from the price equation

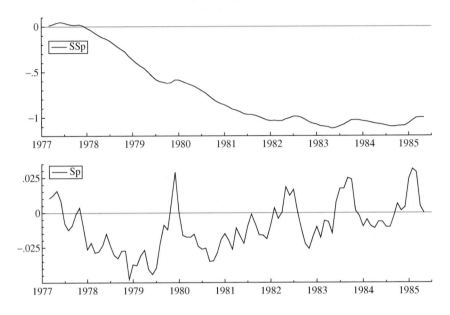

the data, it seems plausible that they have been generated from the nominal shocks. We will, therefore, tentatively assume that the second-order long-run stochastic trend t_s in Equation (4.4) is described by the twice cumulated nominal shocks, $\sum_{s=1}^{t} \sum_{i=1}^{s} u_{1i}$. The long cyclical components c_1 in the data will then be described by a combination of the once cumulated nominal shocks, $\sum_{i=1}^{t} u_{1i}$, and the once cumulated real shocks, $\sum_{i=1}^{t} u_{2i}$. This allows us to distinguish empirically between the long-run stochastic trend in nominal levels, $\sum_{s=1}^{t} \sum_{i=1}^{s} u_{1i}$, the medium-run stochastic trend in nominal growth rates, $\sum_{i=1}^{t} u_{1i}$, and the medium-run stochastic trend in real activity, $\sum_{i=1}^{t} u_{2i}$. Figure 4.5 illustrates.

The trend-cycle formulation below illustrates the ideas:

$$
\begin{bmatrix} m_t \\ p_t \\ s_t^b \\ y_t^r \end{bmatrix} = \begin{bmatrix} c_1 \\ c_2 \\ c_3 \\ 0 \end{bmatrix} \left[\sum_{s=1}^{t} \sum_{i=1}^{s} u_{1i} \right] + \begin{bmatrix} d_{11} & d_{12} \\ d_{21} & d_{22} \\ d_{31} & d_{32} \\ d_{41} & d_{42} \end{bmatrix} \begin{bmatrix} \sum_{i=1}^{t} u_{1i} \\ \sum_{i=1}^{t} u_{2i} \end{bmatrix} + \begin{bmatrix} g_1 \\ g_2 \\ g_3 \\ g_4 \end{bmatrix} [t] \qquad (4.7)
$$

$+$ stat. comp.

Figure 4.5. The graphs of trend-adjusted M3 in levels and differences (upper and lower panel) and trend-adjusted industrial production (lower panel)

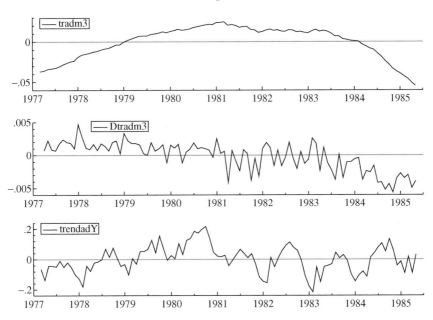

The deterministic trend component, $t_d = t$, is needed to account for linear growth trends present in the levels of the variables. If $g_4 = 0$ and $d_{41} = 0$ in Equation (4.7), then $\sum_{i=1}^{t} u_{2,i}$ is likely to describe the long-run trend in industrial production. In this case, it may be possible to interpret $\sum_{i=1}^{t} u_{2,i}$ as a 'structural' unit root process (cf. the discussion in King *et al.*, 1991 on stochastic vs. deterministic real growth models).

If, on the other hand, $g_4 \neq 0$, then it seems plausible that the long-run real trend can be approximated by a linear deterministic time trend. In this case, $\sum_{i=1}^{t} u_{2,i}$ is likely to describe medium-run deviations from the linear trend, i.e. the long business cycle. The graph of the trend-adjusted industrial production in the lower panel of Figure 4.5 illustrates such a long cycle starting from the long upturn from 1977 to 1980:6 and ending with the downturn from 1980:6 to 1984. Note also the shorter cycles of approximately a year's duration imbedded in the long cycle.

Therefore, the possibility of interpreting the second stochastic trend, $\sum_{i=1}^{t} u_{2,i}$, as a long-run structural trend depends crucially on whether one includes a linear trend in Equation (4.7) or not.

The trend components of m_t, p_t, s_t, and y_t in Equation (4.7) can now be represented by:

$$m_t = c_1 \sum\sum u_{1i} + d_{11}\sum u_{1i} + d_{12}\sum u_{2i} + g_1 t + \text{stat. comp}$$

$$p_t = c_2 \sum\sum u_{1i} + d_{21}\sum u_{1i} + d_{22}\sum u_{2i} + g_2 t + \text{stat. comp}$$

$$\hspace{6cm}(4.8)$$

$$s_t = c_3 \sum\sum u_{1i} + d_{31}\sum u_{1i} + d_{32}\sum u_{2i} + g_3 t + \text{stat. comp}$$

$$y_t = +d_{41}\sum u_{1i} + d_{42}\sum u_{2i} + g_4 t + \text{stat. comp}$$

If $(c_1, c_2, c_3) \neq 0$ then $\{m_t, p_t, s_t\} \sim I(2)$. If, in addition, $c_1 = c_2 = c_3$ then

$$m_t - p_t = (d_{11} - d_{21})\sum u_{1i} + (d_{12} - d_{22})\sum u_{2i} + (g_1 - g_2)t$$
$$+ \text{stat. comp}$$

$$p_t - s_t = (d_{21} - d_{31})\sum u_{1i} + (d_{22} - d_{32})\sum u_{2i} + (g_2 - g_3)t$$
$$+ \text{stat. comp} \hspace{3cm}(4.9)$$

$$m_t - s_t = (d_{11} - d_{31})\sum u_{1i} + (d_{12} - d_{32})\sum u_{2i} + (g_1 - g_3)t$$
$$+ \text{stat. comp}$$

$$y_t = +d_{41}\sum u_{1i} + d_{42}\sum u_{2i} + g_4 t + \text{stat.comp.}$$

The real variables are at most $I(1)$ but, unless $(g_1 = g_2)$, $(g_2 = g_3)$, and $(g_1 = g_3)$, they are $I(1)$ around a linear trend. Figure 4.5 illustrates the trend-adjusted behavior of real M3 and industrial production.

Long-run price homogeneity among all the variables implies that both the long-run stochastic $I(2)$ trends and the linear deterministic trends should cancel in Equation (4.9). But, even if overall long-run homogeneity is rejected, some of the individual components of $\{m_t - p_t, p_t - s_t, m_t - s_t\}$ can, nevertheless, exhibit long-run price homogeneity. For example, the case $(m_t - p_t) \sim I(1)$ is a testable hypothesis which implies that money stock and prices are moving together in the long-run, though not necessarily in the medium-run (over the business cycle).

The condition for long-run and medium-run price homogeneity is $\{c_{11} = c_{21}, \text{ and } d_{11} = d_{21}\}$, i.e. that the nominal shocks u_{1t} affect nominal money and prices in the same way both in the long run and in the medium run. Because the real stochastic trend $\sum u_{2i}$ is likely to enter m_t but not necessarily p_t, testing long-run and medium-run price homogeneity jointly is not equivalent to testing $(m_t - p_t) \sim I(0)$. Testing the composite hypothesis is more involved than the long-run price homogeneity alone.

It is important to note that $(m_t - p_t) \sim I(1)$ implies $(\Delta m_t - \Delta p_t) \sim I(0)$, i.e. long-run price homogeneity implies a stationary spread between price inflation and money growth. In this case, the stochastic trend in inflation is the same as the stochastic trend in money growth. The econometric formulation of long-run and medium-run price-homogeneity in the $I(2)$ model will be discussed in Section 4.7.

When overall long-run price homogeneity holds it is convenient to transform the nominal system (4.8) to a system consisting of real variables and a nominal growth rate, for example:

$$
\begin{bmatrix} m_t - p_t \\ s_t - p_t \\ \Delta p_t \\ y_t \end{bmatrix} = \begin{bmatrix} d_{11} - d_{21} & d_{12} - d_{22} \\ d_{21} - d_{31} & d_{22} - d_{32} \\ c_{21} & 0 \\ d_{41} & d_{42} \end{bmatrix} \begin{bmatrix} \sum_{i=1}^{t} u_{1,i} \\ \sum_{i=1}^{t} u_{2,i} \end{bmatrix}
$$

$$
+ \begin{bmatrix} g_1 - g_2 \\ g_2 - g_3 \\ 0 \\ g_4 \end{bmatrix} [t] + \cdots \tag{4.10}
$$

Given long-run price homogeneity, all variables are at most $I(1)$ in Equation (4.10). The nominal growth rate (measured by Δp_t, Δm_t, or Δs_t) is only affected by the once cumulated nominal trend, $\sum_{i=1}^{t} u_{1,i}$, but all the other variables can (but need not) be affected by both stochastic trends, $\sum_{i=1}^{t} u_{1,i}$ and $\sum_{i=1}^{t} u_{2,i}$.

The case $(m_t - p_t - y_t) \sim I(0)$, i.e. the inverse velocity of circulation is a stationary variable, requires that $d_{11} - d_{21} - d_{41} = 0$, $d_{12}d_{22} - d_{42} = 0$ and $g_1 - g_2 - g_4 = 0$. If $d_{11} = d_{21}$ (i.e. medium run price homogeneity), $d_{22} = 0$ (real stochastic growth does not affect prices), $d_{41} = 0$ (medium-run inflationary movements do not affect real income), and $d_{12} = d_{42}$ then $m_t - p_t - y_t \sim I(0)$. In this case, real money stock and real aggregate income share one common trend, the real stochastic trend $\sum u_{2i}$. The stationarity of money velocity, implying common movements in money, prices, and income, would then be consistent with the conventional monetarist assumption as stated by Friedman (1970) that "inflation always and everywhere is a monetary problem". This case would correspond to model (4.1) in Section 4.2.

The case $(m_t - p_t - y_t) \sim I(1)$, implies that the two common stochastic trends affect the level of real money stock and real income differently. Cagan's model of money demand in a high (hyper) inflation period suggests that the non-stationarity of the liquidity ratio is related to the expected rate of inflation $E_t(\Delta p_{t+1})$. The latter is generally not observable, but as long as $E_t(\Delta p_{t+1}) - \Delta p_t$ is a stationary disturbance, one can replace the unobserved expected inflation with actual inflation without losing co-integration. The condition that $\{E_t(\Delta p_{t+1}) - \Delta p_t\} \sim I(0)$ seems plausible considering that $\{\Delta p_{t+1} - \Delta p_t\} \sim I(0)$ when $p_t \sim I(2)$. It amounts to assuming that $\{E_t(\Delta p_{t+1}) - \Delta p_{t+1}\} \sim I(0)$, i.e. agents' inflationary expectations do not systematically deviate from actual inflation. Therefore, from a co-integration point of view we can replace the expected inflation with the actual inflation:

$$m_t - p_t - y_t + a_1\Delta p_t \sim I(0),$$

or, equivalently:

$$(m_t - p_t - y_t) + a_2\Delta s_t \sim I(0). \tag{4.11}$$

where under the Cagan model $a_1 > 0$, $a_2 > 0$.

4.4. Diagnosing I(2)

VAR models are widely used in empirical macroeconomics based on the assumption that data are $I(1)$ without first testing for $I(2)$ or checking whether a near unit root remains in the model after the co-integration rank has been imposed. Unfortunately, when the data contains a double unit root essentially all inference in the $I(1)$ model is affected. To avoid making wrong inference it is, therefore, important to be able to diagnose typical $I(2)$ symptoms in the $I(1)$ VAR model.

For the Brazilian data, the unrestricted VAR model was specified as:

$$\Delta x_t = \Gamma_1\Delta x_{t-1} + \Pi x_{t-2} + \mu_1 t + \mu_0 + \Phi_p Dp83.8_t + \Phi_s Qs_t$$
$$+ \varepsilon_t, \varepsilon_t \sim N_p(0, \Omega), \quad t = 1, ..., T \tag{4.12}$$

where $x_t = [m_t, p_t, s_t^b, y_t^r]$, $m_t = \ln(H3_t)$, $p_t = \ln(CPI_t)$, $s_t^b = \ln(Exch_t^b)$, $y_t^r = \ln(\text{industrial production})$, $t = 1977 : 1, ..., 1985 : 5$, $\Pi = \alpha\beta'$, $\mu_1 = \alpha\beta_1$, $\mu_{01} = \alpha\beta_{01}$, and $(\Gamma_1, \mu_0, \Phi_p, \Phi_s, \Omega)$ are unrestricted. The estimates have been calculated using CATS for RATS, Hansen and Juselius (1995). Misspecification tests are reported in Appendix A.

The data are distinctly trending and we need to allow for linear trends both in the data and in the co-integration relations when testing for co-integration rank (Nielsen and Rahbek, 2000). The industrial production, y_t^r, exhibits strong seasonal variation and we include 11 seasonal dummies,

Qs_t, and a constant, μ_0 in the VAR model. Finally, the graphs of the differenced black market exchange rate and nominal M3 money stock exhibited an extraordinary large shock at 1983:8, which was accounted for by an unrestricted impulse dummy $Dp83.8_t = 1$ for $t = 1983 : 8$ and 0 otherwise. A permanent shock to the changes corresponds to a level shift in the variables, which may or may not cancel in the co-integration relations. To account for the latter possibility the shift dummy, $Ds83.8_t = 0$ for $t = 1983 : 8$ and 1 otherwise, was restricted to be in the co-integration relations. It was found to be insignificant (p-value 0.88) and was left out.

The $I(1)$ estimation procedure is based on the so called R-model in which the short-run effects have first been concentrated out:

$$R_{0t} = \alpha\beta' R_{1t} + \varepsilon_t. \tag{4.13}$$

where R_{0t} and R_{1t} are defined by:

$$\underbrace{\Delta x_t}_{I(1)} = \hat{B}_{11} \underbrace{\Delta x_{t-1}}_{I(1)} + \text{const} + B_{13}Dp_t + \underbrace{R_{0t}}_{I(0)} \tag{4.14}$$

and

$$\underbrace{x_{t-1}}_{I(2)} = \hat{B}_{21} \underbrace{\Delta x_{t-1}}_{I(1)} + \text{const} + B_{23}Dp_t + \underbrace{R_{1t}}_{I(2)}. \tag{4.15}$$

and Dp_t is a catch-all for all the dummy variables. If $x_t \sim I(2)$ then $\Delta x_t \sim I(1)$ and Equation (4.14) is a regression of an $I(1)$ process on its own lag. Thus, the regressand and the regressor contain the same common trend, which will cancel in regression. This implies that $R_{0t} \sim I(0)$, even if $x_t \sim I(2)$. On the other hand, Equation (4.15) is a regression of an $I(2)$ variable, x_{t-1}, on an $I(1)$ variable, Δx_{t-1}. Because an $I(2)$ trend cannot be cancelled by regressing on an $I(1)$ trend, it follows that $R_{1t} \sim I(2)$.

Therefore, when $x_t \sim I(2)$, Equation (4.13) is a regression of an $I(0)$ variable (R_{0t}) on an $I(2)$ variable (R_{1t}). Under the (testable) assumption that $\varepsilon_t \sim I(0)$, either $\beta' R_{1t} = 0$ or $\beta' R_{1t} \sim I(0)$ for the Equation (4.13) to hold. Because the linear combination $\beta' R_{1t}$ transforms the process from $I(2)$ to $I(0)$, the estimate $\hat{\beta}$ is super–super consistent (Johansen, 1992). Even though β is precisely estimated in the $I(1)$ model when data are $I(2)$, the interpretation of $\beta' x_t$ as a stationary long-run relation has to be modified as will be demonstrated below.

It is easy to demonstrate the connection between $\beta'\tilde{x}_{t-1}$ and $\beta'R_{1t}$ by inserting Equation (4.15) into Equation (4.13):

$$R_{0t} = \alpha\beta'R_{1t} + \varepsilon_t\alpha\beta'(\tilde{x}_{t-1} - B_2\Delta x_{t-1}) + \varepsilon_t$$

$$= \alpha(\beta'\tilde{x}_{t-1} - \beta'B_2\Delta x_{t-1}) + \varepsilon_t$$

$$= \alpha(\underbrace{\underbrace{\beta'\tilde{x}_{t-1}}_{I(1)} - \underbrace{\omega'\Delta x_{t-1}}_{I(1)}}_{I(0)}) + \varepsilon_t \qquad (4.16)$$

where $\omega = \beta'B_2$. It appears that the stationary relations $\beta'R_{1t}$ consists of two components $\beta'\tilde{x}_{t-1}$ and $\omega'\Delta x_{t-1}$ both of which are generally $I(1)$. The stationarity of $\beta'R_{1t}$ is, therefore, a consequence of co-integration between $\beta'\tilde{x}_{t-1} \sim I(1)$ and $\omega\Delta x_{t-1} \sim I(1)$.

Thus, when data are $I(2)$, $\beta'_i\tilde{x}_t \sim I(1)$, while $\beta'_iR_{1t} \sim I(0)$ for at least one i, $i = 1, ..., r$. It is, therefore, a clear sign of double unit roots (or, alternatively, a unit root and an explosive root) in the model when the graphs of $\beta'_i\tilde{x}_t$ exhibits non-stationary behaviour whereas β'_iR_{1t} looks stationary. As an illustration we have reported the graphs of all four co-integration relations (of which β'_1R_{1t} and β'_2R_{1t} are stationary) in Figures 4.6–4.9. The upper panels contain the relations, $\beta'_i\tilde{x}_t$, and the lower panels the co-integration relations corrected for short-run dynamics, β'_iR_{1t}.

Among the graphs in Figures 4.6 and 4.7, $\beta'_1\tilde{x}_t$ and $\beta'_2\tilde{x}_t$ exhibit distinctly non-stationary behaviour whereas the graphs of the corresponding $\beta'_iR_{1,t}$ look reasonably stationary. This is strong evidence of double roots in the data. As all the remaining graphs seem definitely non-stationary, this suggests $r = 2$ and at least one $I(2)$ trend in the data.

Another way of diagnosing $I(2)$ behaviour is to calculate the characteristic roots of the VAR model for different choices of the co-integration rank r. When $x_t \sim I(2)$ the number of unit roots in the characteristic polynomial of the VAR model is $s_1 + 2s_2$, where s_1 and s_2 are the number of autonomous $I(1)$ and $I(2)$ trends, respectively and $s_1 + s_2 = p - r$.

The characteristic roots contain information on unit roots associated with both Γ and Π, whereas the standard $I(1)$ trace test is only related to the number of unit roots in the Π matrix. If the data are $I(1)$ the number of unit roots (or near unit roots) should be $p - r$, otherwise $p - r + s_2$. Therefore, if for any reasonable choice of r there are still (near) unit roots in the model, it is a clear sign of $I(2)$ behaviour in at least some of the variables. Because the additional unit root(s) are related to Δx_{t-1}, i.e. belong to the

Figure 4.6. **The graphs of $\beta'_1 x_t$ (upper panel) and $\beta'_1 R_{1t}$ (lower panel)**

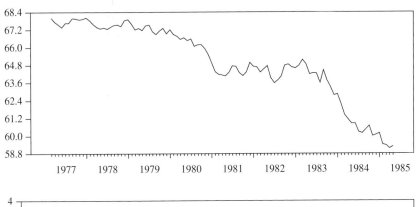

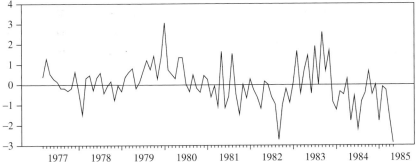

matrix $\Gamma = I - \Gamma_1$, lowering the value of r does not remove the s_2 additional unit root associated with the $I(2)$ behaviour.

In the Brazilian nominal model, there are altogether $p \times k = 4 \times 2 = 8$ eigenvalue roots in the characteristic polynomial, which are reported below for $r = 1, ..., 4$. Unrestricted near unit roots are indicated with bold face.

VAR(p)	**1.002**	**0.97**	**0.90**	**0.90**	0.38	0.33	0.06	0.06
$r = 3$	1.0	**1.002**	**0.91**	**0.91**	0.38	0.33	0.06	0.06
$r = 2$	1.0	1.0	**0.99**	**0.86**	0.38	0.32	0.09	0.07
$r = 1$	1.0	1.0	1.0	**1.001**	0.61	0.33	0.09	0.00

In the unrestricted model, two of the roots are very close to the unit circle, one is larger than unity possibly indicating explosive behaviour, the other is a stable near unit root. In addition, there is a complex pair of two fairly large roots. The presence of an unstable root can be seen in the graph of the first co-integration relation $\beta'_1 \tilde{x}_t$ in Figure 4.6: the equilibrium error

Figure 4.7.   The graphs of $\beta'_2 x_t$ (upper panel) and $\beta'_2 R_{1t}$ (lower panel)

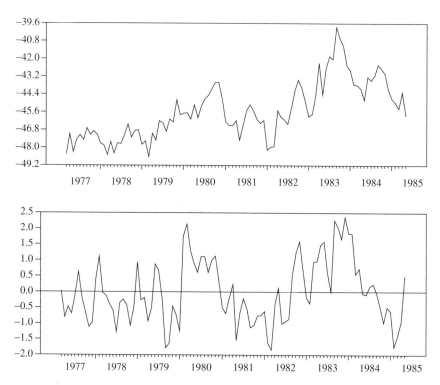

in the 'steady-state' relation in levels grows in an unstable manner at the end of the period, but is 'compensated' by a similar increase in the inflation rate, so $\beta'_1 R_{1,t}$ looks stationary. This suggests that the seed to the Brazilian hyper inflation in the subsequent period can already be found in the present data.

However, the explosive part of the root is very small and might not be statistically significant. In such a case, we would expect the unstable root to disappear when restricting the rank. We notice that for $r = 3$ and $r = 1$, the explosive root is still left in the model, whereas for $r = 2$ it has disappeared. Independently of the choice of r, a near unit root remains in the model consistent with $I(2)$, or moderately explosive, behaviour. Therefore, we continue with $r = 2$ and disregard the possibility of an explosive root in the econometric analysis. Subsequently, we will use the empirical results to demonstrate where in the model the seed to the subsequent hyper inflationary behaviour can be found.

In most cases, a graphical inspection of the data is sufficient to detect $I(2)$ behaviour and it might seem meaningless to estimate the $I(1)$ model

Figure 4.8. **The graphs of $\beta_3' x_t$ (upper panel) and $\beta_3' R_{1t}$ (lower panel)**

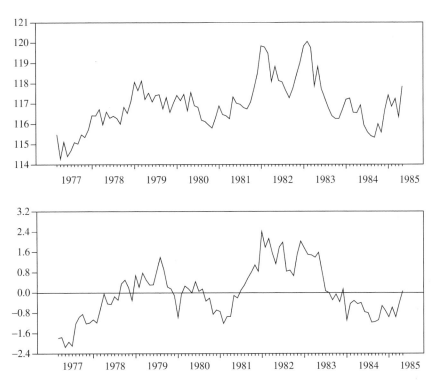

when x_t is in fact $I(2)$. However, a variety of hypotheses can be adequately tested using the $I(1)$ procedure with the caveat that the interpretation of the co-integration results should be in terms of CI(2, 1) relations, i.e. relations which co-integrated from $I(2)$ to $I(1)$, and not from $I(1)$ to $I(0)$. One of the more important hypotheses that can be tested is the long-run price homogeneity of β to be discussed in Section 4.7.

4.5. Defining the I(2) model

It is useful to reformulate the VAR model defined in the previous section in acceleration rates, changes and levels:

$$\Delta^2 x_t = \Gamma \Delta x_{t-1} + \Pi x_{t-1} + \Phi_p D_{p,t} + \Phi_s Q_{s,t} + \mu_0 + \mu_1 t$$
$$+ \varepsilon_t, \varepsilon_t \sim N_p(0, \Omega), \quad t = 1, ..., T \tag{4.17}$$

where $\Gamma = -(I - \Gamma_1)$ and $\mu_1 = \alpha \mu_{1.0}$ is restricted to lie in $sp(\alpha)$ (cf. Section 4.5.3).

Figure 4.9. The graphs of $\beta'_4 x_t$ (upper panel) and $\beta'_4 R_{1t}$ (lower panel)

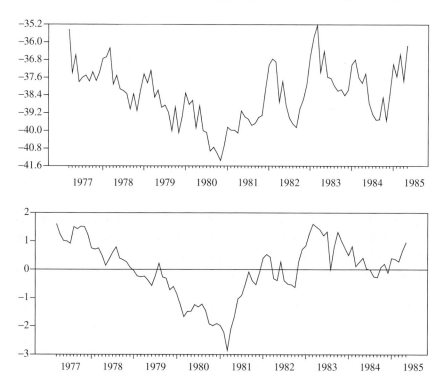

4.5.1. The AR formulation

The hypothesis that x_t is $I(2)$ is formulated in Johansen (1992) as two reduced rank hypotheses:

$$\Pi = \alpha\beta', \text{ where } \alpha, \beta \text{ are } p \times r \tag{4.18}$$

and

$$\alpha'_{\perp}\Gamma\beta_{\perp} = \zeta\eta', \text{ where } \zeta, \eta \text{ are } (p-r) \times s_1. \tag{4.19}$$

The first condition is the usual $I(1)$ reduced rank condition associated with the variables in levels, whereas the second condition is associated with the variables in differences. The intuition is that the differenced process also contains unit roots when data are $I(2)$. Note, however, that Equation (4.19) is formulated as a reduced rank condition on the transformed Γ. The intuition behind this can be seen by pre-multiplying Equation (4.17) with $\alpha_{\perp}$ (and post-multiplying by $\beta_{\perp}$). This makes the levels component

$\alpha\beta' x_{t-2}$ disappear and reduces the model to a $((p-r)\times(p-r))$-dimensional system of equations in first- and second-order differences. In this system, the hypothesis of reduced rank of the matrix $\alpha'_{\perp}\Gamma\beta_{\perp}$ is tested in the usual way. Thus, the second reduced rank condition is similar to the first except that the reduced rank regression is on the $p-r$ common driving trends. Using Equation (4.19) it is possible to decompose $\alpha_{\perp}$ and $\beta_{\perp}$ into the $I(1)$ and $I(2)$ directions:

$$\alpha_{\perp} = \{\alpha_{\perp 1}, \alpha_{\perp 2}\} \text{ and } \beta_{\perp} = \{\beta_{\perp 1}, \beta_{\perp 2}\}, \tag{4.20}$$

where $\alpha_{\perp 1} = \alpha_{\perp}(\alpha'_{\perp}\alpha_{\perp})^{-1}\zeta$ and $\beta_{\perp,1} = \beta_{\perp}(\beta'_{\perp}\beta_{\perp})^{-1}\eta$ is $p\times s_1$, $\alpha_{\perp 2} = \alpha_{\perp}\zeta_{\perp}$ and $\beta_{\perp 2} = \beta_{\perp}\eta_{\perp}$ is $p\times s_2$, and $\zeta_{\perp}, \eta_{\perp}$ are the orthogonal complements of ζ and η, respectively. Note that the matrices $\alpha_{\perp 1}$, $\alpha_{\perp 2}$, $\beta_{\perp 1}$, and $\beta_{\perp 2}$ are called α_1, α_2, β_1 and β_2 in the many papers on $I(2)$ by Johansen and co-authors. The reason why we deviate here from the simpler notation is that we need to distinguish between different β and α vectors in the empirical analysis and, hence, use the latter notation for this purpose.

While the $I(1)$ model is only based on the distinction between r co-integrating relations and $p-r$ non-cointegrating relations, the $I(2)$ model makes an additional distinction between s_1 $I(1)$ trends and s_2 $I(2)$ trends. Furthermore, when $r > s_2$, the r co-integrating relations can be divided into $r_0 = r - s_2$ directly stationary $CI(2,2)$ relations (co-integrating from $I(2)$ to $I(0)$) and s_2 polynomially co-integrating relations. This distinction will be illustrated in Section 6 based on the Brazilian data.

4.5.2. The moving average representation

The moving average representation of Equation (4.17) describes the variables as a function of stochastic and deterministic trends, stationary components, initial values and deterministic dummy variables. It is given by:

$$x_t = C_2 \sum_{s=1}^{t}\sum_{i=1}^{s}\varepsilon_i + C_2\frac{1}{2}\mu_0 t^2 + C_2\Phi_p\sum_{s=1}^{t}\sum_{i=1}^{s}Dp_i$$

$$+ C_2\Phi_s\sum_{s=1}^{t}\sum_{i=1}^{s}Qs_i + C_1\sum_{s=1}^{t}\varepsilon_s + C_1\Phi_p\sum_{s=1}^{t}Dp_s$$

$$+ C_2\Phi_s\sum_{s=1}^{t}Qs_s + \left(C_1 + \tfrac{1}{2}C_2\right)\mu_0 t + \gamma_1 t + Y_t + A + Bt, \quad t = 1,\dots,T$$

$$\tag{4.21}$$

where Y_t defines the stationary part of the process, A and B are functions of the initial values $x_0, x_{-1}, \ldots, x_{-k+1}$, and the coefficient matrices satisfy:

$$C_2 = \beta_{\perp 2}(\alpha'_{\perp 2}\Psi\beta_{\perp 2})^{-1}\alpha'_{\perp 2}, \qquad \beta'C_1 = -\bar{\alpha}'\Gamma C_2,$$

$$\beta'_{\perp 1}C_1 = -\bar{\alpha}'_{\perp 1}(I - \Psi C_2) \tag{4.22}$$

where $\Psi = \Gamma\bar{\beta}\bar{\alpha}'\Gamma + I - \Gamma_1$ and the shorthand notation $\bar{\alpha} = \alpha(\alpha'\alpha)^{-1}$ is used. See Johansen (1992, 1995).

We denote $\tilde{\beta}_{\perp 2} = \beta_{\perp 2}(\alpha'_{\perp 2}\Psi\beta_{\perp 2})^{-1}$ so that

$$C_2 = \tilde{\beta}_{\perp 2}\alpha'_{\perp 2} \tag{4.23}$$

i.e. the C_2 matrix has a similar reduced rank representation as C_1 in the $I(1)$ model. It is, therefore, natural to interpret $\alpha'_{\perp 2}\sum\sum\varepsilon_i$ as the second-order stochastic trend that has affected the variables x_t with weights $\tilde{\beta}_{\perp 2}$. However, the C_1 matrix cannot be decomposed similarly. It is a more complex function of the AR parameters of the model and the C_2 matrix and the interpretation of the parameters $\alpha_{\perp 1}$ and $\beta_{\perp 1}$ is less intuitive.

The MA representation (4.22) together with (4.23) can be used to obtain ML estimates of the stochastic and deterministic trends and cycles and their loadings in the intuitive scenario (4.8) of Section 4.3. This will be illustrated in Section 4.6.

4.5.3. Deterministic components in the I(2) model

It appears from Equation (4.21) that an unrestricted constant in the model is consistent with linear and quadratic trends in the data. Johansen (1992) suggested the decomposition of the constant term μ_0 into the α, $\alpha_{\perp 1}$, $\alpha_{\perp 2}$ projections:

$$\mu_0 = \alpha\gamma_0 + \gamma_1 + \gamma_2,$$

where

- γ_0 is a constant term in the stationary co-integration relations,
- γ_1 is the slope coefficient of linear trends in the variables, and
- γ_2 is the slope coefficient of quadratic trends in the variables.

Quadratic trends in the levels of the variables is consistent with linear trends in the growth rates, i.e. in inflation rates, which generally does not seem plausible (not even as a local approximation). Therefore, the empirical model will be based on the assumption that the data contain linear but no quadratic trends, i.e. that $\gamma_2 = 0$.

Similar arguments can be given for the dummy variables. An unrestricted shift dummy, such as $Ds83.8_t$, in the model is consistent with a broken quadratic trend in the data, whereas an unrestricted blip dummy, such as $Dp83.8_t = \Delta Ds83.8_t$, is consistent with a broken linear trend in the data. Thus, a correct specification of dummies is important as they are likely to strongly affect both the model estimates and the asymptotic distribution of the rank test.

In many cases, it is important to allow for trend-stationary relations in the $I(2)$ model (Rahbek *et al.*, 1999). In this case, $\mu_1 t \neq 0$ and the vector μ_1 needs to be decomposed in a similar way as the constant term:

$$\mu_1 = \alpha' \delta_0 + \delta_1 + \delta_2,$$

where

- δ_0 is the slope coefficient of a linear trend in the co-integration relations,
- δ_1 is the slope coefficient of quadratic trends in the variables, and
- δ_2 is the slope coefficient of cubic trends in the variables.

Since the presence of deterministic quadratic or cubic trends are not very plausible, we will assume that $\delta_1 = \delta_2 = 0$.

4.5.4. The determination of the two rank indices

The co-integration rank r can be determined either by the two-step estimation procedure in Johansen (1995) based on the polynomial co-integration property of $\beta' x_t$, or by the *FIML* procedure in Johansen (1997) based on the CI(2, 1) property of $\beta' x_t$ and $\beta'_{\perp 1} x_t$. The idea of the two-step procedure is as follows: the first step determines $r = \bar{r}$ based on the trace test in the standard $I(1)$ model and the estimates $\hat{\alpha}$ and $\hat{\beta}$. The second step determines $s_1 = \bar{s}_1$ by solving the reduced rank problem for the matrix $(\hat{\alpha}'_{\perp} \Gamma \hat{\beta}_{\perp})$. The practical procedure is to calculate the trace test for all possible combinations of r and s_1 so that the joint hypothesis (r, s_1) can be tested using the procedure in Paruolo (1996).

Based on a broad simulation study, Nielsen and Rahbek (2003) show that the FIML procedure has better size properties than the two-step procedure. The estimates here are, therefore, based on the *FIML* procedure using the new version 2.D of CATS for RATS developed by Jonathan Dennis.

Table 4.1 reports the test of the joint hypothesis (r, s_1) with the 95% quantiles of the simulated distribution given in brackets. They are derived for a model with a linear trend restricted to be in the co-integration space.

**Table 4.1.	Testing the two rank indices in the I(2) model**

$p-r$	r	FIML Test Procedure: $Q(s_1, r)$				$Q(r)$	λ_i
4	0	323.87 (0.00)	220.09 (0.00)	149.68 (0.00)	99.01 (0.00)	95.91 (0.00)	0.43
3	1		141.95 (0.00)	73.89 (0.02)	51.69 (0.08)	44.16 (0.04)	0.24
2	2			48.92 (0.05)	24.14 (0.47)	19.67 (0.25)	0.12
1	3				13.40 (0.34)	7.29 (0.32)	0.05
s_2		4	3	2	1	0	

The test procedure starts with the most restricted model $(r = 0, s_1 = 0, s_2 = 4)$ in the upper left-hand corner, continues to the end of the first row $(r = 0, s_1 = 4, s_2 = 0)$, and proceeds similarly row-wise from left to right until the first acceptance. The first acceptance is at $(r = 1, s_1 = 1, s_2 = 1)$ with a p-value of 0.08. However, the case $(r = 2, s_1 = 1, s_2 = 1)$ is accepted with a much higher p-value 0.47 and will be our preferred choice. As a matter of fact, the subsequent results will demonstrate that the second relation plays a crucial role in the price mechanisms, which led to hyper inflation.

To improve the small sample properties of the test procedures, a Bartlett correction can be employed (Johansen, 2002). Even though it significantly improves the size of the co-integration rank, the power of the tests is generally very low for $I(2)$ or near $I(2)$ data.

The Paruolo procedure delivers a correct size asymptotically, but does not solve the problem of low power. Because economic theory is often consistent with few rather than many common trends, a reversed order of testing might be preferable from an economic point of view. However, in that case the test will no longer deliver a correct asymptotic size.

Furthermore, when the $I(2)$ model contains intervention dummies that cumulate to trends in the *DGP*, standard asymptotic tables are no longer valid. For example, an unrestricted impulse dummy, like $Dp83.8_t$, will cumulate to a broken linear trend in the data. The asymptotic distributions for the $I(2)$ model do not account for this feature. Since the null of a unit root is not necessarily reasonable from an economic point of view, the low power and the impact of the dummies on the distributions can be a serious problem. This can sometimes be a strong argument for basing the choice of r and s_1 on prior information given by the economic insight as well as the statistical information in the data. As demonstrated in Section 4.4, such information can be a graphical inspection and the number of (near) unit roots in the characteristic polynomial of the VAR.

For the present choice of rank $(r = 2, s_1 = 1, s_2 = 1)$ the characteristic roots of the *VAR* model became

$$1.0 \quad 1.0 \quad 1.0 \quad 0.89 \quad 0.39 \quad 0.06 \quad -0.09 \quad -0.32$$

leaving a fairly large root in the model. Therefore, another possibility would have been to choose $r = 2$, $s_1 = 0$, $s_2 = 2$.

4.6. Interpreting the I(2) structure

It is no easy task to give the intuition for the different levels of integration and co-integration in the $I(2)$ model and how they can be translated into economically relevant relationships. Table 4.2 illustrates the $I(2)$ decomposition of the Brazilian data, which is based on the following assumptions (anticipating the subsequent results):

$$m_t \sim I(2), p_t \sim I(2), s_t^b \sim I(2), y_t^r \sim I(1)$$

and

$$\underbrace{r = 2}_{r_0 = 1, r_1 = 1}, \text{ and } \underbrace{p - r}_{s_1 = 1, s_2 = 1} = 2$$

The left-hand side of Table 4.2 illustrates the decomposition of x_t into two β and two $\beta_\perp$ directions corresponding to $r = 2$ and $p - r = 2$. This decomposition defines two stationary polynomially co-integrating relations, $\beta_1' x_t + \omega_1' \Delta x_t$ and $\beta_2' x_t + \omega_2' \Delta x_t$, and two non-stationary relations, $\beta_{\perp 1}' x_t \sim I(1)$ and $\beta_{\perp 2}' x_t \sim I(2)$. Note that $\beta_{\perp 1}' x_t$ is co-integrating from $I(2)$ to $I(1)$, and can become $I(0)$ by differencing once, whereas $\beta_{\perp 2}' x_t$ is not co-integrating at all and, thus, can only become $I(0)$ by differencing twice.

Table 4.2. Decomposing the data vector using the I(2) model

	The $\beta, \beta_\perp$ Decomposition of x_t	The $\alpha, \alpha_\perp$ Decomposition
$r = 2$	$[\underbrace{\beta_1' x_t}_{I(1)} + \underbrace{\omega_1' \Delta x_t}_{I(1)}] \sim I(0)$	α_1: short-run adjustment coefficients
	$[\underbrace{\beta_2' x_t}_{I(1)} + \underbrace{\omega_2' \Delta x_t}_{I(1)}] \sim I(0)$	α_2: short-run adjustment coefficients
$s_1 = 1$	$\beta_{\perp 1}' x_t \sim I(1)$	$\alpha_{\perp 1}' \sum_{i=1}^t \varepsilon_i$: $I(1)$ stochastic trend
$s_2 = 1$	$\beta_{\perp 2}' x_t \sim I(2)$	$\alpha_{\perp 2}' \sum_{s=1}^t \sum_{i=1}^s \varepsilon_i$: $I(2)$ stochastic trend

When $r > s_2$ the polynomially co-integrating relations can be further decomposed into $r_0 = r - s_2 = 1$ directly co-integrating relations, $\beta'_0 x_t$, and $r_1 = r - r_0 = s_2 = 1$ polynomially co-integrating relations, $\beta'_1 x_t + \kappa' \Delta x_t$, where κ is a $p \times s_2$ matrix proportional $\beta_{\perp 2}$.

The right-hand side of Table 4.2 illustrates the corresponding decomposition into the α and the $\alpha_\perp$ directions, where α_1 and α_2 measure the short-run adjustment coefficients associated with the polynomially co-integrating relations, whereas $\alpha_{\perp 1}$ and $\alpha_{\perp 2}$ measure the loadings to the first- and second-order stochastic trends.

Both $\beta' x_t$ and $\beta'_{\perp 1} x_t$ are CI(2, 1) but they differ in the sense that the former can become stationary by polynomial co-integration, whereas the latter can only become stationary by differencing. Thus, even in the $I(2)$ model, the interpretation of the reduced rank of the matrix Π is that there are r relations that can become stationary either by co-integration or by multi-co-integration, and $p - r$ relations that only become stationary by differencing.

Thus, the $I(2)$ model can distinguish between the CI(2, 1) relations between levels $\{\beta' x_t, \beta'_{\perp 1} x_t\}$, the CI(1, 1) relations between levels and differences $\{\beta' x_{t-1} + \omega' \Delta x_t\}$, and finally the CI(1, 1) relations between differences $\{\beta'_{\perp 1} \Delta x_t\}$. As a consequence, when discussing the economic interpretation of these components, we need to modify the generic concept of "long-run" steady-state relations accordingly. Here, we will use the interpretation of

- $\beta'_0 x_t$ as a *static long-run equilibrium relation*,
- $\beta'_1 x_t + \kappa' \Delta x_t$ as a *dynamic long-run equilibrium relation*,
- $\beta'_{\perp 1} \Delta x_t$ as a *medium-run equilibrium relation*.

As mentioned above, the parameters of Table 4.2 can be estimated either by the two-step procedure or by the FIML procedure. Paruolo (2000) showed that the two-step procedure gives asymptotically efficient ML estimates. The FIML procedure solves just one reduced rank problem in which the eigenvectors determine the space spanned by $(\beta, \beta_{\perp 1})$, i.e. the $p - s_2$ $I(1)$ directions of the process. Independently of the estimation procedure, the crucial estimates are $\{\hat{\beta}, \hat{\beta}_{\perp 1}\}$, because for given values of these it is possible to derive the estimates of $\{\alpha, \alpha_{\perp 1}, \alpha_{\perp 2}, \beta_{\perp 2}\}$ and, if $r > s_2$, to further decompose β and α into $\beta = \{\beta_0, \beta_1\}$ and $\alpha = \{\alpha_0, \alpha_1\}$.

The parameter estimates in Table 4.3 are based on the two-step procedure for $r = 2$, $s_1 = 1$ and $s_2 = 1$. We have imposed identifying restrictions on two co-integration relations by distinguishing between the directly stationary relation, $\beta'_0 x_t$, and the polynomially co-integrated relation, $\beta'_1 x_t + \kappa \Delta x_t$, where κ is proportional to $\beta_{\perp 2}$. Note, however,

Table 4.3. Unrestricted estimates of the I(0), I(1), and I(2) directions of α and β

	m	p	s^b	y^r
The stationary co-integrating relations				
$\hat{\beta}_0$	1.00	−0.07	−0.91	−1.22
$\hat{\beta}_1$	−0.67	1.00	−0.06	0.37
κ	−4.87	−3.78	−5.48	−0.30
The adjustment coefficients				
$\hat{\alpha}_0$	0.04	−0.03	0.17	0.01
$\hat{\alpha}_1$	0.10	0.04	0.11	−0.01
The non-stationary relations				
$\hat{\beta}_{\perp 1}$	4.54	0.46	−3.99	6.69
$\hat{\beta}_{\perp 2}$	0.52	0.40	0.58	−0.03
The common stochastic trends				
$\hat{\alpha}_{\perp 1}$	0.038	−0.007	−0.012	0.122
$\hat{\alpha}_{\perp 2}$	−0.053	−0.078	−0.016	−0.023
$\hat{\sigma}_\varepsilon$	0.016	0.010	0.054	0.028

that this is just one of many identification schemes which happen to be possible because $r - s_2 = 1$. In Section 4.8, we will present another identified structure where both relations are polynomially co-integrating.

The $\hat{\beta}'_{\perp 1} x_t$ relation is a CI(2, 1) co-integrating relation which only can become stationary by differencing. We interpret such a relation as a medium long-run steady-state relation. The estimated coefficients of $\hat{\beta}_{\perp 1}$ suggest a first tentative interpretation:

$$\Delta y^r_t = 0.60\Delta s^b_t - 0.68\Delta m_t$$

i.e. real industrial production has increased in the medium run with the currency depreciation relative to the growth of money stock.

The estimate of $\alpha_{\perp 2}$ determines the stochastic I(2) trend $\hat{\alpha}'_{\perp 2}\sum\sum\hat{\varepsilon}_i = \sum\sum\hat{u}_{2i}$, where $\hat{\varepsilon}_i$ is the vector of estimated residuals from Equation (4.17) and $\hat{u}_{2t} = \hat{\alpha}'_{\perp 2}\hat{\varepsilon}_t$. Permanent shocks to money stock relative to price shocks, to black market exchange rates and to industrial production seem to have generated the I(2) trend in this period. The standard deviations of the VAR residuals are reported in the bottom row of the table.

The estimate of $\alpha_{\perp 1}$ describes the second I(1) stochastic trend, $\sum\hat{u}_{2i} = \hat{\alpha}'_{\perp 1}\sum\hat{\varepsilon}_i$. The coefficient to real industrial production has by far the largest

**Figure 4.10.   The graphs of the estimated I(2) trend in the upper panel,
the nominal I(1) trend (i.e. the differenced I(2) trend) in the middle panel
and the real I(1) trend in the lower panel**

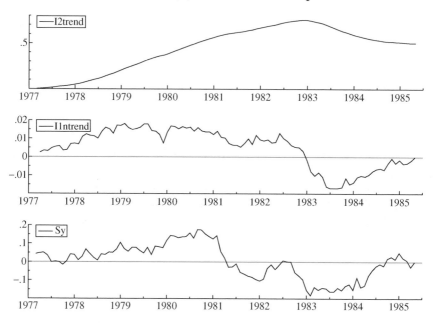

weight in $\hat{\alpha}_{\perp 1}$ suggesting that it measures an autonomous real shock. This
is consistent with the hypothetical scenario (4.7) of Section 4.3.

Figure 4.10, upper panel, shows the graph of the $I(2)$ stochastic trend,
$\hat{\alpha}'_{\perp 2}\sum\sum\hat{\varepsilon}_i$, where $\hat{\alpha}_{\perp 2}$ is from Table 4.3. The graph in the middle panel is
the differenced $I(2)$ trend and the graph in the lower panel is the real
stochastic trend given by $\sum\hat{\varepsilon}_{y,i}$.

The vector $\hat{\beta}_{\perp 2}$ describes the weights c_i, $i = 1, ..., 4$ of the $I(2)$ trend in
the scenario (4.7) of Section 4.3 for the Brazilian variables. Nominal
money, prices and exchange rates have large coefficients of approximately
the same size, whereas the coefficient to real income is very small. This
suggests that only the nominal variables are $I(2)$ consistent with the
assumption behind the scenario in (4.7).

4.7. Nominal growth in the long run and the medium run

The notion of price homogeneity plays an important role for the analysis of
price adjustment in the long run and the medium run. Both in the $I(1)$ and
the $I(2)$ models, long-run price homogeneity can be defined as a zero sum
restriction on β. Under the assumption that industrial production is not

affected by the $I(2)$ trend, long-run price homogeneity for the Brazilian data can be expressed as:

$$\beta_i' = [a_i, -\omega_i a_i, -(1 - \omega_i)a_i, *, *], \quad i = 1, ..., 2,$$
$$\beta_{\perp 1}' = [b, -\omega_3 b, -(1 - \omega_3)b,^*] \tag{4.24}$$
$$\beta_{\perp 2}' = [c, c, c, 0].$$

where β and $\beta_{\perp 1}$ define CI(2, 1) relations and $\beta_{\perp 2}$ define the variables which are affected by the $I(2)$ trends. Overall price homogeneity is testable either as a joint hypothesis of the first two conditions or as a single hypothesis of the last condition in Equation (4.24) (see, Kongsted, 2004). The first condition in (4.24) describes price homogeneity between the levels of the nominal variables. It can be easily tested in the standard $I(1)$ model as a linear hypothesis on β either expressed as $R'\beta_i = 0, i = 1, ..., r,$ where for the Brazilian data $R' = [1, 1, 1, 0, 0]$ or, equivalently, as $(\beta = H\varphi$ where φ is a $(p1 - 1) \times r$ matrix of free coefficients and

$$H = \begin{bmatrix} 1 & 0 & 0 & 0 \\ -1 & -1 & 0 & 0 \\ 0 & 1 & 0 & 0 \\ 0 & 0 & 1 & 0 \\ 0 & 0 & 0 & 1 \end{bmatrix}$$

The hypothesis of price homogeneity was strongly rejected based on an LR test statistic of 41.9, asymptotically distributed as $(\chi^2(2)$. We note that the first three coefficients of $\hat{\beta}_1$ in Table 4.3 do not even approximately sum to zero, whereas those of $\hat{\beta}_0$ are much closer to zero.

The $\hat{\beta}_{\perp 2}$ estimates in Table 4.3 suggest that nominal money stock and black market exchange rate have been similarly affected by the $I(2)$ trend, whereas the CPI price index has a smaller weight. Furthermore, the coefficient to industrial production is close to zero, consistent with the hypothesis that the latter has not been affected by the $I(2)$ trend. This can be formally tested based on the LR procedure (Johansen, 2004) as an hypothesis that industrial production is $I(1)$. The test, distributed as $\chi^2(1)$, was accepted based a test statistic of 1.30 and a p-value of 0.25.

In the $I(2)$ model, there is the additional possibility of medium-run price homogeneity defined as homogeneity between nominal growth rates. This is, in general, associated with real variables being $I(1)$. For example, if $(m - p) \sim I(1)$ and $(s^b - p) \sim I(1)$, then $(\Delta m - \Delta p) \sim I(0)$ and $(\Delta s^b - \Delta p) \sim I(0)$ and there is medium-run price homogeneity in the sense of nominal growth rates being pairwise co-integrated $(1, -1)$. Hence, a rejection of long-run price homogeneity implies a rejection of homogeneity between the nominal growth rates. We note that the first three coefficients of $\hat{\beta}_{\perp 1}$ in Table 4.3 do not even roughly sum to zero consistent with the rejection of long-run price homogeneity.

The previous section demonstrated that the levels component, Πx_{t-2} and the differences component, $\Gamma \Delta x_{t-1}$ in Equation (4.17) are closely tied together by polynomial co-integration. In addition, $\Gamma \Delta x_{t-1}$ contains information about $\beta'_{\perp} \Delta x_{t-1}$, i.e. about the medium long-run relation between growth rates. Relying on results in Johansen (1995), the levels and difference components of model (4.17) can be decomposed as:

$$\Gamma \Delta x_{t-1} + \Pi x_{t-1}$$

$$= (\Gamma \bar{\beta}) \underbrace{\beta' \Delta \mathbf{x}_{t-1}}_{I(0)} + (\alpha \bar{\alpha}' \Gamma \bar{\beta}_{\perp 1} + \alpha_{\perp 1}) \underbrace{\beta'_{\perp 1} \Delta \mathbf{x}_{t-1}}_{I(0)}$$

$$+ (\alpha \bar{\alpha}' \Gamma \bar{\beta}_{\perp 2}) \underbrace{\beta'_{\perp 2} \Delta \mathbf{x}_{t-1}}_{I(0)} + \alpha_1 \underbrace{\beta'_1 \mathbf{x}_{t-1}}_{I(1)} + \alpha_0 \underbrace{\beta'_0 \mathbf{x}_{t-1}}_{I(0)} \qquad (4.25)$$

where $\bar{\beta} = \beta(\beta'\beta)^{-1}$ and $\bar{\alpha}$ is similarly defined. The Γ matrix is decomposed into three parts describing different dynamic effects from the growth rates, and the Π matrix into two parts describing the effects from the stationary relation, $\beta'_0 x_{t-1}$, and the non-stationary relation, $\beta'_1 x_{t-1}$. The matrices in brackets correspond to the adjustment coefficients.

The interpretation of the first component in Equation (4.25), $(\Gamma \bar{\beta}) \beta' \Delta x_{t-1}$, is that prices are not just adjusting to the equilibrium error between the price levels, $\beta' x_{t-2}$, but also to the change in the equilibrium error, $\beta' \Delta x_{t-1}$. Under long-run price homogeneity, it would have represented a homogeneous effect in inflation rates.

The second component, $(\alpha \bar{\alpha}' \Gamma \bar{\beta}_{\perp 1} + \alpha_{\perp 1}) \beta'_{\perp 1} \Delta \mathbf{x}_{t-1}$, corresponds to a stationary medium long-run relation between growth rates of nominal magnitudes. Because of the rejection of long-run price homogeneity, this represents a non-homogeneous effect in nominal growth rates.

The third component, $(\alpha \bar{\alpha}' \Gamma \bar{\beta}_{\perp 2}) \beta'_{\perp 2} \Delta \mathbf{x}_{t-1}$, and the fourth component, $\alpha_1 \beta'_1 x_t$, are both $I(1)$ relations which combine to a stationary polynomial co-integration relation, $\alpha_1 (\beta'_1 x_{t-1} + \kappa' \Delta x_{t-1}) \sim I(0)$, where $\alpha_1 \kappa' = (\alpha \bar{\alpha}' \Gamma \bar{\beta}_{\perp 2}) \beta'_{\perp 2}$.

The long-run matrix Π is the sum of the two levels components measured by:

$$\Pi = \alpha_0 \beta'_0 + \alpha_1 \beta'_1.$$

Table 4.4. The unrestricted parameter estimates

The estimated $\Gamma = \alpha'_\perp \Gamma \beta_\perp$ matrix

	Δm_t	Δp_t	Δs_t^b	Δy_t^r
$\Delta^2 m_t$	-1.07	-0.06	0.00	0.02
$\Delta^2 p_t$	-0.02	-0.55	0.01	-0.01
$\Delta^2 s_t^b$	-0.42	0.42	-0.92	0.03
$\Delta^2 y_t^r$	-0.13	0.20	0.04	-1.32

The estimated $\Pi = \alpha\beta'$ matrix

	m_{t-1}	p_{t-1}	s_{t-1}^b	y_{t-1}^r	Trend
$\Delta^2 m_t$	$-0.03\ (-1.7)$	**0.11** (7.5)	$-\mathbf{0.05}\ (-3.3)$	$0.00\ (0.4)$	$-0.001\ (-6.6)$
$\Delta^2 p_t$	$-\mathbf{0.05}\ (-5.1)$	**0.03** (3.3)	**0.03** (3.1)	**0.05** (4.8)	$0.00\ (0.1)$
$\Delta^2 s_t^b$	**0.11** (1.9)	**0.15** (2.8)	$-\mathbf{0.19}\ (-3.9)$	$-\mathbf{0.15}\ (-2.6)$	**0.002** (4.2)
$\Delta^2 y_t^r$	$0.02\ (0.7)$	$-0.01\ (-0.3)$	$-0.01\ (-0.5)$	$-0.02\ (-0.6)$	$-0.00\ (-0.1)$

Hypothetically, the Π matrix is likely to satisfy the condition for long-run price homogeneity in a regime where inflation is under control. Thus, the lack of price homogeneity is likely to be the first sign of inflation running out of control.

The growth-rates matrix Γ is the sum of the three different components measured by

$$\Gamma = (\Gamma\bar{\beta})\beta' + (\alpha\bar{\alpha}'\Gamma\bar{\beta}_{\perp1} + \alpha_{\perp1})\beta'_{\perp1} + (\alpha\bar{\alpha}'\Gamma\bar{\beta}_{\perp2})\beta'_{\perp2}.$$

The Γ matrix is, however, not likely to exhibit medium-run price homogeneity, even under the case of long-run price homogeneity. This is because $R'\beta = 0$ implies $R'\beta_{\perp2} \neq 0$. The intuition is as follows: when $\beta'x_t \sim I(0)$, a non-homogeneous reaction in nominal growth rates is needed to achieve an adjustment towards a stationary long-run equilibrium position. Therefore, medium-run price homogeneity interpreted as a zero sum restriction of rows of Γ would in general be inconsistent with overall long-run price homogeneity.

Table 4.4 reports the estimates of $\Gamma = -(I - \Gamma_1) = \alpha'_\perp \Gamma \beta_\perp$ and $\Pi = \alpha\beta'$. We notice that the coefficients of each row do not sum to zero. The next section will show that the difference is statistically significant. The diagonal elements of the Π matrix are particularly interesting as they provide information of equilibrium correction behaviour, or the lack of it, of the variables in this system. We notice a significant positive coefficient in the diagonal element of the domestic prices, which in a single equation model would imply accelerating prices. In a VAR model, absence of equilibrium correction in one variable can be compensated by a sufficiently strong counteracting reaction from the other variables in the system. It is noticeable that the only truly market determined variable, the black market exchange rate, is the significantly equilibrium-correcting variable, whereas money stock is only borderline so.

Section 4.3 demonstrated that the unrestricted characteristic roots of the VAR model contained a small explosive root, which disappeared when two unit roots were imposed. Nevertheless, the positive diagonal element of prices suggest that the spiral of price increases, which subsequently became hyper inflation had already started at the end of this sample.

4.8. Money growth, currency depreciation, and price inflation in Brazil

Long-run price homogeneity is an important property of a nominal system and rejecting it is likely to have serious implications both for the interpretation of the results and for the validity of the nominal to real transformation. The empirical analysis of Durevall (1998) was based on a nominal to real transformation without first testing its validity. We will here use the $I(2)$ model for the empirical investigation of the money-price spiral without having to impose invalid long-run price homogeneity.

4.8.1. Identifying the β relations

The estimates of β_0, β_1 and κ in Table 4.3 are uniquely identified by the CI(2, 2) property of $\beta_0' x_t$. However, other linear combinations of β_0 and β_1 may be more relevant from an economic point of view, but these will be $I(1)$ and will, therefore, have to be combined with the differenced $I(2)$ variables to become stationary.

To obtain more interpretable results, three overidentifying restrictions have been imposed on the two β relations (see Johansen and Juselius, 1994). The LR test of overidentifying restrictions, distributed as $\chi^2(3)$ became 1.41 and the restrictions were accepted based on a p-value of 0.70. The estimates of the two identified relations became:

$$\beta_{1,t}^{c'} x_t = m_{t-1} - s_{t-1}^b - y_{t-1}^r - \underset{(-2.5)}{0.005} \text{ trend}$$

$$\beta_{2,t}^{c'} x_t = p_{t-1} - \underset{(18.3)}{0.64} (m_{t-1} - y_{t-1}^r) - \underset{(-2.5)}{0.008} \text{ trend} \tag{4.26}$$

The first relation is essentially describing a trend-adjusted liquidity ratio, except that the black market exchange rate is used instead of the CPI as a measure of the price level. The liquidity ratio with CPI instead of the

Figure 4.11. *The graphs of inverse velocity with CPI as a price variable (upper panel) and with nominal exchange rate (lower panel)*

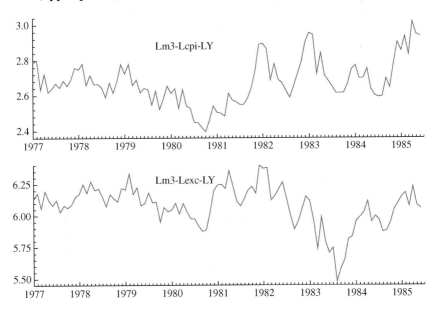

exchange rate was strongly rejected. This suggests that inflationary expectations were strongly affected by the expansion of money stock and that these expectations influenced the rise of the black market nominal exchange rate.

Both relations need a linear deterministic trend. The estimated trend coefficient of the first relation in (4.26) suggests that 'the liquidity ratio' grew on average with 6% ($0.005 \times 12 \times 100$) per year in this period. The second relation shows that prices grew less than proportionally with the expansion of M3 money stock relative to industrial production after having accounted for an average price increase of approximately 9% ($0.008 \times 12 \times 100$) per year.

The graphs in Figure 4.11 of the liquidity ratio based on the nominal exchange rate and on the CPI index, respectively, may explain why nominal exchange rates instead of domestic prices were empirically more relevant in the first relation. It is interesting to note that the graphs are very similar until the end of 1980, whereafter the black market exchange rate started to grow faster than CPI prices. Thus, the results suggest that money stock grew faster than prices in the crucial years before the first hyper inflation episode, but also that the depreciation rate of the black market currency was more closely related to money stock expansion. This period coincided with the Mexican moratorium, the repercussions of which were strongly and painfully felt in the Brazilian economy. The recession and the major decline of Brazilian exports caused the government to abandon its previous more orthodox policy of fighting inflation by maintaining a revalued currency and, instead, engage in a much looser monetary policy. For a comprehensive review of the Brazilian exchange rate policy over the last four decades, see Bonomo and Terra (1999).

Under the assumption that the black market exchange rate is a fairly good proxy for the 'true' value of the Brazilian currency, the following scenario seems plausible: the expansion of money stock needed to finance the recession and devaluations in the first case increased inflationary expectations in the black market, which then gradually spread to the whole domestic economy. Because of the widespread use of wage and price indexation in this period there were no effective mechanisms to prevent the accelerating price inflation.

4.8.2. Dynamic equilibrium relations

This scenario can be further investigated by polynomial co-integration. In the $I(2)$ model $\beta'x_t \sim I(1)$ has to be combined with the nominal growth rates to yield a stationary dynamic equilibrium relation. The two identified relations, $\beta'_{1,1}x_t$ and $\beta'_{1,2}x_t$ in Equation (4.26) need to be combined with nominal growth rates to become stationary. Table 4.5 reports various versions of the estimated dynamic equilibrium relations.

The first dynamic steady-state relation corresponds essentially to Cagan's money demand relation in periods of hyper inflation. However, the price level is measured by the black market nominal exchange rate and the opportunity cost of holding money is measured both by the CPI inflation and by the currency depreciation. The coefficient to inflation corresponds to Cagan's α coefficient, which defines the average inflation rate $(1/\alpha)$ at which the government can obtain maximum seignorage. The present estimate

Table 4.5. Estimates of the dynamic equilibrium relations $\beta'x_t + \omega'\Delta x_t$

	$\hat{\beta}'_{1,1}x_t$	$\omega_{1,1}\Delta m_t$	$\omega_{1,2}\Delta p_t$	$\omega_{1,3}\Delta s_t^b$
(1)	1.0	-0.62 (1.1)	2.52 (3.4)	0.59 (2.7)
(2)	1.0	$-$	2.02 (3.4)	0.53 (2.5)

	$\hat{\beta}'_{1,2}x_t$	$\omega_{2,1}\Delta m_t$	$\omega_{2,2}\Delta p_t$	$\omega_{2,3}\Delta s_t^b$
(3)	1.0	-5.80 (67)	-11.32 (9.9)	-0.34 (1.0)
(4)	1.0	-6.02 (7.1)	-11.38 (10.0)	$-$
(5)	1.0	$-$	-16.57 (15.4)	$-$
(6)	1.0	-11.42 (12.4)	$-$	$-$

suggests average inflation rates of an order of magnitude of 0.40–0.50 which corresponds to the usual definition of hyper inflation periods.

The second relation is more difficult to interpret from a theoretical point of view but seems crucial for the mechanisms behind the increasingly high inflation of this period and the hyper inflation of the subsequent periods. Equation (4.3) shows that the 'gap' between prices and 'excess' money as measured by $\beta_{1,2}'x_t$ is co-integrated with changes in money stock and prices, but not with currency depreciation. Equation (4.4) combines $\beta_{1,2}'x_t$ with money growth, Δm, and price inflation, Δp, Equation (4.5) with Δp and Equation (4.6) with Δm. Although, both nominal growth rates are individually co-integrating with $\beta_{1,2}'x_t$, there is an important difference between them: the relationship between money growth and the relation $\beta_{1,2}'x_t$ suggests error-correcting behaviour in money stock, whereas the one between price inflation and $\beta_{1,2}'x_t$ indicates lack error-correcting behaviour in prices. The latter would typically describe a price mechanism leading ultimately to hyper inflation unless counterbalanced by other compensating measures, such as currency control.

4.8.3. The short-run dynamic adjustment structure

The inflationary mechanisms will now be further investigated based on the estimated short-run dynamic adjustment structure. Current as well as lagged changes of industrial production were insignificant in the system and were, therefore, left out. Thus, real growth rates do not seem to have had any significant effect on the short-run adjustment of nominal growth

Table 4.6. Dynamic adjustment and feed-back effects in the nominal system

Reference	Regressors	Equation		
		Δm_t	Δp_t	Δs_t^b
	Δm_{t-1}	0.33 (4.2)	0.11 (2.4)	0.91 (2.7)
	Δp_{t-1}	0.59 (5.6)	0.76 (12.1)	–
Table 4.5 (2)	$(\hat{\beta}_{1,1}x - \hat{w}_{1,1}\Delta x)_{t-1}$	−0.03 (−2.3)	−0.03 (−2.9)	0.08 (1.9)
Table 4.5 (4)	$(\hat{\beta}_{1,2}x - \hat{w}_{1,2}\Delta x)_{t-1}$	0.06 (6.4)	0.02 (4.3)	0.06 (2.0)
Table 4.3	$\hat{\beta}_{\perp 1}'\Delta x_t$	+0.008 (−2.2)	−0.005 (2.1)	–
	Residual correlations	1.0		
		−0.02	1.0	
		0.08	−0.12	1.0

rates, which is usually assumed to be the case in a high inflation regime. Furthermore, based on an F-test the lagged depreciation rate was also found insignificant in the system and was similarly left out. Table 4.6 reports the estimated short-run structure of the simplified model. Most of the significant coefficients describe feed-back effects from the dynamic steady-state relations defined by Models (2) and (4) in Table 4.5 and the medium-run steady-state relation between growth rates, $\beta'_{\perp 1}\Delta x_t$ defined in Table 4.3. It is notable that the residual correlations are altogether very small, so that interpretation of the results would be robust to linear transformations of the system.

The short-run adjustment results generally confirm the previous findings. Price inflation has not been equilibrium correcting in the second steady-state relation, whereas the growth in money stock has been so in both of the two dynamic steady-state relations. The depreciation of the black market exchange rate has been equilibrium correcting to the first steady-state relation measuring the liquidity ratio relation and has been strongly affected by the second price 'gap' relation. Furthermore, it has reacted strongly to changes in money stock confirming the above interpretation of the important role of inflationary expectations (measured by changes in money stock) for the currency depreciation rate.

After the initial expansion of money stock at around 1981 (which might have been fatal in terms of the subsequent hyper inflation experience), money supply seems primarily to have accommodated the increasing price inflation. The lack of equilibrium correction behaviour in the latter was probably related to the widespread use of wage and price indexation in this period. Thus, the lack of market mechanism to correct for excessive price changes allowed domestic price inflation to gain momentum as a result of high inflationary expectations in the foreign exchange market.

4.9. Concluding remarks

The purpose of this chapter was partly to give an intuitive account of the co-integrated $I(2)$ model and its rich (but also complicated) statistical structure, partly to illustrate how this model can be used to address important questions related to inflationary mechanisms in high inflation periods. The empirical analysis was based on data from the Brazilian high inflation period, 1977:1–1985:5. An additional advantage of this period was that it was succeeded by almost a decade of hyper-inflationary episodes. The chapter demonstrates empirically that it is possible to uncover certain features in the data and the model, which at an early stage may suggest a lack of control in the price mechanism. Thus, a violation of two distinct properties, price homogeneity and equilibrium correction, usually prevalent in periods of controlled inflation, seemed to have a high signal value as a means to detect an increasing risk for a full-blown hyper inflation. The chapter demonstrates that:

1. prices started to grow in a non-homogeneous manner at the beginning of the eighties when the repercussions of the Mexican moratorium strongly and painfully hit the Brazilian economy. The expansion of money stock needed to finance the recession and the subsequent devaluations increased inflationary expectations in the black market, which then spread to the whole domestic economy;
2. the widespread use of wage and price indexation in this period switched off the natural equilibrium correction behaviour of the price mechanism. Without other compensating control measures, which might have dampened inflationary expectations, it was not possible to prevent price inflation to accelerate.

Acknowledgements

Useful comments from Michael Goldberg, Saren Johansen, and Mikael Juselius are gratefully acknowledged. The article was produced with financial support from the Danish Social Sciences Research Council.

References

Bonomo, M. and C. Terra (1999), "The political economy of exchange rate policy in Brazil: 1964–1997", Graduate School of Economics, Getulio Vargas Foundation, Rio de Janeiro, Brazil.

Cagan, P. (1956), "The monetary dynamic of hyperinflation", in: M. Friedman, editor, *Studies in the Quantity Theory of Money*, Chicago: University Press.

Doornik, J.A. (1996), "Testing vector error autocorrelation and heteroscedasticity", Available at http://www.nuff.ox.ac.uk/users/doornik

Doornik, J.A. and H. Hansen (1994), "An ominbus test for univariate and multivariate normality", Technical report, Nuffield College, Oxford.

Durevall, D. (1998), "The dynamics of chronic inflation in Brazil, 1968–1985", *Journal of Business and Economic Statistics*, Vol. 16, pp. 423–432.

Friedman, M. (1970), "The counterrevolution in monetary theory", Institute of Economic Affairs, Occasional Paper 33.

Hansen, H. and K. Juselius (1995), "CATS in RATS", Manual to Cointegration Analysis of Time Series, Evanston: Estima.

Johansen, S. (1992), "A representation of vector autoregressive processes integrated of order 2", *Econometric Theory*, Vol. 8, pp. 188–202.

Johansen, S. (1995), "A statistical analysis of cointegration for *I*(2) variables", *Econometric Theory*, Vol. 11, pp. 25–59.

Johansen, S. (1997), "A likelihood analysis of the $I(2)$ model", *Scandinavian Journal of Statistics*, Vol. 24, pp. 433–462.

Johansen, S. (2002), "A small sample correction of the test for cointegrating rank in the vector autoregressive model", *Econometrica*, Vol. 70, pp. 1929–1961.

Johansen, S. (2004), "Statistical analysis of hypotheses on the cointegrating relations in the $I(2)$ model", *Journal of Econometrics* (forthcoming).

Johansen, S. and K. Juselius (1994), "Identification of the long-run and the short-run structure. An application to the ISLM model", *Journal of Econometrics*, Vol. 63, pp. 7–36.

Juselius, K. (1999a), "Models and relations in economics and econometrics", *Journal of Economic Methodology*, Vol. 6(2), pp. 259–290.

Juselius, K. (1999b), "Price convergence in the long run and the medium run. An $I(2)$ analysis of six price indices" in: R. Engle and H. White, editors, 'Cointegration, Causality, and Forecasting' Festschrift in Honour of Clive W.J: Granger' ', Oxford University press, 1999.

Juselius, K. and Z. Vuojosevic (2003), "High inflation, hyper inflation, and explosive roots", *The Case of Yugoslavia*, Institute of Economics, University of Copenhagen (preprint).

King, R.G., C.I. Plosser, J.H. Stock and M.W. Watson (1991), "Stochastic trends and economic fluctuations", *American Economic Review*, Vol. 81, pp. 819–840.

Kongsted, H.C. (2004), "Testing the nominal-to-real transformation", *Journal of Econometrics* (forthcoming).

Nielsen, B. and A. Rahbek (2000), "Similarity issues in cointegration analysis", *Oxford Bulletin of Economics and Statistics*, Vol 62(1), pp. 5–22.

Nielsen, H.B. and A. Rahbek (2003), "Likelihood ratio testing for cointegration ranks in $I(2)$ models", Discussion Paper 2003-42, Institute of Economics, University of Copenhagen.

Omtzigt, P. (2003), "Me2: A computer package for the maximum likelihood estimation of $I(2)$ systems", Techanical report, University of Amsterdam.

Paruolo, P. (1996), "On the determination of integration indices in $I(2)$ systems", *Journal of Econometrics*, Vol. 72, pp. 313–356.

Parulo, P. (2000), "Asymptotic efficiency of the two stage estimator in $I(2)$ systems", *Econometric Theory*, Vol. 16(4), pp. 524–550.

Rahbek, A., H.C. Kongsted and C. Jørgensen (1999), "Trend-stationarity in the $I(2)$ cointegration model", *Journal of Econometrics*, Vol. 90, pp. 265–289.

Romer, D. (1996), *Advanced Macroeconomics*, New York: McGraw Hill.

Sargent, T. (1977), "The demand for money during hyperinflation under rational expectations: I", *International Economic Review*, Vol. 18(1), pp. 59–82.

Appendix A. Misspecification diagnostics

The univariate normality test in Table A4.1 is a Jarque–Bera test, distributed as $\chi^2(2)$. The multivariate normality test is described in Doornik and Hansen (1995) distributed as $\chi^2(8)$. The AR-test is the F-test described in Doornik (1996, p. 4). P-values are in brackets.

Table A4.1. Misspecification tests

Univariate misspecification tests

	y^r	s^b	m	p
Normality, $\chi^2(2)$	0.66 (0.72)	1.71 (0.43)	0.36 (0.84)	1.67 (0.43)
AR(1)	0.19 (0.66)	0.00 (0.95)	0.03 (0.87)	1.27 (0.26)
Skewness	− 0.13	0.21	0.09	− 0.21
Kurtosis	3.06	3.29	2.62	3.27

Multivariate misspecification tests

Normality, $\chi^2(8)$	4.43 (0.82)
AR(1)	5.59 (0.99)
AR(4)	62.21 (0.54)

Figure A4.1. Residual autocorrelograms and cross-correlograms with 95% confidence bands

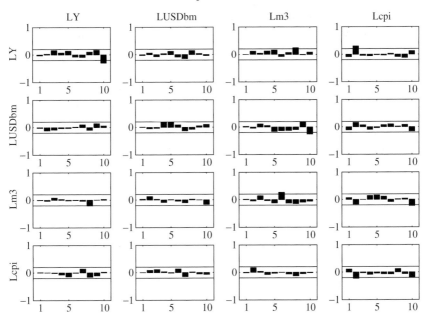

K. Juselius

Figure A4.2. Residual histograms for the four equations

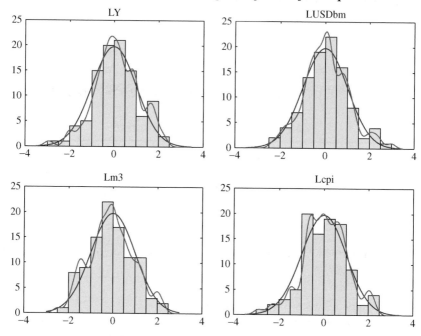

Figure A4.1 shows the residual auto-correlograms and cross-correlo-grams of order 10 for all four equations. Figure A4.2 shows the residual histograms compared to the normal distribution for all equations. Both figures have been produced with the program, Me2, described in Omtzigt (2003).

New Directions in Macromodelling
A. Welfe (Editor)
DOI: 10.1016/S0573-8555(04)69005-5

CHAPTER 5

Recent Advances in Cointegration Analysis

Helmut Lütkepohl

Department of Economics, European University Institute, Via della Piazzuola 43,
I-50133 Firenze, Italy

Abstract

A small system of German economic variables consisting of the money stock M3, Gross National Product (GNP) and a bond rate is used to illustrate the power of cointegration analysis and the usefulness of some recently developed tools for this kind of analysis. Testing for the cointegrating rank and specifying a VECM, estimating the cointegrating relations and other parameters as well as model checking are discussed. The estimated model is analysed with an impulse response analysis and a forecast error variance decomposition is performed. A quite reasonable long-run money demand relation is found.

Keywords: cointegration, German monetary system, vector error correction model

JEL classification: C32

5.1. Introduction

The cointegration framework has been developed rapidly over the last years. Its fast progress is to a large extent due to its usefulness for applied work. Cointegration is a concept for modelling equilibrium or long-run relations of economic variables. Many economic issues have been reanalysed using the cointegration toolkit with partly very interesting new findings and insights. In this study I will use a small German macrosystem consisting of the three variables log real M3 (m_t), log real GNP (gnp_t) and a long-term bond rate (R_t) to illustrate the power of cointegration analysis. The system was previously analysed by Lütkepohl (2004b). It is modelled around a possible money demand relation. Thus, one would expect to find one long-run relation representing a money demand function. Hence, the cointegration framework is potentially useful for analysing this system. The need for some of the recent developments will be demonstrated in the analysis.

In performing a cointegration analysis, the first step is to determine the order of integration of the individual variables. This part of the analysis will be discussed in Section 5.3. Then the number of cointegration relations has to be investigated. This issue is dealt with in Section 5.4. When the number of cointegration relations is known, their parameters can be estimated and restrictions may be placed on them as appropriate. This step is considered in Section 5.5. Although the cointegration relations often form the central part of interest, a complete model is necessary for assessing the general quality of the modelling exercise and for subsequent further investigations or forecasting. Therefore specifying and estimating the short-run part of the model for the DGP is discussed in Section 6. Model checking is treated in Section 7. Once a satisfactory complete model is available the dynamic interactions between the variables can be studied in more detail with the help of an impulse response analysis or a forecast error variance decomposition. These tools are presented in Section 8 and Section 9 concludes with a brief summary of some other interesting lines of research related to cointegration.

Throughout the issues are illustrated and the methods are guided by the small German monetary system sketched in the foregoing. The special data features call for special methods that have only recently been developed. Therefore, the example system is useful for motivating the specific recent developments presented in this review. The data are discussed in more detail in the next section. The computations are performed with the software JMulTi (Lütkepohl and Krätzig, 2004; web page www.jmulti.de).

The following general notation will be used. The differencing and lag operators are denoted by Δ and L, respectively, i.e. for a stochastic process y_t, $\Delta y_t = y_t - y_{t-1}$ and $Ly_t = y_{t-1}$. Convergence in distribution is signified by $\overset{d}{\to}$ and log denotes the natural logarithm. The trace, determinant and rank of the matrix A are denoted by $\mathrm{tr}(A)$ $\det(A)$ and $\mathrm{rk}(A)$, respectively. The symbol vec is used for the column vectorization operator so that $\mathrm{vec}(A)$ is the vector of columns of the matrix A. An $(n \times n)$ identity matrix is denoted by I_n. DGP, ML, LS, GLS, RR and LR are used to abbreviate data generation process, maximum likelihood, least squares, generalized least squares, reduced rank and likelihood ratio, respectively.

VAR and VECM stand for vector autoregression and vector error correction model, respectively.

5.2. The data

As mentioned in the introduction, an example model built around a money demand relation for Germany will be used for illustrative purposes throughout. The money demand relation is especially important for a monetary policy that targets the money stock growth. Such a monetary policy was conducted by the Bundesbank (German central bank) in Germany since the middle of the 1970s. Therefore, investigating whether a stable money demand relation has existed for Germany for the period of monetary targeting by the Bundesbank is of interest.

According to economic theory real money demand should depend on the real transactions volume and a nominal interest rate. The latter variable represents opportunity costs of holding money. Because the quantity theory suggests a log-linear relationship, the three-dimensional system (m_t, gnp_t, R_t) is considered, where m_t is the log of real M3, gnp_t the log of real GNP and R_t is the nominal long-term interest rate. The money stock measure M3 is used because the Bundesbank announced a target growth rate for that variable since 1988. In addition to currency holdings and sight deposits, M3 also includes savings deposits and time deposits for up to 4 years. Therefore, it seems plausible to use a long-term interest rate as a measure for opportunity costs. Specifically, the so-called 'Umlaufsren-dite', an average bond rate will be used in the following. GNP represents the transactions volume. Clearly, in a system of this type there may be other important related variables. For instance, inflation or an exchange rate may be considered in addition to our three variables. A small three-dimensional system is preferable for illustrative purposes, however. An analysis of a related larger system was performed by Lütkepohl and Wolters (2003).

Our sample period is 1975Q1–1998Q4 because the Bundesbank started its monetary targeting policy in 1975 and at the beginning of 1999 the Euro was introduced so that the European Central Bank became responsible for the monetary policy. Quarterly, seasonally unadjusted data is used. Both M3 and GNP are deflated by the GNP deflator.[1] The series m_t, gnp_t and R_t are plotted in Figure 5.1. The variables m_t and gnp_t have a seasonal pattern and a level shift in the third quarter of 1990 when the monetary unification

---

[1] Details of the data sources are given in the Appendix of Lütkepohl and Wolters (2003).

Figure 5.1. Seasonally unadjusted, quarterly German log real M3 (m), log real GNP (gnp) and average bond rate (R), 1975Q1–1998Q4

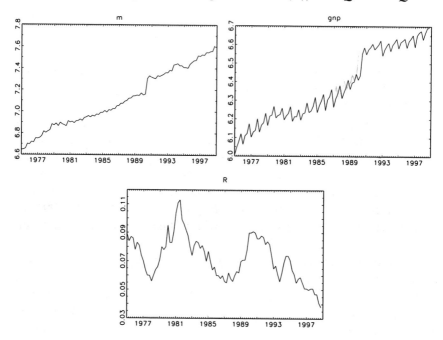

of East and West Germany occurred. Before that date, the series only refer to West Germany and afterwards they refer to the unified Germany. The special data features and in particular the level shifts will be taken into account in the subsequent analysis.

5.3. Unit root analysis

We start by investigating the unit roots in the DGPs of the three individual series. In other words, their order of integration is determined.

5.3.1. The Augmented Dickey–Fuller test

The point of departure is an $AR(p)$ with deterministic term ν_t, $y_t = \alpha_1 y_{t-1} + \cdots + \alpha_p y_{t-p} + \nu_t + u_t$. This process has a unit root and is hence integrated if $\alpha(1) = 1 - \alpha_1 - \cdots - \alpha_p = 0$. The objective is, therefore, to test this null hypothesis against the alternative of stationarity of the process (i.e. $\alpha(1) > 0$). For this purpose the model is reparameterized by subtracting y_{t-1} on both sides and rearranging terms,

$$\Delta y_t = \pi y_{t-1} + \sum_{j=1}^{p-1} \gamma_j \Delta y_{t-j} + v_t + u_t, \tag{5.1}$$

where $\pi = -\alpha(1)$ and $\gamma_j = -(\alpha_{j+1} + \cdots + \alpha_p)$. The so-called *augmented Dickey–Fuller* (ADF) *test* for the pair of hypotheses $H_0 : \pi = 0$ vs. $H_1 : \pi < 0$ is based on the t-statistic of the coefficient π from an OLS estimation of Equation (5.1) (Fuller, 1976; Dickey and Fuller, 1979). Its limiting distribution is nonstandard and depends on the deterministic terms in the model. Critical values have been simulated for different deterministic terms (see, e.g. Fuller, 1976; Davidson and MacKinnon, 1993). In these tests the number of lagged differences of y_t may be based on model selection criteria such as AIC, HQ or SC (see Lütkepohl, 1991 for definitions) or a sequential testing procedure which eliminates insignificant coefficients (see, e.g. Ng and Perron (1995)).

If the time series under study may have more than one unit root, the series should first be differenced sufficiently often to make it stationary. Then an ADF test may be applied to the differenced series. If a unit root is rejected, an ADF test is applied to the series which is differenced one time less than in the previous test. This procedure is repeated until a unit root cannot be rejected. Suppose for instance that a series y_t is possibly $I(2)$. Then a unit root test is applied to $\Delta^2 y_t$ first. If it rejects, a unit root test is applied to Δy_t. If the unit root cannot be rejected in Δy_t this result confirms that y_t is indeed best modelled as an $I(2)$ series. If, however, a unit root is also rejected for Δy_t, the original series y_t is better not treated as $I(2)$. This approach for determining the number of unit roots was proposed by Pantula (1989). It is therefore sometimes called the *Pantula principle*.

For the German bond rate (R_t) ADF test results are given in Table 5.1. From Figure 5.1 one may conclude that the variable may be $I(1)$.

Table 5.1.   ADF tests for interest rate series

Variable	Deterministic Term	No. of Lagged Differences	Test Statistic	5% Critical Value
ΔR_t	None	0	-8.75	-1.94
		2	-4.75	
R_t	constant	1	-1.48	-2.86
		3	-1.93	

Note: Critical values from Davidson and MacKinnon (1993, Table 20.1)

Therefore, the first differences are tested first. For both lag orders given in Table 5.1 the test clearly rejects the unit root. A deterministic term is not included in the test regression because a linear trend term is not regarded as plausible for the original series and a constant term vanishes upon differencing. The tests for a unit root in the original series do not reject the null hypothesis regardless of the lag order. Thus we conclude that the series should be treated as an $I(1)$ variable in the subsequent analysis.

Both m_t and gnp_t have level shifts and therefore the deterministic term should be modified accordingly (Perron, 1989). Suitable extensions of the ADF tests have been proposed recently and will be discussed next.

5.3.2. Unit root tests for series with structural breaks

Perron (1989, 1990) considers models with deterministic terms $\mu_t = \mu_0 + \mu_0^s d_{tT_B} + \mu_1 t + \mu_1^s (t - T_B) d_{tT_B}$, where $d_{tT_B} = 0$ for $t \le T_B$ and $d_{tT_B} = 1$ for $t > T_B$. Thus, if $\mu_0^s \ne 0$, there is a level shift after time T_B and a change in the trend slop occurs at the same time, if $\mu_1^s \ne 0$ (see also Perron and Vogelsang, 1992; Amsler and Lee, 1995 for tests allowing for such deterministic terms). Lanne et al. (2002) and Saikkonen and Lütkepohl (2002) argue that a shift may not occur in a single period but may be spread out over a number of periods. Moreover, there may be a smooth transition to a new level. They consider shift functions of the general nonlinear form $f_t(\theta)' \gamma$ which are added to the deterministic term. Hence, if there is, e.g. a linear trend term and a shift, we have a model

$$y_t = \mu_0 + \mu_1 t + f_t(\theta)' \gamma + x_t, \tag{5.2}$$

where θ and γ are unknown parameters or parameter vectors and the errors x_t are assumed to be generated by an AR(p) process, $\alpha(L)x_t = u_t$ with $\alpha(L) = 1 - \alpha_1 L - \cdots - \alpha_p L^p$.

Shift functions may, e.g. be based on a simple shift dummy, d_{tT_B} or an exponential function such as $f_t(\theta) = 1 - \exp\{-\theta(t - T_B)\}$ for $t \ge T_B$ and zero elsewhere. The simple shift dummy function does not involve any extra parameter θ and the parameter γ is a scalar. The exponential shift function allows for a nonlinear gradual shift to a new level, starting at time T_B. For this type of shift, both θ and γ are scalar parameters. The first one is confined to the positive real line ($\theta > 0$), whereas the second one may assume any value.

Saikkonen and Lütkepohl (2002) and Lanne et al. (2002) propose unit root tests for the model (5.2) which are based on estimating the deterministic term first by a generalized least squares procedure and subtracting it from the original series. Then an ADF type test is performed on the adjusted series $\hat{x}_t = y_t - \hat{\mu}_0 - \hat{\mu}_1 t - f_t(\hat{\theta})'\hat{\gamma}$ based on a model which accounts for the estimation errors in the nuisance parameters and worked quite well in small sample simulations (Lanne *et al.*, 2002). As in the case of the ADF statistic, the asymptotic null distribution is nonstandard. Critical values are tabulated in Lanne *et al.* (2002). Again a different asymptotic distribution is obtained if the deterministic linear trend term is excluded a priori. Because the power of the test tends to improve when the linear trend is not present, it is advisable to use any prior information regarding the deterministic term. If the series of interest has seasonal fluctuations, it is also possible to include seasonal dummies in addition in the model (5.2). Another advantage of this approach is that it can be extended easily to the case where the break date is unknown (see Lanne *et al.*, 2003).

We have applied tests with a simple shift dummy and an exponential shift function to check the integration properties of the gnp_t and m_t series. It is known that the break has occurred in the third quarter of 1990 at the time of the German monetary unification. The break date T_B is therefore fixed accordingly. In Table 5.2 the test values for the two test statistics are given. They are all quite similar and do not provide evidence against a unit root in gnp_t and m_t.

In Figure 5.2 the gnp series together with the estimated deterministic term and the adjusted series as well as the estimated exponential shift function are plotted. It turns out that in this case the exponential shift function looks almost like a shift dummy due to the large estimated value for θ. The sum of squared errors objective function, which is minimized in estimating the deterministic parameters is also plotted as a function of θ in the lower right hand panel of Figure 5.2. Obviously, this function is decreasing in θ. Given that for large values of θ the exponential shift function is the same as a shift dummy for practical purposes, the shape of

*Table 5.2. **Unit root tests in the presence of structural shifts for gnp$_t$ and m$_t$ using four lagged differences, a constant, seasonal dummies and a linear trend***

Variable	Shift Function	Test Statistic	5% Critical Value
gnp_t	$d_{tT_B}\gamma$	-1.41	-3.03
	Exponential	-1.36	
m_t	$d_{tT_B}\gamma$	-1.70	-3.03
	Exponential	-1.69	

Note: Critical value from Lanne *et al.* (2002).

**Figure 5.2.   Deterministic terms and adjusted series used in unit root
tests for log GNP series, based on a model with four lagged differences,
sample period 1976Q2–1996Q4 (Note: the figure is extracted from
Figure 2.18 of Lütkepohl (2004a))**

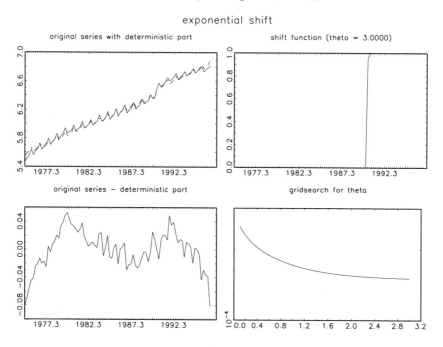

the shift function is not surprising. In the estimation procedure we have
actually constrained the range of θ to the interval from zero to three
because for $\theta = 3$ the exponential shift function almost represents an
instantaneous shift to a new level. Therefore, there is no need to consider
larger values.

An analysis of the first differences of the two variables rejects unit roots
in these series. Hence, there is some evidence that the variables are well
modelled as $I(1)$. The results for the first differences are not presented
because the main purpose of this analysis is to illustrate the tests for series
with level shifts. The first differences of the variables do not have a level
shift anymore but just an outlying value for the third quarter of 1990 which
is captured by using an impulse dummy variable in the tests.

5.4. Cointegration rank tests

The next step of the analysis is to investigate the number of cointegration
relations between the series. A great number of proposals have been made

for this purpose. Many of them are reviewed and compared in Hubrich *et al.* (2001). Generally, there is a good case for using the Johansen (1995a) likelihood ratio (LR) approach based on Gaussian assumptions and its modifications because all other approaches were found to have severe shortcomings in some situations. Even if the actual DGP is non-Gaussian, the resulting pseudo LR tests for the cointegrating rank may have better properties than many competitors. Only if specific data properties make this approach problematic, using other tests may be worth trying. However, even in the LR approach special data properties such as level shifts should be taken into account. Suitable modifications exist and will be outlined in the following after the standard setup has been presented.

5.4.1. The model setup

It is assumed that the DGP of a given K-dimensional vector of time series y_t can be decomposed in a deterministic part, μ_t, and a stochastic part, x_t,

$$y_t = \mu_t + x_t. \tag{5.3}$$

The deterministic part will only be of secondary interest. It may contain, e.g. a constant, a polynomial trend, seasonals and other dummy variables. The stochastic part x_t is an $I(1)$ process generated by a VECM of the form

$$\Delta x_t = \alpha\beta'x_{t-1} + \Gamma_1\Delta x_{t-1} + \cdots + \Gamma_{p-1}\Delta x_{t-p+1} + u_t, \tag{5.4}$$

where u_t is a K-dimensional unobservable zero mean white noise process with positive definite covariance matrix $E(u_t u_t') = \Sigma_u$. The parameter matrices α and β have dimensions $(K \times r)$ and rank r. They specify the long-run part of the model with β containing the *cointegrating relations* and α representing the *loading coefficients*. The Γ_i $(i = 1, ..., p - 1)$ are $(K \times K)$ short-run parameter matrices.

If there are deterministic terms in the DGP of the variables of interest, the x_ts are unobserved whereas the y_ts will be the observable variables. Left-multiplying y_t in Equation (5.3) by the operator $\Delta I_K - \alpha\beta'L - \Gamma_1\Delta L - \cdots - \Gamma_{p-1}\Delta L^{p-1}$, it is easy to see that y_t has the VECM representation

$$\Delta y_t = \alpha(\beta'y_{t-1} + \delta^{co'}d_{t-1}^{co}) + \Gamma_1\Delta y_{t-1} + \cdots + \Gamma_{p-1}\Delta y_{t-p+1} + Cd_t^s + u_t.$$

$$= \alpha\beta^{*'}y_{t-1}^* + \Gamma_1\Delta y_{t-1} + \cdots + \Gamma_{p-1}\Delta y_{t-p+1} + Cd_t^s + u_t, \tag{5.5}$$

where d_t^{co} is a vector of deterministic variables which can be absorbed into the cointegration relations. The corresponding coefficient matrix is denoted by δ^{co}. The vector d_t^s includes the remaining deterministic variables with coefficient matrix C. The matrix $\beta^{*'} = [\beta' : \delta^{co'}]$ is $(r \times K^*)$ and $y_{t-1}^* = [y_{t-1}', d_{t-1}^{co'}]'$ is $(K^* \times 1)$ with $K^* = K +$ dimension (d_t^{co}). This is the form of the process on which much of the inference is based.

In practice, it is necessary to determine the lag order p and the cointegrating rank r, the former quantity may be chosen by model selection criteria or sequential testing procedures. If r is still unknown at that stage, the least restricted form of the model should be used. In other words, lag order selection may be based on Equation (5.5) with cointegration rank K or, equivalently, on the corresponding levels VAR representation. In the following section it is assumed that the lag order p has been chosen in a previous step of the analysis and the determination of the cointegrating rank is discussed for a given lag order.

5.4.2. The tests

Denoting the matrix $\alpha\beta'$ in the error correction term by Π, the following sequence of hypotheses is considered in the Johansen approach:

$$H_0(i) : \text{rk}(\Pi) = i \text{ vs. } H_1(i) : \text{rk}(\Pi) > i, \qquad i = 0, \ldots, K - 1. \qquad (5.6)$$

The cointegrating rank specified in the first null hypothesis which cannot be rejected is then chosen as cointegrating rank r. If $H_0(0)$, the first null hypothesis in this sequence, cannot be rejected, a VAR process in first differences is considered. If all the null hypotheses can be rejected including $H_0(K - 1)$, $\text{rk}(\Pi) = K$ and the process is $I(0)$. Given that the variables are supposed to be $I(1)$, the process cannot really be $I(0)$. In other words, under the present assumptions, there is strictly speaking no need to consider a test of $H_0(K - 1)$. However, it may serve as a check of the unit root analysis.

Using (pseudo) LR tests is attractive because, for any given lag order p, they are easy to compute if the short-run parameters, $\Gamma_1, \ldots, \Gamma_{p-1}$, are unrestricted, as shown by Johansen (1995a) (see also Section 5.5). The LR statistics under their respective null hypotheses have nonstandard asymptotic distributions, however. They depend on the difference $K - r_0$ and on the deterministic terms included in the DGP but not on the short-run dynamics.

Although the asymptotic theory for quite general situations is available, a possible problem arises in practice because the small sample properties of the tests can be improved by specifying the deterministic terms as tightly as possible (see also Saikkonen and Lütkepohl (1999) for an asymptotic analysis of this problem). For example, if there is no deterministic linear trend term, it is desirable to perform the cointegration rank tests without such terms. On the other hand, leaving them out if they are part of the DGP can lead to major distortions in the tests. Johansen (1995a) also provides the asymptotic theory for testing hypotheses regarding the deterministic terms which can be helpful in this respect. Interestingly, under standard assumptions these tests have asymptotic χ^2 distributions with the number of degrees of freedom corresponding to the number of restrictions imposed under the null hypothesis.

A case which is not easily handled in this framework is a deterministic term with shift dummy variables of the form $d_{tT_B} = 0$ for $t \le T_B$ and $d_{tT_B} = 1$ for $t > T_B$, as specified before. Shift dummy variables may be necessary to capture a level shift in the variables in time period T_B, as in the example series m_t and gnp_t. If such dummy variables belong to the deterministic term, the asymptotic null distribution of the LR test statistic for the cointegrating rank also depends on the shift period T_B. This is problematic if T_B is unknown.

In that case, a variant of an LR test for the cointegrating rank suggested in a series of papers by Saikkonen and Lütkepohl is convenient (e.g. Saikkonen and Lütkepohl, 2000c). The idea is to estimate the parameters of the model under the null hypothesis in a first step using a model such as Equation (5.5) by Johansen's ML procedure with the shift dummy included in d_t^{co} (see Section 5.5). Then the estimated α, β and Γ_i ($i = 1, ..., p - 1$) are used to construct an estimator of the covariance matrix of x_t and a feasible GLS estimation is performed to estimate the parameters of the deterministic part from a model such as Equation (5.3) with shift dummy in the deterministic term. For example, if the deterministic term has the form $\mu_t = \mu_0 + \mu_1 t + \delta d_{tT_B}$, the parameter vectors μ_0, μ_1 and δ are estimated by feasible GLS applied to $y_t = \mu_0 + \mu_1 t + \delta d_{tT_B} + x_t$. Using these estimates y_t may be adjusted for deterministic terms to obtain $\tilde{x}_t = y_t - \hat{\mu}_0 - \hat{\mu}_1 t - \hat{\delta} d_{tT_B}$ and the Johansen LR test for the cointegrating rank is applied to $\tilde{x}_t$.

The advantage of this procedure is that the asymptotic null distribution of the resulting test statistic does not depend on the shift dummy or the shift date. Therefore, the procedure can be used even if the shift date is unknown. In that case, the shift date can be estimated first and the whole procedure may be based on an estimated T_B (see Lütkepohl *et al.*, 2004).

Although the short-run dynamics do not matter for the asymptotic theory, they have a substantial impact in small and moderate samples. Therefore the choice of the lag order p is quite important. Choosing p rather large to be on the safe side as far as missing out on important short-run dynamics is concerned, may lead to a drastic loss in power of the cointegrating rank tests. On the other hand, choosing the lag order too small may lead to dramatic size distortions even for well-behaved DGPs. In a small sample simulation study, Lütkepohl and Saikkonen (1999) found that using the AIC criterion for order selection may be a good compromise. It is also a good idea to use a few different lag orders and check the robustness of the results.

Because the dimension of the system also has an important impact on the test results (Gonzalo and Pitarakis, 1999), it is useful to apply cointegration tests to all possible subsystems as well and check whether the results are consistent with those for a higher-dimensional model. For example, in a system of three $I(1)$ variables, if all pairs of variables are found to be cointegrated, the cointegrating rank of the three-dimensional system must be 2.

There are many interesting suggestions for modifying and improving the Johansen approach to cointegration testing. For example, to improve the performance of the Johansen cointegration tests in small samples, Johansen (2002) presents a Bartlett correction. Also there are a number of proposals based on different ideas. As mentioned previously, much of the earlier literature is reviewed in Hubrich et al. (2001). Generally, at present it appears that the Johansen approach should be the default and only if there are particular reasons other proposals are worth contemplating.

5.4.3. Cointegration tests for the example system

As suggested in the previous section, the rank of all pairs of series is investigated in addition to the rank of the three-dimensional system. Knowing the cointegrating ranks of the subsystems can also be helpful in finding a proper normalization of the cointegration matrix for the estimation stage (Section 5.5). Because of the shift in the m_t and gnp$_t$ series in the third quarter of 1990 a shift dummy variable will be allowed for and the cointegration tests proposed by Saikkonen and Lütkepohl (S&L tests) are used. The results are shown in Table 5.3

The deterministic terms in addition to the shift dummies and the number of lagged differences in the model have to be specified before the tests can be carried out. Because m_t and gnp$_t$ both have some seasonality and a trending behaviour that may perhaps be captured with a linear trend term, seasonal dummy variables and a linear trend term are included in the models used in the tests. To avoid a decision whether the trend is just in the variables and, hence, orthogonal to the cointegration relations or fully

Table 5.3. **S&L cointegration tests for German macrosystem, sample period: 1975Q1–1998Q4**

Variables	Deterministic Terms	No. of Lagged Differences	$H_0 : \mathrm{rk}(\Pi) = r_0$	Test Statistic	5% Critical Value
m_t, gnp_t	c, tr, sd, shift	0	$r_0 = 0$	6.86	15.92
			$r_0 = 1$	0.37	6.83
		4	$r_0 = 0$	4.91	15.92
			$r_0 = 1$	1.75	6.83
	c, orth tr, sd, shift	0	$r_0 = 0$	9.13	9.79
m_t, R_t	c, tr, sd, shift	0	$r_0 = 0$	26.71	15.92
			$r_0 = 1$	0.00	6.83
	c, orth tr, sd, shift	0	$r_0 = 0$	22.98	9.79
gnp_t, R_t	c, tr, sd, shift	0	$r_0 = 0$	8.26	15.92
			$r_0 = 1$	0.20	6.83
		6	$r_0 = 0$	8.42	15.92
			$r_0 = 1$	0.56	6.83
	c, orth tr, sd, shift	0	$r_0 = 0$	4.04	9.79
		6	$r_0 = 0$	9.36	9.79
m_t, gnp_t, R_t	c, tr, sd, shift	0	$r_0 = 0$	38.36	28.47
			$r_0 = 1$	9.07	15.92
			$r_0 = 2$	0.00	6.83
		4	$r_0 = 0$	19.58	28.47
			$r_0 = 1$	4.93	15.92
			$r_0 = 2$	4.53	6.83
	c, orth tr, sd, shift	0	$r_0 = 0$	33.62	20.66
			$r_0 = 1$	9.47	9.79
		4	$r_0 = 0$	20.14	20.66
			$r_0 = 1$	4.53	9.79

Notes: c: constant, tr: linear trend, orth tr: linear trend orthogonal to the cointegration relations, sd: seasonal dummies, shift: shift dummy variable $S90Q3$; critical values from Lütkepohl and Saikkonen (2000, Table 1) for models with unrestricted trend and from Saikkonen and Lütkepohl (2000b, Table 1) for models with trend orthogonal to the cointegration relations. This table is adapted from Lütkepohl (2004b).

general, both types of tests are performed. Notice that if the trend is orthogonal to the cointegration relations, it is captured by an intercept term in the specification (5.5).

An easy way to choose the number of lagged differences to be included in the model is to apply model selection criteria. Using a maximum lag order of 10, the lag orders specified in Table 5.3 were suggested by AIC and HQ. The larger number of lagged differences is always the one chosen by AIC and the lower lag order is obtained with the HQ criterion. Considering different orders is useful in this context because choosing the order too small can lead to size distortions for the tests while selecting too large an order may result in power reductions.

In Table 5.3 the sample period is 1975Q1–1998Q4, including presample values needed in the estimation. There is strong evidence for a cointegration rank of zero for the (m_t, gnp_t) and (gnp_t, R_t) systems so that the two variables in each of these systems are not likely to be cointegrated. On the other hand, one cointegration relation is found for the (m_t, R_t) system under both alternative trend specifications. Thus, one would also expect to find at least one cointegration relation in the three-dimensional system of all variables. If no cointegration relation exists between m_t and gnp_t as well as between gnp_t and R_t as suggested by the bivariate analysis, then there cannot be a second cointegration relation between the three variables. If two linearly independent cointegration relations exist between the three variables, they can always be transformed so that they both involve just two of the variables, as we will see in Section 5. Consistent with the results for the bivariate models, there is some evidence of just one cointegration relation in the three-dimensional system.

5.5. Estimating the cointegration relations

5.5.1. Estimation methods

5.5.1.1. Reduced rank ML estimation

For a given cointegrating rank and lag order, the VECM (5.5) can be estimated by RR regression as shown in Johansen (1991, 1995a). Assuming that a sample of size T and p presample values are available, the estimator may be determined by denoting the residuals from regressing Δy_t and y_{t-1}^* on $\Delta Y_{t-1}' = [\Delta y_{t-1}', \ldots, \Delta y_{t-p+1}', d_t^{s'}]$ by R_{0t} and R_{1t}, respectively, defining $S_{ij} = T^{-1} \sum_{t=1}^{T} R_{it} R_{jt}', i,j = 0,1$, and solving the generalized eigenvalue problem

$$\det(\lambda S_{11} - S_{10} S_{00}^{-1} S_{01}) = 0. \tag{5.7}$$

Let the ordered eigenvalues be $\lambda_1 \geq \cdots \geq \lambda_{K^*}$ with corresponding matrix of eigenvectors $B = [b_1, \ldots, b_{K^*}]$ satisfying $\lambda_i S_{11} b_i = S_{01}' S_{00}^{-1} S_{01} b_i$ and normalized such that $B' S_{11} B = I_{K^*}$. Estimators of β^* and α are then given by

$$\hat{\beta}^* = [b_1, \ldots, b_r] \quad \text{and} \quad \hat{\alpha} = S_{01} \hat{\beta}^* (\hat{\beta}^{*'} S_{11} \hat{\beta}^*)^{-1}. \tag{5.8}$$

The corresponding estimator of $\Gamma = [\Gamma_1, \ldots, \Gamma_{p-1}, C]$ is

$$\hat{\Gamma} = \left(\sum_{t=1}^{T} (\Delta y_t - \hat{\alpha}\hat{\beta}^{*'} y_{t-1}^{*}) \Delta Y_{t-1}' \right) \left(\sum_{t=1}^{T} \Delta Y_{t-1} \Delta Y_{t-1}' \right)^{-1}.$$

Under Gaussian assumptions these estimators are ML estimators conditional on the presample values (Johansen, 1995a). The estimator of Γ is consistent and asymptotically normal under general assumptions and, if there are no deterministic terms,

$$\sqrt{T}\,\mathrm{vec}(\hat{\Gamma} - \Gamma) \xrightarrow{d} N(0, \Sigma_{\hat{\Gamma}}).$$

Here the asymptotic distribution of $\hat{\Gamma}$ has a nonsingular covariance matrix $\Sigma_{\hat{\Gamma}}$ so that standard inference may be used for the short-run parameters Γ_j. The convergence rate for the deterministic terms may be different if polynomial trends are included.

For the estimators $\hat{\alpha}$ and $\hat{\beta}^{*}$, the product $\hat{\Pi}^{*} = \hat{\alpha}\hat{\beta}^{*'}$ is also a consistent and asymptotically normally distributed estimator,

$$\sqrt{T}\,\mathrm{vec}(\hat{\Pi}^{*} - \Pi^{*}) \xrightarrow{d} N(0, \Sigma_{\hat{\Pi}^{*}}).$$

The $(KK^{*} \times KK^{*})$ covariance matrix $\Sigma_{\hat{\Pi}^{*}}$ is singular if $r < K$, however. The matrices α and β are only identified individually with further restrictions. Identifying and overidentifying restrictions for these matrices have been the subject of some recent research (see, e.g. Johansen and Juselius, 1992, 1994; Boswijk, 1995, 1996; Johansen, 1995a; Elliott, 2000; Boswijk and Doornik, 2002; Pesaran and Shin, 2002). The latter article allows for very general nonlinear restrictions. For our purposes imposing restrictions on α, β and other parameters may be useful either for reducing the parameter space and thereby improving estimation precision or to identify the cointegration relations to associate them with economic relations. Imposing just-identifying restrictions on α and/or β does not do any damage. Therefore, we are free to impose just-identifying restrictions on the cointegration parameters.

A triangular form has received some attention in the literature (see, e.g. Phillips, 1991). It assumes that the first part of β is an identity matrix, $\beta' = [I_r : \beta_{(K-r)}']$ and, hence, $\beta^{*'} = [I_r : \beta_{(K^{*}-r)}^{*'}]$, where $\beta_{(K-r)}$ is $((K - r) \times r)$ and $\beta_{(K^{*}-r)}^{*}$ is a $((K^{*} - r) \times r)$ matrix. For $r = 1$, this restriction amounts to normalizing the coefficient of the first variable to be one. Given that $\mathrm{rk}(\beta) = r$, there exists a nonsingular $(r \times r)$ submatrix of β' which motivates the normalization. Notice that $\Pi^* = \alpha\beta^{*\prime} = \alpha\Phi\Phi^{-1}\beta^{*\prime}$ for any nonsingular $(r \times r)$ matrix Φ. Hence, choosing Φ such that it corresponds to the nonsingular $(r \times r)$ submatrix of β' results in a decomposition of Π^* where β and, hence, β^* contains an identity submatrix. By a suitable rearrangement of the variables it can be ensured that β' is of the form $[I_r : \beta'_{(K-r)}]$. It should be clear, however, that such a normalization requires a suitable order of the variables. Some care is necessary in choosing this order to make sure that only valid cointegration relations result. In practice, it is usually fairly easy to choose the order of the variables properly if the cointegrating ranks of all subsystems are known as well. In other words, in the initial analysis it will be useful to not only check the cointegrating rank of the system of interest but also of all smaller dimensional subsystems, as was done for the example system. There are also formal statistical tests for normalizing restrictions (e.g. Luukkonen et al., 1999).

The normalization ensures identified parameters $\beta^*_{(K^*-r)}$ so that inference becomes possible. To simplify matters, it is now assumed that there are no deterministic terms in the model. The estimators for the parameters $\beta_{(K-r)}$ have an asymptotic distribution which is multivariate normal upon appropriate normalization. Partitioning R'_{1t} as $R'_{1t} = [R^{(1)\prime}_{1t}, R^{(2)\prime}_{1t}]$ where $R^{(1)}_{1t}$ and $R^{(2)}_{1t}$ are $(r \times 1)$ and $((K-r)\times 1)$, respectively, it holds that

$$\text{vec}\left\{(\hat{\beta}'_{(K-r)} - \beta'_{(K-r)})\left(\sum_{t=1}^T R^{(2)}_{1t}R^{(2)\prime}_{1t}\right)^{1/2}\right\}$$

$$= \left[\left(\sum_{t=1}^T R^{(2)}_{1t}R^{(2)\prime}_{1t}\right)^{1/2}\otimes I_{K-r}\right]\text{vec}(\hat{\beta}'_{(K-r)} - \beta'_{(K-r)})$$

$$\xrightarrow{d} N(0, I_{K-r}\otimes(\alpha'\Sigma_u^{-1}\alpha)^{-1}) \tag{5.9}$$

(e.g. Reinsel, 1993, Chapter 6). The asymptotic distribution of the untransformed estimator is mixed normal (Johansen, 1995a). The present result is useful for deriving t-tests or Wald tests for restrictions on the parameters $\beta_{(K-r)}$.

Using that $T^{-2}\sum_{t=1}^T R^{(2)}_{1t}R^{(2)\prime}_{1t}$ converges weakly, it can be seen from this result that $T\text{vec}(\hat{\beta}'_{(K-r)} - \beta'_{(K-r)})$ has an asymptotic distribution. In other words, the estimator $\hat{\beta}'_{(K-r)}$ converges at a rate T rather than $\sqrt{T}$.

Imposing identifying restrictions on β, expressions for the asymptotic covariances of the other parameters are also readily available:

$$\sqrt{T}\text{vec}([\hat{\alpha}, \hat{\Gamma}_1, ..., \hat{\Gamma}_{p-1}] - [\alpha, \Gamma_1, ..., \Gamma_{p-1}]) \xrightarrow{d} N(0, \Omega^{-1}\otimes\Sigma_u),$$

where

$$\Omega = \text{plim } T^{-1} \sum_{t=1}^{T} \left(\begin{bmatrix} \beta' y_{t-1} \\ \Delta Y_{t-1} \end{bmatrix} [y'_{t-1}\beta, \Delta Y'_{t-1}] \right).$$

Asymptotically these parameters are distributed independently of $\hat{\beta}_{(K-r)}$.

Deterministic terms can be included by just extending the relevant quantities in the foregoing formulas. For example deterministic terms not included in the cointegration relations are taken into account by adding the components to ΔY_{t-1} and extending the parameter matrix Γ accordingly. Deterministic terms which are restricted to the cointegration relations are accounted for by using y^*_{t-1} and β^* instead of y_{t-1} and β in the error correction term. The convergence rates of the deterministic terms depend on the specific components included.

5.5.1.2. A two-step estimator

Ahn and Reinsel (1990), Reinsel (1993, Chapter 6) and Saikkonen (1992) proposed another estimator for the cointegration parameters. To focus on the latter parameters, we consider the concentrated model corresponding to the VECM (5.5),

$$R_{0t} = \alpha \beta^{*'} R_{1t} + \tilde{u}_t. \tag{5.10}$$

Using the normalization $\beta^{*'} = [I_r : \beta^{*'}_{(K^*-r)}]$, this model can be written in the form

$$R_{0t} - \alpha R_{1t}^{(1)} = \alpha \beta^{*'}_{(K^*-r)} R_{1t}^{(2)} + \tilde{u}_t, \tag{5.11}$$

where $R_{1t}^{(1)}$ and $R_{1t}^{(2)}$ again consist of the first r and last $K^* - r$ components of R_{1t}, respectively. Premultiplying Equation (5.11) by $(\alpha' \Sigma_u^{-1} \alpha)^{-1} \alpha' \Sigma_u^{-1}$ and defining $w_t = (\alpha' \Sigma_u^{-1} \alpha)^{-1} \alpha' \Sigma_u^{-1} (R_{0t} - \alpha R_{1t}^{(1)})$, gives

$$w_t = \beta^{*'}_{(K^*-r)} R_{1t}^{(2)} + v_t, \tag{5.12}$$

where $v_t = (\alpha' \Sigma_u^{-1} \alpha)^{-1} \alpha' \Sigma_u^{-1} \tilde{u}_t$ is an r-dimensional error vector. The corresponding error term of the unconcentrated model is a white noise process with mean zero and covariance matrix $\Sigma_v = (\alpha' \Sigma_u^{-1} \alpha)^{-1}$.

From this model $\beta^{*'}_{(K^*-r)}$ can be estimated by a two step procedure. In the first step, the parameters in the model $R_{0t} = \Pi^* R_{1t} + \tilde{u}_t$ are estimated by unrestricted OLS. The first r columns of Π^* are equal to α and hence these columns from the estimated matrix are used as an estimator $\tilde{\alpha}$. This estimator and the usual residual covariance estimator are used to obtain a feasible version of w_t, say $\tilde{w}_t = (\tilde{\alpha}' \tilde{\Sigma}_u^{-1} \tilde{\alpha})^{-1} \tilde{\alpha}' \tilde{\Sigma}_u^{-1} (R_{0t} - \tilde{\alpha} R_{1t}^{(1)})$. This quantity is substituted for w_t in Equation (5.12) in the second step and

$\beta^{*\prime}_{(K^*-r)}$ is estimated from that model by OLS. The resulting two step estimator has the same asymptotic distribution as the ML estimator (Ahn and Reinsel, 1990; Reinsel 1993, Chapter 6).

5.5.1.3. Other estimators

So far we have started from a parametrically specified model setup. If interest centres on the cointegration parameters only, it is always possible to find a transformation of the variables such that the system of transformed variables can be written in so-called triangular form,

$$y_{1t} = \beta'_{(K-r)}y_{2t} + z_{1t} \qquad \text{and} \qquad \Delta y_{2t} = z_{2t},$$

where $z_t = [z'_{1t}, z'_{2t}]'$ is a general stationary linear process. Phillips (1991) considers inference for the cointegration parameters in this case and shows that the covariance structure of z_t has to be taken into account for optimal inference. Very general nonparametric estimators are sufficient, however, to obtain asymptotic optimality. Hence, it is not necessary to assume a specific parametric structure for the short-run dynamics.

There are also other systems methods for estimating the cointegrating parameters. For example, Stock and Watson (1988) consider an estimator based on principal components and Bossaerts (1988) uses canonical correlations. These estimators were shown to be inferior to Johansen's ML method in a comparison by Gonzalo (1994) and are therefore not further considered here.

5.5.1.4. Restrictions for the cointegration relations

In case just identifying restrictions for the cointegration relations are available, estimation may proceed by RR regression and then the identified estimator of β may be obtained by a suitable transformation of $\hat{\beta}$. For example, if β is just a single vector, a normalization of the first component may be obtained by dividing the vector $\hat{\beta}$ by its first component, as discussed previously.

Sometimes over-identifying restrictions are available for the cointegration matrix. They can be handled easily if they can be written in the form $\beta^* = H\varphi$, where H is some known, fixed $(K^* \times s)$ matrix and φ is $(s \times r)$ with $s \geq r$. In this case R_{1t} is simply replaced by $H'R_{1t}$ in the quantities entering the generalized eigenvalue problem (5.7), that is, we have to solve

$$\det(\lambda H'S_{11}H - H'S_{10}S_{00}^{-1}S_{01}H) = 0 \qquad (5.13)$$

for λ to get $\lambda_1^H \geq \cdots \geq \lambda_s^H$. The eigenvectors corresponding to $\lambda_1^H, \ldots, \lambda_r^H$ are the estimators of the columns of φ. Denoting the resulting estimator by $\hat{\varphi}$ gives a restricted estimator $\hat{\beta}^* = H\hat{\varphi}$ for β^* and corresponding estimators of α and Γ as previously.

More generally, restrictions may be available in the form $\beta^* = [H_1\varphi_1, \ldots, H_r\varphi_r]$, where H_j is $(K \times s_j)$ and φ_j is $(s_j \times 1)$ $(j = 1, \ldots, r)$. In that case, restricted ML estimation is still not difficult but requires an iterative optimization whereas the two-step estimator is available in closed form, as will be shown now.

In general, if the restrictions can be represented in the form

$$\text{vec}(\beta^{*'}_{(K^*-r)}) = \mathcal{H}\eta + h,$$

where $\mathcal{H}$ is a fixed matrix, h a fixed vector and η a vector of free parameters, the second step of the two-step estimator given in Equation (5.12) may be adapted using the vectorized form

$$w_t = (R^{(2)'}_{1t} \otimes I_r)\text{vec}(\beta^{*'}_{(K^*-r)}) + v_t$$
$$= (R^{(2)'}_{1t} \otimes I_r)(\mathcal{H}\eta + h) + v_t$$

so that

$$\tilde{w}_t - (R^{(2)'}_{1t} \otimes I_r)h = (R^{(2)'}_{1t} \otimes I_r)\mathcal{H}\eta + v_t$$

can be used in the second step. The feasible GLS estimator of η, say $\tilde{\tilde{\eta}}$, has an asymptotic normal distribution upon appropriate normalization so that t-ratios can be obtained and interpreted in the usual manner.

5.5.2. *Estimating the example cointegration relation*

Using the results of Section 5.4.3, we consider a VECM for the example series with cointegrating rank one, four lagged differences and seasonal dummy variables. Moreover, the shift dummy is included in differenced form only because it turned out to be unnecessary in the cointegration relation. In other words, an impulse dummy variable $I90Q3_t = \Delta S90Q3_t$ is included instead of the shift dummy. A linear trend term was also included initially but was found to be insignificant. The money variable m_t is the first variable in our model because we want its coefficient to be normalized to one in the cointegration relation. The resulting ML estimator of the cointegration relation with standard errors in parentheses is

$$\text{ec}^{\text{ML}}_t = m_t - \underset{(0.090)}{1.093}\,\text{gnp}_t + \underset{(1.267)}{6.514}\,R_t$$

or

$$m_t = \underset{(0.090)}{1.093} \, \mathrm{gnp}_t - \underset{(1.267)}{6.514} \, R_t + \mathrm{ec}_t^{\mathrm{ML}}.$$

This equation is easily interpreted as a money demand relation, where increases in the transactions volume increase money demand and increases in the opportunity costs (R_t) reduce the demand for money. The coefficient 1.093 of gnp_t is the estimated output elasticity because m_t and gnp_t appear in logarithms. For a constant velocity of money a 1% increase in the transactions volume is expected to induce a 1% increase in money demand. In other words, the output elasticity is expected to be one in a simple theoretical model. Therefore, it is appealing that the gnp_t coefficient is close to 1. In fact, taking into account its standard deviation of 0.090, it is not significantly different from 1 at common significance levels. Using the two-step estimator for estimating the cointegration relation with unit income elasticity gives

$$m_t = \mathrm{gnp}_t - \underset{(0.742)}{3.876} \, R_t + \mathrm{ec}_t^{2S}. \tag{5.14}$$

Notice that in this relation the coefficient of R_t is a semi-elasticity because the interest rate is not in logarithms.

Taking into account the results of the cointegrating rank tests in Section 5.4.3, it may be puzzling that we found a cointegration relation between m_t and R_t that does not involve gnp_t in testing the bivariate system. This result suggests that the single cointegration relation found in the three-dimensional analysis may be one between m_t and R_t only which does not fit together with our money demand function (5.14). Because gnp_t enters significantly in the cointegration relation there is indeed a slight inconsistency between the bivariate and the three-dimensional analysis. Maintaining all three variables in the cointegration relation may still be reasonable because eliminating gnp_t from the cointegration relation imposes a restriction on the model which is rejected by the full three-dimensional information set.

5.6. Estimation of short-run parameters and model reduction

A VECM may also be estimated with restrictions on the loading coefficients (α), the short-run (Γ) and other parameter matrices. Restrictions for α are typically zero constraints, meaning that some cointegrating relations are excluded from some of the equations of the system. Usually it is possible to estimate β^* in a first stage. For example, ignoring the restrictions for the short-run parameters, the RR regression ML procedure or the two-step procedure may be used.

The first stage estimator $\hat{\beta}^*$, say, may be treated as fixed in a second-stage estimation of the restricted VECM, because the estimators of the cointegrating parameters converge at a better rate than the estimators of the short-run parameters. In other words, a systems estimation procedure may be applied to

$$\Delta y_t = \alpha\hat{\beta}^{*\prime} y_{t-1}^* + \Gamma_1\Delta y_{t-1} + \cdots + \Gamma_{p-1}\Delta y_{t-p+1} + Cd_t^s + \hat{u}_t. \quad (5.15)$$

If only exclusion restrictions are imposed on the parameter matrices in this form, standard econometric systems estimation procedures such as feasible GLS or SURE (e.g. Judge *et al.*, 1985) or similar methods may be applied which result in estimators of the short-run parameters with the usual asymptotic properties. A substantial number of articles deals with estimating models containing integrated variables. Examples are Phillips and Durlauf (1986), Phillips (1987, 1991), Phillips and Hansen (1990) and Phillips and Loretan (1991). A textbook treatment is given in Davidson (2000).

Some care is necessary with respect to the treatment of deterministic variables. For the parameters of those terms that are properly restricted to the cointegration relations, the properties can be recovered from a result similar to that given in Equation (5.9). Thus, e.g. *t*-ratios can be interpreted in the usual way. The properties of the estimators corresponding to d_t^s are not treated in detail here because in a subsequent analysis of the model, the parameters of the deterministic terms are often of minor interest (see, however, Sims *et al.*, 1990).

The standard *t*-ratios and *F*-tests retain their usual asymptotic properties if they are applied to the short-run parameters in a VECM. Hence, individual zero coefficients can be imposed based on the *t*-ratios of the parameter estimators and one may sequentially eliminate those regressors with the smallest absolute values of *t*-ratios until all *t*-ratios (in absolute value) are greater than some threshold value γ. Alternatively, restrictions for individual parameters or groups of parameters in VECMs may be based on model selection criteria. Brüggemann and Lütkepohl (2001) discuss the relation between sequential testing procedures and using model selection criteria in this context.

Using the cointegration relation in Equation (5.14) I have performed a model reduction starting from a model with four lagged differences of the variables. The model reduction procedure was based on a sequential selection of variables and the AIC. The following estimated model was obtained:

$$
\begin{bmatrix} \Delta m_t \\ \Delta gnp_t \\ \Delta R_t \end{bmatrix} = \begin{bmatrix} \underset{(-3.1)}{-0.04} \\ 0 \\ \underset{(-1.6)}{-0.01} \end{bmatrix} (m_{t-1} - gnp_{t-1} + 3.876 R_{t-1})
$$

$$
+ \begin{bmatrix} \underset{(2.5)}{0.15} & \underset{(-2.9)}{-0.18} & \underset{(-3.4)}{-0.58} \\ \underset{(2.8)}{0.22} & \underset{(-4.2)}{-0.36} & 0 \\ 0 & 0 & \underset{(1.8)}{0.18} \end{bmatrix} \begin{bmatrix} \Delta m_{t-1} \\ \Delta gnp_{t-1} \\ \Delta R_{t-1} \end{bmatrix} + \begin{bmatrix} 0 & 0 & \underset{(-1.6)}{-0.30} \\ \underset{(3.1)}{0.25} & \underset{(-2.4)}{-0.22} & \underset{(1.5)}{0.37} \\ 0 & 0 & 0 \end{bmatrix} \begin{bmatrix} \Delta m_{t-2} \\ \Delta gnp_{t-2} \\ \Delta R_{t-2} \end{bmatrix}
$$

$$
+ \begin{bmatrix} 0 & \underset{(-1.8)}{-0.09} & 0 \\ 0 & 0 & 0 \\ 0 & 0 & \underset{(1.8)}{0.18} \end{bmatrix} \begin{bmatrix} \Delta m_{t-3} \\ \Delta gnp_{t-3} \\ \Delta R_{t-3} \end{bmatrix} + \begin{bmatrix} 0 & 0 & 0 \\ 0 & \underset{(4.0)}{0.28} & 0 \\ 0 & 0 & 0 \end{bmatrix} \begin{bmatrix} \Delta m_{t-4} \\ \Delta gnp_{t-4} \\ \Delta R_{t-4} \end{bmatrix}
$$

$$
+ \begin{bmatrix} \underset{(17.5)}{0.15} & \underset{(4.9)}{0.07} & \underset{(-5.4)}{-0.03} & \underset{(-3.5)}{-0.02} & \underset{(-4.4)}{-0.02} \\ \underset{(8.9)}{0.11} & \underset{(7.7)}{0.04} & \underset{(-9.1)}{-0.07} & \underset{(-4.2)}{-0.03} & \underset{(-3.5)}{-0.03} \\ 0 & \underset{(1.5)}{0.01} & 0 & 0 & 0 \end{bmatrix} \begin{bmatrix} 190Q3_t \\ c \\ s_{1,t} \\ s_{2,t} \\ s_{3,t} \end{bmatrix} + \begin{bmatrix} \hat{u}_{1,t} \\ \hat{u}_{2,t} \\ \hat{u}_{3,t} \end{bmatrix}.
$$

$$(5.16)$$

Here estimation of the final model was done by feasible GLS applied to the full system and the t-values are given in parentheses. For the residuals the following covariance and correlation matrices were estimated:

$$
\tilde{\Sigma}_u = \begin{bmatrix} 6.85 & -0.01 & 0.40 \\ \cdot & 13.3 & 1.12 \\ \cdot & \cdot & 2.59 \end{bmatrix} \times 10^{-5} \quad \text{and}
$$

$$
\widetilde{\text{Corr}} = \begin{bmatrix} 1 & -0.00 & 0.10 \\ \cdot & 1 & 0.19 \\ \cdot & \cdot & 1 \end{bmatrix}.
$$

The off-diagonal elements of $\widetilde{\text{Corr}}$ are all quite small, given the effective sample size of $T = 91$ observations. Clearly, they are all smaller than $2/\sqrt{T} = 0.21$. Hence, they may be classified as not significantly different from zero. This result is good to remember at a later stage when an impulse response analysis is performed (see Section 5.8).

5.7. Model checking

5.7.1. Some tools

Various checks of the adequacy of a given model are available for VECMs. One group of checks considers the estimated residuals and another one investigates the time invariance of the model parameters. Residual based tests for autocorrelation, nonnormality, conditional heteroskedasticity etc. are available for stationary VAR models (e.g. Lütkepohl, 1991; Doornik and Hendry, 1997). Many of the tests have been extended to VECMs with cointegrated variables as well. The modifications relative to the stationary VAR case are usually straightforward. Therefore these tests will not be discussed here. The situation is somewhat different with respect to checks of parameter constancy. In addition to more classical tests, specific tools for this purpose have been developed which are especially suitable for VECMs. Some of them will be presented in the following.

5.7.1.1. Chow tests for structural stability

Chow tests check the null hypothesis of time invariant parameters throughout the sample period against the possibility of a change in the parameter values in period T_B. The model under consideration is estimated from the full sample of T observations and from the first T_1 and the last T_2 observations, where $T_1 < T_B$ and $T_2 \leq T - T_B$. The test is constructed using the LR principle based on Gaussian assumptions. In other words, the likelihood maximum from the constant parameter model is compared to the one with different parameter values before and after period T_B, leaving out the observations between T_1 and $T - T_2 + 1$. Denoting the conditional log-density of the tth observation vector by $l_t = \log f(y_t | y_{t-1}, \ldots, y_1)$, the Chow test statistic can be written as

$$\lambda_{\text{Chow}} = 2 \left[\sup\left(\sum_{t=1}^{T_1} l_t \right) + \sup\left(\sum_{t=T-T_2+1}^{T} l_t \right) - \left(\sum_{t=1}^{T_1} l_t^* + \sum_{t=T-T_2+1}^{T} l_t^* \right) \right],$$

where l_t^* is the log-likelihood increment for observation t evaluated at the parameter values which maximize the likelihood over the full sample. If the model is time invariant, the statistic has an asymptotic χ^2-distribution. The degrees of freedom are given by the number of restrictions imposed by assuming a constant coefficient model for the full sample period, i.e. it is the difference between the sum of the number of free coefficients estimated in the first and last subperiods and the number of free coefficients in the full sample model (Hansen, 2003). The parameter constancy hypothesis is rejected if the value of the test statistic is large.

From the point of view of asymptotic theory there is no need to leave out any observations between the two subsamples. So $T_1 = T_B - 1$ and $T_2 = T - T_B$ is a possible choice. In practice, if the parameter change has not occurred instantaneously at the beginning of period T_B, but is spread out over a few periods or its exact timing is unknown, leaving out some observations may improve the small sample power of the test.

Various generalizations of these tests are possible. For example, one could test for more than one break or one could check constancy of a subset of parameters keeping the remaining ones fixed. Moreover, there may be deterministic terms in the cointegration relations or the number of cointegration relations may change in different subperiods. These generalizations are also treated by Hansen (2003). A Chow forecast test version for multivariate time series models was considered by Doornik and Hendry (1997). It tests the null hypothesis that the forecasts from a model fitted to the first T_B observations are in line with the actually observed data. Doornik and Hendry (1997) also proposed small sample corrections of the tests which may be used in conjunction with critical values from F distributions.

Candelon and Lütkepohl (2001) pointed out that especially for multivariate time series models the asymptotic χ^2 distribution may be an extremely poor guide for small sample inference. Even adjustments based on F approximations can lead to drastically distorted test sizes. Therefore, they proposed to use bootstrap versions of the Chow tests in order to improve their small sample properties.

Chow tests are sometimes performed repeatedly for a range of potential break points T_B. If the test decision is based on the maximum of the test statistics, the test is effectively based on the test statistic $\sup_{T_B \in T} \lambda_{Chow}$, where $T \subset \{1, \ldots, T\}$ is the set of periods for which the test statistic is determined. The asymptotic distribution of this test statistic is not χ^2. Distributions of test statistics of this kind are discussed by Andrews (1993), Andrews and Ploberger (1994) and Hansen (1997).

5.7.1.2. Recursive eigenvalues

For parameter constancy analysis, Hansen and Johansen (1999) proposed recursive statistics based on the eigenvalues that were encountered in the RR ML estimation procedure. Let $\lambda_i^{(\tau)}$ be the ith largest eigenvalue based on sample moments from the first τ observations only. Hansen and Johansen (1999) presented approximate 95% confidence intervals (CIs) for the nonzero true eigenvalues corresponding to

$\lambda_1^{(\tau)}, \ldots, \lambda_r^{(\tau)}$ under the assumption of time invariance of the DGP. The plots of the intervals for consecutive sample sizes $\tau = T_{\min}, \ldots, T$, can reveal structural breaks in the DGP.

Hansen and Johansen (1999) also proposed formal tests for parameter constancy. The following notation will be used in stating them:

$$\xi_i^{(\tau)} = \log\left(\frac{\lambda_i^{(\tau)}}{1 - \lambda_i^{(\tau)}}\right)$$

and

$$\mathcal{T}(\xi_i^{(\tau)}) = \frac{\tau}{T}|(\xi_i^{(\tau)} - \xi_i^{(T)})/\hat{\sigma}_{ii}|,$$

where $\hat{\sigma}_{ii}$ is a suitable estimator of the standard deviation of $(\xi_i^{(\tau)} - \xi_i^{(T)})$. The statistic $\mathcal{T}(\xi_i^{(\tau)})$ compares the ith eigenvalue obtained from the full sample to the one estimated from the first τ observations only and Hansen and Johansen (1999) have shown that the maximum over all τ,

$$\sup_{T_{\min} \leq \tau \leq T} \mathcal{T}(\xi_i^{(\tau)}),$$

has a limiting distribution which depends on a Brownian bridge. Critical values were tabulated by Ploberger *et al.* (1989). If the difference between the eigenvalues based on the subsamples and the full sample gets too large so that $\mathcal{T}(\xi_i^{(\tau)})$ exceeds the relevant critical value, the parameter constancy is rejected.

An alternative test considers the sum of the r largest recursive eigenvalues. It is based on the statistic

$$\mathcal{T}\left(\sum_{i=1}^{r} \xi_i^{(\tau)}\right) = \frac{\tau}{T}\left|\left[\sum_{i=1}^{r}(\xi_i^{(\tau)} - \xi_i^{(T)})\right]\middle/\hat{\sigma}_{1-r}\right|.$$

Here $\hat{\sigma}_{1-r}$ is an estimator of the standard deviation of the quantity $\sum_{i=1}^{r}(\xi_i^{(\tau)} - \xi_i^{(T)})$. The limiting distribution of

$$\sup_{T_{\min} \leq \tau \leq T} \mathcal{T}\left(\sum_{i=1}^{r} \xi_i^{(\tau)}\right)$$

is also given by Hansen and Johansen (1999).

5.7.2. Checking the example model

Estimating a VECM as in Equation (5.16) with cointegrating rank one but otherwise unrestrictedly by the RR ML procedure and checking the residuals with autocorrelation and nonnormality tests, it turned out that the model is a quite satisfactory representation of the DGP. Detailed results are not shown to save space. Also a stability analysis based an the recursive eigenvalues and the $\mathcal{T}(\xi_1^{(\tau)})$ statistic for 1986Q1–1998Q4 did not give rise to concern. The value of the test statistic did not exceed the critical value for a 5% level test.

The sample-split Chow tests in Figure 5.3 show a somewhat different picture, however. The p-values are computed by a bootstrap on the assumption that a test is made for a single break point only. The cointegration relation is fixed throughout the sample. Moreover, the test assumes a time invariant residual covariance matrix. Notice that the test statistic is only computed for the centre part of the sample because sufficiently many degrees of freedom have to be available for estimation in the two subsamples. Clearly, quite small p-values are estimated for part of the sample. Thus, one may conclude that there is a stability problem for the model parameters. A closer investigation reveals, however, that there is a possible ARCH problem in the residuals of the interest rate equation. ARCH effects in the residuals of financial data series such as interest rates are fairly common in practice. They are not necessarily a signal for inadequate modelling of the conditional mean of the DGP. Because

Figure 5.3.   Chow test p-values for unrestricted VECM with cointe-grating rank one, four lagged differences, constants, impulse dummy and seasonal dummies for German money demand system; sample period: 1975Q1–1998Q4 (including presample values)

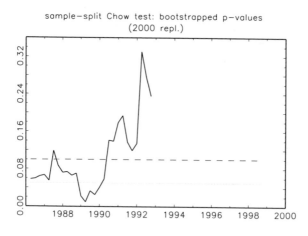

interest centres on the latter part in the present analysis, the possibly remaining ARCH in the residuals of the interest rate equation is ignored. ARCH in the residuals signals volatility clusters that can lead to significant values of Chow tests because these tests compare the residual variability in different subperiods to decide on parameter instability. Higher volatility is indeed found in the first part of the sample and may be responsible for the significant sample-split Chow tests.

The usual diagnostic tests for autocorrelation in the residuals of the restricted model (5.16) did not give rise to concern about the adequacy of the subset model either. Given the results of the stability test based on the recursive eigenvalues, the model is used as a basis for further analysis in the following section. Possible tools for such an analysis are considered next.

5.8. Impulse response analysis

5.8.1. Background

For an $I(0)$ process y_t, the effects of shocks in the variables are easily seen in its Wold moving average (MA) representation,

$$y_t = \mu_t + u_t + \Phi_1 u_{t-1} + \Phi_2 u_{t-2} + \cdots. \tag{5.17}$$

The coefficient matrices of this representation may be obtained by recursive formulas from the coefficient matrices A_j of the levels VAR representation, $y_t = A_1 y_{t-1} + \cdots + A_p y_{t-p} + \nu_t + u_t$, where ν_t contains all deterministic terms (Lütkepohl, 1991, Chapter 2). The elements of the Φ_ss may be interpreted as the responses to impulses hitting the system. In particular, the ijth element of Φ_s represents the expected marginal response of $y_{i,t+s}$ to a unit change in y_{jt} holding constant all past values of the process. Because u_{it} is the forecast error in y_{it} given $\{y_{t-1}, y_{t-2}, \ldots\}$, the elements of Φ_s represent the impulse responses of the components of y_t with respect to the u_t innovations. Because these quantities are just the 1-step ahead forecast errors the corresponding impulse responses are sometimes referred to as *forecast error impulse responses* (Lütkepohl, 1991). In the presently considered $I(0)$ case, $\Phi_s \to 0$ as $s \to \infty$. Consequently, the effect of an impulse vanishes over time and is hence transitory.

These impulse responses have been criticized on the grounds that the underlying shocks may not occur in isolation if the components of u_t are instantaneously correlated. Therefore, orthogonal innovations are preferred in an impulse response analysis. Using a Choleski decomposition of the covariance matrix $E(u_t u_t') = \Sigma_u$ is one way to obtain uncorrelated innovations. Let B be a lower-triangular matrix with the property that $\Sigma_u = BB'$. Then orthogonalized shocks are given by $\varepsilon_t = B^{-1}u_t$. Substituting in Equation (5.17) and defining $\Psi_i = \Phi_i B\,(i = 0, 1, 2, ...)$ gives

$$y_t = \mu_t + \Psi_0 \varepsilon_t + \Psi_1 \varepsilon_{t-1} + \cdots. \tag{5.18}$$

Notice that $\Psi_0 = B$ is lower triangular so that the first shock may have an instantaneous effect on all the variables, whereas the second shock can only have an instantaneous effect on y_{2t} to y_{Kt} but not on y_{1t}. This way a recursive Wold causal chain is obtained. The effects of ε shocks are sometimes called *orthogonalized impulse responses* because they are instantaneously uncorrelated (orthogonal).

A drawback of these shocks is that many matrices B exist which satisfy $BB' = \Sigma_u$. The Choleski decomposition is to some extent arbitrary if there are no good reasons for a particular recursive structure. Clearly, if a lower triangular Choleski decomposition is used to obtain B, the actual innovations will depend on the ordering of the variables in the vector y_t so that different shocks and responses may result if the vector y_t is rearranged. In response to this problem, Sims (1981) recommended to consider different triangular orthogonalizations and check the robustness of the results if no particular ordering is suggested by economic theory. Taking into account subject matter theory in identifying the relevant impulses is the idea underlying structural VAR modelling. I do not discuss that issue here in detail but refer the reader to Breitung *et al.* (2004) for a recent introduction.

For nonstationary cointegrated processes the Wold representation does not exist. Still the Φ_s impulse response matrices can be computed as for stationary processes from the levels version of a VECM (Lütkepohl, 1991, Chapter 11; Lütkepohl and Reimers, 1992). Generally Φ_s will not converge to zero as $s \rightarrow \infty$ in this case. Consequently, some shocks may have permanent effects. Distinguishing between shocks with permanent and transitory effects can also help in finding identifying restrictions for the innovations and impulse responses of a VECM. For an introduction to structural VECMs see also Breitung *et al.* (2004).

5.8.2. Statistical inference for impulse responses

5.8.2.1. Asymptotic theory considerations

Suppose an estimator $\hat{\theta}$, say, of the model parameters θ is available. Then an impulse response coefficient $\phi = \phi(\theta)$, say, can be estimated as $\hat{\phi} = \phi(\hat{\theta})$. If $\hat{\theta}$ has an asymptotic normal distribution, $\sqrt{T}(\hat{\theta} - \theta) \xrightarrow{d} N(0, \Sigma_{\hat{\theta}})$, then $\hat{\phi}$ is also asymptotically normally distributed. Denoting by $\partial\phi/\partial\theta$ the vector of first order partial derivatives of ϕ with respect to the elements of θ and using the delta method gives

$$\sqrt{T}(\hat{\phi} - \phi) \xrightarrow{d} N(0, \sigma_{\hat{\phi}}^2), \tag{5.19}$$

where $\sigma_{\hat{\phi}}^2 = (\partial\phi/\partial\theta')\Sigma_{\hat{\theta}}(\partial\phi/\partial\theta)$. This result holds if $\sigma_{\hat{\phi}}^2$ is nonzero which is guaranteed if $\Sigma_{\hat{\theta}}$ is nonsingular and $\partial\phi/\partial\theta \neq 0$. The covariance matrix $\Sigma_{\hat{\theta}}$ may be singular if the system contains $I(1)$ variables. The partial derivatives will also usually be zero in some points of the parameter space because the ϕ generally consist of sums of products of the VAR coefficients. Then the partial derivatives will also be sums of products of such coefficients which may be zero. The partial derivatives are nonzero if all elements of θ are nonzero. Therefore, fitting subset models where all those coefficients are restricted to zero which are actually zero, helps to make the asymptotics for impulse responses work (Benkwitz *et al.*, 2001).

5.8.2.2. *Bootstrapping impulse responses*

In practice, CIs for impulse responses are often constructed by bootstrap methods because they have some advantages over asymptotic CIs. In particular, they were found to be more reliable in small samples than those based on asymptotic theory (e.g. Kilian, 1998). Moreover, precise expressions for the asymptotic variances of the impulse response coefficients are not needed if a bootstrap is used. The asymptotic variances are rather complicated (e.g. Lütkepohl, 1991, Chapter 3) and it may therefore be an advantage if they can be avoided.

Typically, a residual based bootstrap is used in this context. Let ϕ, $\hat{\phi}$ and $\hat{\phi}^*$ denote some general impulse response coefficient, its estimator implied by the estimators of the model coefficients and the corresponding bootstrap estimator, respectively. The *standard percentile interval* is perhaps the most common method in setting up CIs for impulse responses in practice. It is given by $[s_{\gamma/2}^*, s_{(1-\gamma/2)}^*]$, where $s_{\gamma/2}^*$ and $s_{(1-\gamma/2)}^*$ are the $\gamma/2$- and $(1-\gamma/2)$-quantiles, respectively, of the empirical distribution of the $\hat{\phi}^*$ (see, e.g. Efron and Tibshirani, 1993). Benkwitz *et al.* (2001) also consider *Hall's percentile interval* (Hall, 1992) which is derived using the principle that the distribution of $\sqrt{T}(\hat{\phi} - \phi)$ is approximately equal to that of $\sqrt{T}(\hat{\phi}^* - \hat{\phi})$ in large samples. The resulting CI is $[\hat{\phi} - t_{(1-\gamma/2)}^*, \hat{\phi} - t_{\gamma/2}^*]$. Here $t_{\gamma/2}^*$ and $t_{(1-\gamma/2)}^*$ are the $\gamma/2$- and $(1-\gamma/2)$-quantiles, respectively, of the empirical distribution of $(\hat{\phi}^* - \hat{\phi})$.

Unfortunately, the bootstrap generally does not overcome the problems due to a singularity in the asymptotic distribution which results from a zero variance in Equation (5.19). In these cases bootstrap CIs may not have the desired coverage probability as discussed by Benkwitz *et al.* (2000). To overcome these problems one may (i) consider bootstrap procedures that adapt to the kind of singularity in the asymptotic distribution, (ii) fit subset models or (iii) assume an infinite VAR order. The first one of these approaches has drawbacks in empirical applications (see Benkwitz *et al.*, 2000). Either they are not very practical for processes of realistic dimension and autoregressive order or they do not perform well in samples of typical size.

Fitting subset models may also be problematic because this only solves the singularity problem if indeed all zero coefficients are found (Benkwitz *et al.*, 2001). Usually there is uncertainty regarding the actual zero restrictions if statistical methods are used for subset modelling, however. The third possible solution to the singularity problem is to assume a VAR or VECM with infinite lag order and letting the model order increase when more sample information becomes available. In this approach, the model order is assumed to go to infinity with the sample size at a suitable rate. Relevant asymptotic theory was developed by Lütkepohl (1988, 1996), Lütkepohl and Poskitt (1991, 1996), Lütkepohl and Saikkonen (1997) and Saikkonen and Lütkepohl (1996, 2000a) based on work by Lewis and Reinsel (1985) and Saikkonen (1992). The disadvantage of this approach is that the greater generality of the models implies an inefficiency relative to the model with finite fixed order, provided the latter is a proper representation of the actual DGP. For practical purposes, subset modelling may be the best solution.

5.8.3. Impulse response analysis of the example system

For illustrative purposes an impulse response analysis is performed based on the subset VECM (Equation (5.16)). Thereby we hope to account for the problems related to constructing bootstrap CIs. Because the estimated instantaneous residual correlations were found to be small, it may be reasonable to consider the forecast error impulse responses. They are shown in Figure 5.4 with standard percentile and Hall's percentile CIs, based on 2000 bootstrap replications. According to the bootstrap literature the number of bootstrap replications has to be quite large in order to obtain reliable results. Therefore, one may wonder if using 2000 replications is adequate. We have also computed CIs with 1000 replications and found that they are not very different from those based on 2000 replications. Hence, 2000 replications should be sufficient for the present example.

The two different methods for constructing CIs result in very similar intervals for the present example system (Figure 5.4). The impulse

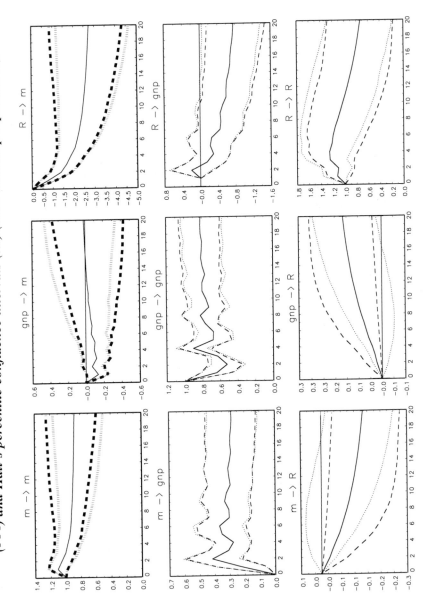

Figure 5.4.   Forecast error impulse responses of German macrosystem based on subset VECM (16) with 95% standard (- - -) and Hall's percentile confidence intervals (...) (2000 bootstrap replications).

responses are all quite plausible. For example, an interest rate impulse leads to a reduction in money demand and in output, whereas a money shock raises output and, in the long-run, tends to decrease the nominal interest rate. Not surprisingly, shocks in all three variables have long-term impacts because the variables are all $I(1)$.

5.8.4. Forecast error variance decomposition

Forecast error variance decompositions are related to impulse responses and may also be used for interpreting dynamic models. The h-step forecast error for the y_t variables in terms of structural innovations $\varepsilon_t = (\varepsilon_{1t}, \ldots, \varepsilon_{Kt})' = B^{-1} u_t$ can be shown to be

$$\Psi_0 \varepsilon_{T+h} + \Psi_1 \varepsilon_{T+h-1} + \cdots + \Psi_{h-1} \varepsilon_{T+1},$$

so that the kth element of the forecast error vector is

$$\sum_{n=0}^{h-1} (\psi_{k1,n} \varepsilon_{1,T+h-n} + \cdots + \psi_{kK,n} \varepsilon_{K,T+h-n}),$$

where $\psi_{ij,n}$ denotes the ijth element of Ψ_n (Lütkepohl, 1991). Because, by construction, the ε_{kt} are contemporaneously and serially uncorrelated and have unit variances, the corresponding forecast error variance is

$$\sigma_k^2(h) = \sum_{n=0}^{h-1} (\psi_{k1,n}^2 + \cdots + \psi_{kK,n}^2) = \sum_{j=1}^{K} (\psi_{kj,0}^2 + \cdots + \psi_{kj,h-1}^2).$$

The quantity $(\psi_{kj,0}^2 + \cdots + \psi_{kj,h-1}^2)$ is interpreted as the contribution of variable j to the h-step forecast error variance of variable k. This interpretation is justified if the ε_{it} can be viewed as shocks in variable i. The percentage contribution of variable j to the h-step forecast error variance of variable k is obtained by dividing the above terms by $\sigma_k^2(h)$,

$$\omega_{kj}(h) = (\psi_{kj,0}^2 + \cdots + \psi_{kj,h-1}^2)/\sigma_k^2(h).$$

The corresponding estimated quantities are often reported for various forecast horizons.

In Figure 5.5, a forecast error variance decomposition of the German macrosystem based on the subset VECM (Equation (5.16)) is shown. It uses orthogonalized innovations obtained via a Choleski decomposition of the covariance matrix. In Figure 5.5 it appears that the interest rate dominates its own development as well as that of m_t at least in the long-run, whereas the gnp_t variable is largely determined by its own innovations. This interpretation relies on the point estimates, however, because the

Figure 5.5. Forecast error variance decomposition of German macrosystem based on subset VECM (Equation (5.16))

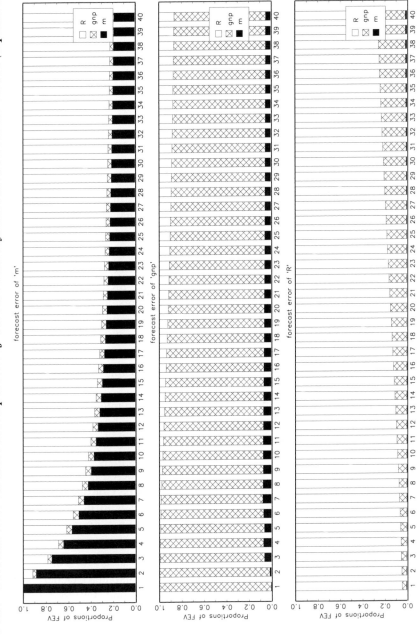

forecast error variance components are computed from estimated quantities. They are therefore uncertain. Also, the ordering of the variables may have an impact on the results. Although the instantaneous residual correlation is small in our subset VECM, it may have some impact on the outcome of a forecast error variance decomposition. This possibility was checked by reversing the ordering of the variables. It turned out that for the present system the ordering of the variables has a very small effect only.

5.9. Conclusions and extensions

Cointegration analysis has become a standard tool in econometrics during the last two decades after its introduction by Granger (1981) and Engle and Granger (1987). In this chapter some recent developments are reviewed. A small German macrosystem around a money demand relation is used to illustrate the methodology. The example data have special features for which new methods have been developed recently. In particular, they have level shifts that have to be taken into account in unit root and cointegration testing and in modelling the DGP. Some recent tools for handling such data properties have been discussed. In addition, methods for parameter estimation and model checking have been presented and applied. A satisfactory model for the example data set is found. This model is then used to study the dynamic interactions between the variables within an impulse response analysis and by means of a forecast error variance decomposition. Some recent developments in using these tools are also discussed.

In this review I have not tried to present all the interesting and exciting developments of cointegration analysis over the last two decades. The present review focuses explicitly on developments related to a specific example data set and on methodology to which I have contributed. An interesting development that has not been considered is, for instance, the analysis of systems with higher integration orders. Considerable progress has been made on the theory for analyzing models of this type (see, e.g. Johansen, 1995b, 1997; Kitamura, 1995; Haldrup, 1998; Paruolo and Rahbek, 1999; Boswijk, 2000; Paruolo, 2000, 2002). Moreover, models for variables with seasonal unit roots have been analysed (Johansen and Schaumburg, 1999; Ghysels and Osborn, 2001, Chapter 3). Generally these models are more complicated than the $I(1)$ case and the theory is not as complete as that of $I(1)$ models. Not surprisingly, there are also fewer applications.

Another generalization of the models considered so far is obtained by allowing the order of integration to be a real number rather than restricting it to an integer value. For real numbers d, one may define the differencing operator Δ^d by the following power series expansion:

$$\Delta^d = \sum_{j=0}^{\infty} L^j \Gamma(j-d)/\Gamma(j+1)\Gamma(-\mathrm{d}),$$

where $\Gamma(\cdot)$ denotes the Gamma function. With this definition, processes y_t may be considered for which $\Delta^d y_t$ is stationary for real values of $d > -1$. The concept of cointegration has been extended to this type of *fractionally integrated* processes (e.g. Breitung and Hassler, 2002; Marmol *et al.*, 2002; Robinson and Yajima, 2002; Velasco, 2003). They allow more flexibility with respect to the persistence of shocks to the system.

It is also possible to extend the linear VECMs by considering nonlinear error correction terms. For example, the term $\alpha\beta'y_{t-1}$ may be replaced by a nonlinear function $f(\beta'y_{t-1})$ or more generally by $g(y_{t-1})$. Such extensions may be of interest because the implications of linear models are not always fully satisfactory. For example, in a linear model a positive deviation from the long-run equilibrium relation has the same effect as a negative deviation of the same magnitude except that it has the opposite sign. Such a reaction is not always realistic in economic systems, where, for instance, the reaction may depend on the state of the business cycle. Models with nonlinear error correction terms have been proposed and considered, for example, by Balke and Fomby (1997), Lo and Zivot (2001), Saikkonen (2001a,b) and Escribano and Mira (2002).

Other forms of nonlinearities may also be considered. For example, nonlinearities may be present in the short-run dynamics in addition or alternatively to the error correction term. For example, Krolzig (1997) extends Markov regime switching models which were originally introduced to econometrics by Hamilton (1989), to systems of cointegrated variables.

Other extensions of the basic model include VECMs with finite order vector MA terms (Lütkepohl and Claessen, 1997; Lütkepohl, 2002) and models which condition on some of the variables (Harbo *et al.*, 1998; Pesaran *et al.*, 2000).

To do a cointegration analysis it is usually not necessary anymore to develop the software because some packages exist which can be used comfortably. Examples are EViews (EViews, 2000), PcFiml (Doornik and Hendry, 1997), Microfit (Pesaran and Pesaran, 1997), CATS (Hansen and Juselius, 1994), JMulTi (Lütkepohl and Krätzig, 2004). The latter program was also used for the computations related to the example discussed in the present chapter.

142   *H. Lütkepohl*

Acknowledgements

I am grateful to Dmitri Boreiko for helping with the figures. An earlier version of the paper was presented at Venice University. I thank the seminar participants for their comments.

References

Ahn, S.K. and G.C. Reinsel (1990), "Estimation of partially nonstationary multivariate autoregressive models", *Journal of the American Statistical Association*, Vol. 85, pp. 813–823.

Amsler, C. and J. Lee (1995), "An LM test for a unit root in the presence of a structural change", *Econometric Theory*, Vol. 11, pp. 359–368.

Andrews, D.W.K. (1993), "Tests for parameter instability and structural change with unknown change point", *Econometrica*, Vol. 61, pp. 821–856.

Andrews, D.W.K. and W. Ploberger (1994), "Optimal tests when a nuisance parameter is present only under the alternative", *Econometrica*, Vol. 62, pp. 1383–1414.

Balke, N.S. and T.B. Fomby (1997), "Threshold cointegration", *International Economic Review*, Vol. 38, pp. 627–645.

Benkwitz, A., H. Lütkepohl and M. Neumann (2000), "Problems related to bootstrapping impulse responses of autoregressive processes", *Econometric Reviews*, Vol. 19, pp. 69–103.

Benkwitz, A., H. Lütkepohl and J. Wolters (2001), "Comparison of bootstrap confidence intervals for impulse responses of German monetary systems", *Macroeconomic Dynamics*, Vol. 5, pp. 81–100.

Bossaerts, P. (1988), "Common nonstationary components of asset prices", *Journal of Economic Dynamics and Control*, Vol. 12, pp. 347–364.

Boswijk, H.P. (1995), "Efficient inference on cointegration parameters in structural error correction models", *Journal of Econometrics*, Vol. 69, pp. 133–158.

Boswijk, H.P. (1996), "Testing identifiability of cointegrating vectors", *Journal of Business & Economic Statistics*, Vol. 14, pp. 153–160.

Boswijk, H.P. (2000), "Mixed normality and ancillarity in I(2) systems", *Econometric Theory*, Vol. 16, pp. 878–904.

Boswijk, H.P. and J.A. Doornik (2002), "Identifying, estimating and testing restricted cointegrated systems: An overview", Paper presented at the Henri Theil Memorial Conference, Universiteit van Amsterdam.

Breitung, J. and U. Hassler (2002), "Inference on the cointegration rank in fractionally integrated processes", *Journal of Econometrics*, Vol. 110, pp. 167–185.

Breitung, J., R. Brüggemann and H. Lütkepohl (2004), "Structural vector autoregressive modelling and impulse responses", pp. 159–196 in: H. Lütkepohl and M. Krätzig, editors, *Applied Time Series Econometrics*, Cambridge: Cambridge University Press.

Brüggemann, R. and H. Lütkepohl (2001), "Lag selection in subset VAR models with an application to a U.S. monetary system", pp. 107–128 in: R. Friedmann, L. Knüppel and H. Lütkepohl, editors, *Econometric Studies: A Festschrift in Honour of Joachim Frohn*, Münster: LIT Verlag.

Candelon, B. and H. Lütkepohl (2001), "On the reliability of Chow-type tests for parameter constancy in multivariate dynamic models", *Economics Letters*, Vol. 73, pp. 155–160.

Davidson, J. (2000), *Econometric Theory*, Oxford: Blackwell.

Davidson, R. and J. MacKinnon (1993), *Estimation and Inference in Econometrics*, London: Oxford University Press.

Dickey, D.A. and W.A. Fuller (1979), "Estimators for autoregressive time series with a unit root", *Journal of the American Statistical Association*, Vol. 74, pp. 427–431.

Doornik, J.A. and D.F. Hendry (1997), *Modelling Dynamic Systems Using PcFiml 9.0 for Windows*, London: International Thomson Business Press.

Efron, B. and R.J. Tibshirani (1993), *An Introduction to the Bootstrap*, New York: Chapman & Hall.

Elliott, G. (2000), "Estimating restricted cointegrating vectors", *Journal of Business & Economic Statistics*, Vol. 18, pp. 91–99.

Engle, R.F. and C.W.J. Granger (1987), "Cointegration and error correction: Representation, estimation and testing", *Econometrica*, Vol. 55, pp. 251–276.

Escribano, A. and S. Mira (2002), "Nonlinear error correction models", *Journal of Time Series Analysis*, Vol. 23, pp. 509–522.

EViews (2000), *EViews 4.0 User's Guide*, Irvine, CA: Quantitative Micro Software.

Fuller, W.A. (1976), *Introduction to Statistical Time Series*, New York: Wiley.

Ghysels, E. and D.R. Osborn (2001), *The Econometric Analysis of Seasonal Time Series*, Cambridge: Cambridge University Press.

Gonzalo, J. (1994), "Five alternative methods of estimating long-run equilibrium relationships", *Journal of Econometrics*, Vol. 60, pp. 203–233.

Gonzalo, J. and J.-Y. Pitarakis (1999), "Dimensionality effect in cointegration analysis", pp. 212–229 in: R. Engle and H. White, editors, *Cointegration, Causality, and Forecasting. A Festschrift in Honour of Clive W. J. Granger*, Oxford: Oxford University Press.

Granger, C.W.J. (1981), "Some properties of time series data and their use in econometric model specification", *Journal of Econometrics*, Vol. 16, pp. 121–130.

Haldrup, N. (1998), "An econometric analysis of I(2) variables", *Journal of Economic Surveys*, Vol. 12, pp. 595–650.

Hall, P. (1992), *The Bootstrap and Edgeworth Expansion*, New York: Springer.

Hamilton, J.D. (1989), "A new approach to the economic analysis of nonstationary time series and the business cycle", *Econometrica*, Vol. 57, pp. 357–384.

Hansen, B.E. (1997), "Approximate asymptotic *p*-values for structural-change tests", *Journal of Business & Economic Statistics*, Vol. 15, pp. 60–67.

Hansen, H. and S. Johansen (1999), "Some tests for parameter constancy in cointegrated VAR-models", *Econometrics Journal*, Vol. 2, pp. 306–333.

Hansen, H. and K. Juselius (1994), *CATS for RATS4: Manual to Cointegration Analysis to Time Series*, Estima.

Hansen, P.R. (2003), "Structural changes in the cointegrated vector autoregressive model", *Journal of Econometrics*, Vol. 114, pp. 261–295.

Harbo, I., S. Johansen, B. Nielsen and A. Rahbek (1998), "Asymptotic inference on cointegrating rank in partial systems", *Journal of Business & Economic Statistics*, Vol. 16, pp. 388–399.

Hubrich, K., H. Lütkepohl and P. Saikkonen (2001), "A review of systems cointegration tests", *Econometric Reviews*, Vol. 20, pp. 247–318.

Johansen, S. (1991), "Estimation and hypothesis testing of cointegration vectors in Gaussian vector autoregressive models", *Econometrica*, Vol. 59, pp. 1551–1581.

Johansen, S. (1995a), *Likelihood-based Inference in Cointegrated Vector Autoregressive Models*, Oxford: Oxford University Press.

Johansen, S. (1995b), "A statistical analysis of cointegration for I(2) variables", *Econometric Theory*, Vol. 11, pp. 25–59.

Johansen, S. (1997), "Likelihood analysis of the I(2) model", *Scandinavian Journal of Statistics*, Vol. 24, pp. 433–462.

Johansen, S. (2002), "A small sample correction for the test of cointegrating rank in the vector autoregressive model", *Econometrica*, Vol. 70, pp. 1929–1961.

Johansen, S. and K. Juselius (1992), "Testing structural hypotheses in a multivariate cointegration analysis of the PPP and UIP for UK", *Journal of Econometrics*, Vol. 53, pp. 211–244.

Johansen, S. and K. Juselius (1994), "Identification of the long-run and the short-run structure. An application to the ISLM model", *Journal of Econometrics*, Vol. 63, pp. 7–36.

Johansen, S. and E. Schaumburg (1999), "Likelihood analysis of seasonal cointegration", *Journal of Econometrics*, Vol. 88, pp. 301–339.

Judge, G.G., W.E. Griffiths, R.C. Hill, H. Lütkepohl and T.-C. Lee (1985), *The Theory and Practice of Econometrics*, 2nd ed., New York: Wiley.

Kilian, L. (1998), "Small-sample confidence intervals for impulse response functions", *Review of Economics and Statistics*, Vol. 80, pp. 218–230.

Kitamura, Y. (1995), "Estimation of cointegrated systems with I(2) processes", *Econometric Theory*, Vol. 11, pp. 1–24.

Krolzig, H.-M. (1997), *Markov-Switching Vector Autoregressions: Modelling, Statistical Inference, and Application to Business Cycle Analysis*, Berlin: Springer.

Lanne, M., H. Lütkepohl and P. Saikkonen (2002), "Comparison of unit root tests for time series with level shifts", *Journal of Time Series Analysis*, Vol. 23, pp. 667–685.

Lanne, M., H. Lütkepohl and P. Saikkonen (2003), "Test procedures for unit roots in time series with level shifts at unknown time", *Oxford Bulletin of Economics and Statistics*, Vol. 65, pp. 91–115.

Lewis, R. and G.C. Reinsel (1985), "Prediction of multivarate time series by autoregressive model fitting", *Journal of Multivariate Analysis*, Vol. 16, pp. 393–411.

Lo, M.C. and E. Zivot (2001), "Threshold cointegration and nonlinear adjustment to the law of one price", *Macroeconomic Dynamics*, Vol. 5, pp. 533–576.

Lütkepohl, H. (1988), "Asymptotic distribution of the moving average coefficients of an estimated vector autoregressive process", *Econometric Theory*, Vol. 4, pp. 77–85.

Lütkepohl, H. (1991), *Introduction to Multiple Time Series Analysis*, Berlin: Springer.

Lütkepohl, H. (1996), "Testing for nonzero impulse responses in vector autoregressive processes", *Journal of Statistical Planning and Inference*, Vol. 50, pp. 1–20.

Lütkepohl, H. (2002), "Forecasting cointegrated VARMA processes", pp. 179–205 in: M.P. Clements and D.F. Hendry, editors, *A Companion to Economic Forecasting*, Oxford: Blackwell.

Lütkepohl, H. (2004a), "Univariate time series analysis", pp. 8–85, in: H. Lütkepohl and M. Krätzig, editors, *Applied Time Series Econometrics*, Cambridge: Cambridge University Press.

Lütkepohl, H. (2004b), "Vector autoregressive and vector error correction models", pp. 86–158 in: H. Lütkepohl and M. Krätzig, editors, *Applied Time Series Econometrics*, Cambridge: Cambridge University Press.

Lütkepohl, H. and H. Claessen (1997), "Analysis of cointegrated VARMA processes", *Journal of Econometrics*, Vol. 80, pp. 223–239.

Lütkepohl, H. and M. Krätzig (eds.) (2004), *Applied Time Series Econometrics*, Cambridge: Cambridge University Press.

Lütkepohl, H. and D.S. Poskitt (1991), "Estimating orthogonal impulse responses via vector autoregressive models", *Econometric Theory*, Vol. 7, pp. 487–496.

Lütkepohl, H. and D.S. Poskitt (1996), "Testing for causation using infinite order vector autoregressive processes", *Econometric Theory*, Vol. 12, pp. 61–87.

Lütkepohl, H. and H.-E. Reimers (1992), "Impulse response analysis of cointegrated systems", *Journal of Economic Dynamics and Control*, Vol. 16, pp. 53–78.

Lütkepohl, H. and P. Saikkonen (1997), "Impulse response analysis in infinite order cointegrated vector autoregressive processes", *Journal of Econometrics*, Vol. 81, pp. 127–157.

Lütkepohl, H. and P. Saikkonen (1999), "Order selection in testing for the cointegrating rank of a VAR process", pp. 168–199 in: R.F. Engle and H. White, editors, *Cointegration, Causality, and Forecasting. A Festschrift in Honour of Clive W.J. Granger*, Oxford: Oxford University Press.

Lütkepohl, H. and P. Saikkonen (2000), "Testing for the cointegrating rank of a VAR process with a time trend", *Journal of Econometrics*, Vol. 95, pp. 177–198.

Lütkepohl, H. and J. Wolters (2003), "The transmission of German monetary policy in the pre-euro period", *Macroeconomic Dynamics*, Vol. 7, pp. 711–733.

Lütkepohl, H., P. Saikkonen and C. Trenkler (2004), "Testing for the cointegrating rank of a VAR process with level shift at unknown time", *Econometrica*, Vol. 72, pp. 647–662.

Luukkonen, R., A. Ripatti and P. Saikkonen (1999), "Testing for a valid normalization of cointegrating vectors in vector autoregressive processes", *Journal of Business & Economic Statistics*, Vol. 17, pp. 195–204.

Marmol, F., A. Escribano and F.M. Aparicio (2002), "Instrumental variable interpretation of cointegration with inference results for fractional cointegration", *Econometric Theory*, Vol. 18, pp. 646–672.

Ng, S. and P. Perron (1995), "Unit root tests in ARMA models with data-dependent methods for the selection of the truncation lag", *Journal of the American Statistical Association*, Vol. 90, pp. 268–281.

Pantula, S.G. (1989), "Testing for unit roots in time series data", *Econometric Theory*, Vol. 5, pp. 256–271.

Paruolo, P. (2000), "Asymptotic efficiency of the two stage estimator in $I(2)$ systems", *Econometric Theory*, Vol. 16, pp. 524–550.

Paruolo, P. (2002), "Asymptotic inference on the moving average impact matrix in cointegrated $I(2)$ VAR systems", *Econometric Theory*, Vol. 18, pp. 673–690.

Paruolo, P. and A. Rahbek (1999), "Weak exogeneity in $I(2)$ VAR systems", *Journal of Econometrics*, Vol. 93, pp. 281–308.

Perron, P. (1989), "The great crash, the oil price shock, and the unit root hypothesis", *Econometrica*, Vol. 57, pp. 1361–1401.

Perron, P. (1990), "Testing for a unit root in a time series with a changing mean", *Journal of Business & Economic Statistics*, Vol. 8, pp. 153–162.

Perron, P. and T.J. Vogelsang (1992), "Nonstationarity and level shifts with an application to purchasing power parity", *Journal of Business & Economic Statistics*, Vol. 10, pp. 301–320.

Pesaran, M.H. and B. Pesaran (1997), *Working with Microfit 4.0: Interactive Econometric Analysis*, Oxford: Oxford University Press.

Pesaran, M.H. and Y. Shin (2002), "Long-run structural modelling", *Econometric Reviews*, Vol. 21, pp. 49–87.

Pesaran, M.H., Y. Shin and R.J. Smith (2000), "Structural analysis of vector error correction models with $I(1)$ variables", *Journal of Econometrics*, Vol. 97, pp. 293–343.

Phillips, P.C.B. (1987), "Time series regression with a unit root", *Econometrica*, Vol. 55, pp. 277–301.

Phillips, P.C.B. (1991), "Optimal inference in cointegrated systems", *Econometrica*, Vol. 59, pp. 283–306.

Phillips, P.C.B. and S.N. Durlauf (1986), "Multiple time series regression with integrated processes", *Review of Economic Studies*, Vol. 53, pp. 473–495.

Phillips, P.C.B. and B.E. Hansen (1990), "Statistical inference in instrumental variables regression with $I(1)$ processes", *Review of Economic Studies*, Vol. 57, pp. 99–125.

Phillips, P.C.B. and M. Loretan (1991), "Estimating long-run economic equilibria", *Review of Economic Studies*, Vol. 58, pp. 407–436.

Ploberger, W., W. Krämer and K. Kontrus (1989), "A new test for structural stability in the linear regression model", *Journal of Econometrics*, Vol. 40, pp. 307–318.

Reinsel, G.C. (1993), *Elements of Multivariate Time Series Analysis*, New York: Springer.

Robinson, P.M. and Y. Yajima (2002), "Determination of cointegrating rank in fractional systems", *Journal of Econometrics*, Vol. 106, pp. 217–241.

Saikkonen, P. (1992), "Estimation and testing of cointegrated systems by an autoregressive approximation", *Econometric Theory*, Vol. 8, pp. 1–27.

Saikkonen, P. (2001a), "Consistent estimation in cointegrated vector autoregressive models with nonlinear time trends in cointegrating relations", *Econometric Theory*, Vol. 17, pp. 296–326.

Saikkonen, P. (2001b), "Statistical inference in cointegrated vector autoregressive models with nonlinear time trends in cointegrating relations", *Econometric Theory*, Vol. 17, pp. 327–356.

Saikkonen, P. and H. Lütkepohl (1996), "Infinite order cointegrated vector autoregressive processes: Estimation and inference", *Econometric Theory*, Vol. 12, pp. 814–844.

Saikkonen, P. and H. Lütkepohl (1999), "Local power of likelihood ratio tests for the cointegrating rank of a VAR process", *Econometric Theory*, Vol. 15, pp. 50–78.

Saikkonen, P. and H. Lütkepohl (2000a), "Asymptotic inference on nonlinear functions of the coefficients of infinite order cointegrated VAR processes", pp. 165–201 in: W.A. Barnett, D.F. Hendry, S. Hylleberg, T. Teräsvirta, D. Tjøstheim and A. Würtz, editors, *Nonlinear Econometric Modeling in Time Series Analysis*, Cambridge: Cambridge University Press.

Saikkonen, P. and H. Lütkepohl (2000b), "Testing for the cointegrating rank of a VAR process with an intercept", *Econometric Theory*, Vol. 16, pp. 373–406.

Saikkonen, P. and H. Lütkepohl (2000c), "Testing for the cointegrating rank of a VAR process with structural shifts", *Journal of Business & Economic Statistics*, Vol. 18, pp. 451–464.

Saikkonen, P. and H. Lütkepohl (2002), "Testing for a unit root in a time series with a level shift at unknown time", *Econometric Theory*, Vol. 18, pp. 313–348.

Sims, C.A. (1981), "An autoregressive index model for the U.S. 1948–1975", pp. 283–327 in: J. Kmenta and J.B. Ramsey, editors, *Large-Scale Macro-Econometric Models*, Amsterdam: North-Holland.

Sims, C.A., J.H. Stock and M.W. Watson (1990), "Inference in linear time series models with some unit roots", *Econometrica*, Vol. 58, pp. 113–144.

Stock, J.H. and M.W. Watson (1988), "Testing for common trends", *Journal of the American Statistical Association*, Vol. 83, pp. 1097–1107.

Velasco, C. (2003), "Gaussian semi-parametric estimation of fractional cointegration", *Journal of Time Series Analysis*, Vol. 24, pp. 345–378.

New Directions in Macromodelling
A. Welfe (Editor)
© 2004 Elsevier B.V. All rights reserved.
DOI: 10.1016/S0573-8555(04)69006-7

CHAPTER 6

The Use of Econometric Models in Economic Policy Analysis

Grayham E. Mizon

Head, School of Social Sciences, Murray Building, University of Southampton,
Southampton SO17 1BJ, UK

Abstract

The potential role of econometric models in economic policy analysis is considered. Necessary conditions for avoiding misleading inferences are presented, and the merits of alternative types of policy analyses are discussed. The case for response analysis via dynamic multipliers in open models that condition on policy instruments is presented. Recent results on robust forecasting using open models subject to structural breaks and policy regime shifts are summarized.

Keywords: causality, co-breaking, congruence, encompassing, exogeneity

JEL classifications: C52, C32, E41

6.1. Introduction

One of the major roles of economists is to assist decision makers in government, international organizations, and in private enterprise to assess the likely effects of alternative policy proposals. For example, the Monetary Policy Committee of the Bank of England, the Board of Governors of the Federal Reserve System in the US, and the Board of the European Central Bank, each month have to form a judgement on the state of the economies for which they are responsible and assess the effects of interest rate changes, prior to taking their interest rate decision. In addition to judgemental and other qualitative information, the quantitative estimates of the response in target variables y_t (such as inflation and unemployment rates) to changes in policy instruments $\mathbf{z}_t$ (such as tax and interest rates) are potentially extremely valuable. Well-specified econometric models that embody a good characterization of the actual linkages between targets and policy instruments are thus an important input into the decision process. The focus of this chapter is on the use of econometric models for economic policy analysis. Despite the doubts raised by the Lucas critique, econometric models may have valuable information about the feasibility and the likely effects of alternative economic policies. However, there are conditions that must be satisfied by an econometric model if it is to provide relevant, reliable, and robust information about economic policies. Further, there are many different ways in which the information contained in econometric models can be used for deciding on appropriate policy actions, and assessing the likely effects on target variables. It is argued below that the evaluation of responses to policy via distributed lag or dynamic multiplier analysis in the context of congruent and encompassing open econometric models, usually is preferable to the more commonly used impulse response analysis in closed models.

Section 6.2 presents notation and defines essential concepts, in particular the data generation process (DGP), the local DGP and the econometric model for the modelled variables, and the objectives of economic policy analysis. Section 6.3 analyses the econometric conditions needed to sustain conditional policy analyses, and shows that the econometric concepts of *causality*, *co-breaking*, *congruence*, *encompassing*, *exogeneity*, and *invariance* play a vital role in determining the usefulness of estimated models for economic policy. Section 6.5 describes alternative types of response analysis, including impulse response analysis in closed and open systems, and dynamic multiplier analysis in open econometric models. Section 6.6 then summarizes recent results on robust forecasting using open models in the presence of structural breaks and economic policy regime shifts. Conclusions are presented in Section 6.7.

6.2. Notation and concepts

Let the joint density $D_{w_t}(\mathbf{w}_t | \mathcal{F}_{t-1})$ of the vector of N real random variables $\mathbf{w}_t$, that characterize the economy under analysis at each point in time $t \in \mathcal{T}$, be the DGP with sample space Ω and event space $\mathcal{F}_{t-1}$. It is assumed that this DGP can be represented as a vector stochastic process, with sufficient continuity to make it meaningful to postulate d parameters $\delta \in \mathcal{D}^d \subseteq \mathbb{R}^d$ that do not depend on $\mathcal{F}_{t-1}$ at any t. The parameters need not be constant over time. Denote the history of the stochastic process $\{\mathbf{w}_t\}$ up to time $(t-1)$ by the notation $\mathbf{W}_{t-1} = (\mathbf{W}_0, \mathbf{w}_1, ..., \mathbf{w}_{t-1}) = (\mathbf{W}_0, \mathbf{W}_{t-1}^1)$, where $\mathbf{W}_0$ is the set of initial conditions. Then, for a sample period $t = 1, ..., T$, the DGP is denoted $D_W(\mathbf{W}_T^1|\mathbf{W}_0, \delta)$, and is sequentially factorized as:

$$D_W(\mathbf{W}_T^1|\mathbf{W}_0, \delta) = \prod_{t=1}^{T} D_{wt}(\mathbf{w}_t|\mathbf{W}_{t-1}, \boldsymbol{\kappa}_t) \tag{6.1}$$

where $\mathbf{g}(\delta) = (\boldsymbol{\kappa}_1...\boldsymbol{\kappa}_T)$ for a $1-1$ function $\mathbf{g}(\cdot)$, so that the $\boldsymbol{\kappa}_t$ may be non-constant over time due to regime shifts and structural breaks – see Hendry and Mizon (1998) and Hendry and Mizon (2000) for discussion of the distinction between these parameter changes.

The aim of economic policy is assumed to be changing the target variables $\mathbf{y}_t$ (or some function of them, e.g. $\Delta\mathbf{y}_t$, $E(\mathbf{y}_t)$ or $E(\Delta\mathbf{y}_t)$) by manipulating policy instruments $\mathbf{z}_t$ (or some function of them) in the DGP, even though the decisions are usually made using an econometric model. In other words, although economic policy analysis is concerned with the relationship between $\mathbf{y}_t$ and $\mathbf{z}_t$ in the DGP, in the absence of knowledge of the DGP this analysis is done using an econometric model for $n < N$ variables $\mathbf{x}_t$ which include $\mathbf{y}_t$ and $\mathbf{z}_t$ which are $n_1 \times 1$ and $n_2 \times 1$, respectively. Before introducing the notation for an econometric model it is important to note that the theory of reduction (see, *inter alia*, Hendry, 1995; Mizon, 1995), implies that there exists a 'local DGP' $D_{x_t}(\mathbf{x}_t|\mathbf{X}_{t-1}, \boldsymbol{\zeta})$ derived from $D_{w_t}(\mathbf{w}_t|\cdot)$ in Equation (6.1) by reduction. Hence there is an important sense in which the aim of econometric modelling is to mimic in the econometric model the salient features of the local DGP. Clearly, the salient features are problem dependent, and are limited by the available information.

An econometric model $f_x(\cdot)$ for $\mathbf{x}_t$ is denoted by:

$$f_x(\mathbf{X}_T^1|\mathbf{X}_0, \theta) = \prod_{t=1}^{T} f_x(\mathbf{x}_t|\mathbf{X}_{t-1}, \theta) \text{ where}$$
$$\theta = (\theta_1, ..., \theta_k)' \in \Theta \subseteq \mathbb{R}^k \tag{6.2}$$

when $f_x(\mathbf{x}_t|\mathbf{X}_{t-1}, \theta)$ is the postulated sequential joint density at time t. It is assumed that $k < d$ and θ represents the constant parameters postulated by the modeller, so any time-dependent effects have been reparameterized accordingly (as in a 'structural time-series model' re-represented as an ARIMA process, e.g. see Harvey, 1993).

When $\mathbf{x}_t$ is partitioned as $\mathbf{x}_t' = (\mathbf{y}_t' : \mathbf{z}_t')$ and correspondingly $\mathbf{X}_{t-1} = (\mathbf{Y}_{t-1}, \mathbf{Z}_{t-1})$, the joint density can be factorized into a conditional density and a marginal density as:

$$f_x(\mathbf{x}_t|\mathbf{X}_{t-1}, \theta) = f_{y|z}(\mathbf{y}_t|\mathbf{z}_t, \mathbf{X}_{t-1}, \boldsymbol{\phi}_1)f_z(\mathbf{z}_t|\mathbf{X}_{t-1}, \boldsymbol{\phi}_2). \tag{6.3}$$

This is achieved by transforming the original model parameters $\boldsymbol{\theta} \in \Theta$ to the set $\boldsymbol{\phi} \in \Phi$ given by:

$$\boldsymbol{\phi} = \mathbf{h}(\boldsymbol{\theta}) \quad \text{where} \quad \boldsymbol{\phi} \in \Phi \quad \text{and} \quad \boldsymbol{\theta} \in \Theta, \tag{6.4}$$

such that $\mathbf{h}(\cdot)$ defines a $1-1$ reparameterization of θs into ϕs designed to sustain the partition $\boldsymbol{\phi}' = (\boldsymbol{\phi}_1' : \boldsymbol{\phi}_2')$, where $\boldsymbol{\phi}_i$ has k_i elements ($k_1 + k_2 = k$), corresponding to the factorization (6.3). Much of the following discussion will consider economic policy analysis using models of the conditional density $f_{y|z}(\mathbf{y}_t | \mathbf{z}_t, \mathbf{X}_{t-1}, \boldsymbol{\phi}_1)$. The condition for inference based on such conditional densities to be without loss of information is that $\mathbf{z}_t$ be weakly exogenous for the parameters of interest $\boldsymbol{\psi}$ (see Engle *et al.*, 1983). This condition requires that $\boldsymbol{\psi}$ can be recovered solely from $\boldsymbol{\phi}_1$, and that $\boldsymbol{\phi}_1$ and $\boldsymbol{\phi}_2$ are variation free. However, weak exogeneity has no causal implications.

If, in the universe of information, deleting the history of one set of variables does not alter the joint distribution of any of the remaining variables, then the omitted variables were defined by Granger (1969) not to cause the remaining variables. Hendry and Mizon (1999) provide formal definitions and discuss the limitations of, and difficulties associated with, applying Granger causality empirically. For example: it is non-operational since its definition relates to the universe of information; Granger causality is specific to each point in time, and thus could change so confounding empirical tests. Again, though causality in the DGP is required for effective policy, in the absence of knowledge of the DGP the relevant concept is empirical Granger causality, which for the information set generated by $\{\mathbf{x}_t\}$ was defined by Hendry and Mizon (1999) as:

Definition 1. If the density $f_z(\cdot)$ does not depend on $\mathbf{Y}_{t-1}$ so that:

$$f_z(\mathbf{z}_t | \mathbf{X}_{t-1}, \cdot) = f_z(\mathbf{z}_t | \mathbf{Z}_{t-1}, \cdot), \tag{6.5}$$

then $\mathbf{y}$ does not empirically Granger cause $\mathbf{z}$.

Thus the absence of feedback from one set of variables to another in the context of an econometric model is captured in the concept of *empirical* Granger non-causality, which is denoted by its acronym EGNC. Whereas the absence of feedback from one set of variables to another in the context of the DGP is captured in the concept of Granger non-causality. When $\mathbf{z}_t$ is weakly exogenous and $\mathbf{y}_t$ is EGNC for $\mathbf{z}_t$ then $\mathbf{z}_t$ is strongly exogenous for $\boldsymbol{\psi}$ (see Engle *et al.*, 1983). This condition is important in the context of forecasting since it sustains forecasting of $\mathbf{y}_t$ conditionally on $\mathbf{z}_t$ without there being any loss of information.

Implicit in the above definitions of weak and strong exogeneity is the assumption that $\boldsymbol{\phi}_1$ and $\boldsymbol{\phi}_2$ are constant. However, there is ample empirical evidence of parameter non-constancies in the processes relevant in modelling for economic policy analysis. Hence it is important to extend the concept of exogeneity to be applicable when there are regime shifts and structural changes, such as those resulting from changes in economic policies. Following the schema of Ericsson *et al.* (1998) policy interventions and parameter invariance can be defined in the following way.

A policy regime shift implemented via a parameter intervention at time t affecting the DGP for $\mathbf{x}_t$:

$$D_x(\mathbf{x}_t|\mathbf{X}_{t-1},\boldsymbol{\zeta}_t) = D_{y|z}(\mathbf{y}_t|\mathbf{z}_t,\mathbf{X}_{t-1},\boldsymbol{\zeta}_{1,t})D_z(\mathbf{z}_t|\mathbf{X}_{t-1},\boldsymbol{\zeta}_{2,t}), \qquad (6.6)$$

is defined as any action $\mathbf{a}_t$ by an agent that alters $\boldsymbol{\zeta}_2$ from its current value ($\boldsymbol{\zeta}_{2,t-1}$) to a different value $\boldsymbol{\zeta}_{2,t} = \varphi(\mathbf{a}_t,\boldsymbol{\zeta}_{2,t-1})$ (say), so $\boldsymbol{\zeta}_t = \boldsymbol{\zeta}_{t-1}$ results when no intervention occurs. Let $C_{\zeta_2}(t)$, the set of interventions at time t on $D_z(\mathbf{z}_t|\mathbf{X}_{t-1},\boldsymbol{\zeta}_{2,t})$ that potentially affect $\boldsymbol{\zeta}_{1,t}$, be defined by:

$$C_{\zeta_2}(t) = \{\mathbf{a}_t : \boldsymbol{\zeta}_{2,t} = \varphi(\mathbf{a}_t,\boldsymbol{\zeta}_{2,t-1})\},$$

with $C_{\zeta_2} = \{C_{\zeta_2}(t), t = 1, ..., T\}$. Possible interventions include changes in monetary, fiscal and exchange-rate policy rules, deregulation, nationalization, and some forms of financial and technological innovations. Since the DGP is the economic mechanism, its parameterization can be affected by many forms of intervention. Indeed, the aim of many economic policies is precisely to affect the DGP. Such changes may affect the parameters of the econometric model, thus calling into question its use for economic policy analysis. If the econometric model does provide a good characterization of the DGP then an intervention belonging to C_{ζ_2} will almost certainly result in $\boldsymbol{\phi}_2$ changing. Hence the extent to which an econometric model will remain useful for economic policy analysis in such situations is determined by the degree of invariance of the conditional model parameters $\boldsymbol{\phi}_1$ to the regime shift.

Definition 2. $\boldsymbol{\phi}_1$ is invariant to a class of interventions C_{ϕ_2} if $\boldsymbol{\phi}_1$ is constant over C_{ϕ_2}.

The combination of weak exogeneity and invariance was defined by Engle *et al.* (1983) as super exogeneity.

Definition 3. $\mathbf{z}_t$ is super exogenous for the identified parameters of interest $\boldsymbol{\psi}$ if $\mathbf{z}_t$ is weakly exogenous for $\boldsymbol{\psi}$, and $\boldsymbol{\phi}_1$ is invariant to C_{ϕ_2}.

Thus the super exogeneity of $\mathbf{z}_t$ provides conditions under which changes in $\boldsymbol{\zeta}_2$ can lead to changes in $\boldsymbol{\phi}_2$ without affecting $\boldsymbol{\phi}_1$, or the efficient estimation of the latter. These are precisely the conditions for the Lucas critique (Lucas, 1976) not to apply. Further, Hendry and Mizon (1998) pointed out that contemporaneous mean co-breaking between $\mathbf{y}_t$ and $\mathbf{z}_t$ ensures that $\boldsymbol{\phi}_1$ is invariant to the class of interventions given by changes in the unconditional means of $\mathbf{z}_t$. Hence they demonstrated that in a world where the only sources of non-stationarity are deterministic, the combination of weak exogeneity of $\mathbf{z}_t$ and co-breaking between $\mathbf{y}_t$ and $\mathbf{z}_t$ is sufficient for a conditional econometric model to predict that an economic policy implemented by shifting the unconditional mean of $\mathbf{z}_t$ will be effective, and for the model to provide an efficient estimate of the response in $\mathbf{y}_t$.

6.3. Econometric models and economic policy

Though economic policies can be categorized in many ways the important distinction for the present analysis is that between within-regime drawings of the policy instruments $\mathbf{z}_t$, and those policies that are effected by a regime shift – that is the difference between the implementation of an existing policy and the introduction of a new policy. Although in practice it might be difficult to determine whether some policy decisions are within-regime or a change of regime, a clear distinction is possible in the present analytical framework. When policy is within-regime there is no change in $\boldsymbol{\zeta}_2$ and the observed value of $\mathbf{z}_t$ is a realization from the instrument process $D_z(\mathbf{z}_t|\mathbf{X}_{t-1}, \boldsymbol{\zeta}_2)$. In such cases a change in $\boldsymbol{\phi}_2$ is unlikely, and so the issue of $\boldsymbol{\phi}_1$ being invariant to policy changes does not arise. Of more interest, are those policies that are implemented via changes in some of the elements of $\boldsymbol{\zeta}_2$, so that a change in $\boldsymbol{\phi}_2$ is likely. Hence the invariance of the conditional model parameters $\boldsymbol{\phi}_1$ to the change is critical if the econometric model of $f_{y|z}(\mathbf{y}_t|\mathbf{z}_t, \mathbf{X}_{t-1}, \boldsymbol{\phi}_1)$ is to be valuable in estimating the response in $\mathbf{y}_t$ to the policy regime shift. Attention in the sequel is focused on policies involving regime shifts, but consideration will also be given to impulses of one period duration. Consideration is now given to the conditions under which economic policies will be effective, and analysis of them using econometric models relevant, reliable, and robust (i.e. valid).

Whether or not a particular policy will be effective depends on its relationship to the DGP. In particular, the pre-requisites include that there is causality between the targets $\mathbf{y}_t$ and the instruments $\mathbf{z}_t$ in the DGP, and that it is possible for the policy agency to manipulate the instruments $\mathbf{z}_t$ (i.e. change the parameters $\boldsymbol{\zeta}_2$). In other words, the policy experiment must be feasible in reality in order to be effective. As discussed by Granger and Deutsch (1992) genuine causal links between the policy instruments $\mathbf{z}_t$ and the targets $\mathbf{y}_t$ are required in the DGP for effective policy analysis, and these causal links may be contemporaneous but they might also involve delayed causality. Indeed, the existence of Granger causality between targets $\mathbf{y}_t$ and instruments $\mathbf{z}_t$ in the DGP will ensure that there is feedback between them, but note that the relationship will only be genuinely causal if in addition it is invariant to policy changes.

Although this implies that the feasibility of an economic policy is determined by the nature of the DGP and the chosen instruments, in the absence of knowledge of the DGP an econometric model will often be used to assess this feasibility. Therefore it is important that the econometric model validly supports the proposed policy experiment (i.e. is relevant), and satisfies other conditions for economic policy analysis based on it to be reliable and robust. In general, $f_x(\cdot) \neq D_{x_t}(\cdot)$, and this divergence has to be taken into account when making inferences about $\mathbf{\theta}$, and more particularly $\mathbf{\phi}_1$ and $\mathbf{\phi}_2$. This observation serves to emphasize that an econometric model must represent the salient attributes of the economy sufficiently closely if its policy implications are to match out-turns. In particular, it is required that the partial response matrix $\partial \mathbf{y}_{t+h}/\partial \mathbf{z}_t'$ in the DGP is well approximated using the available evidence by $\partial \mathbf{y}_{t+h}/\partial \mathbf{z}_t'$ in the econometric model for $h \geqslant 0$. Sufficient econometric conditions for this to hold are congruence and encompassing (Hendry (1995); Mizon (1995); Bontemps and Mizon (2003)). An econometric model is congruent when there is no evidence in the information set chosen to develop and evaluate the model to indicate that it differs from the DGP. In other words a congruent model is fully coherent with available information. Precisely because it is possible to design econometric models to have this property, and because different investigators often choose different information sets (perhaps associated with different economic theories), it is possible for there to be more than one econometric model satisfying the empirical conditions for congruence. Noting that the alternative econometric models that are congruent with their information sets will often have different policy implications – this was illustrated using simple monetarist and Keynesian models of inflation in Mizon (1989) – draws attention to the importance of having a means of discriminating between such alternative congruent models. In fact there is no shortage of suggestions for such model discrimination, ranging from random selection, economic theory based selection, goodness of fit criteria, to degrees of freedom adjusted information criteria. However, a limitation that is shared by these selection criteria is that they confine attention, and hence selection, to the set of congruent models. In particular, these selection criteria do not allow for the possibility that their shared corroboration could imply their shared inadequacy (Ericsson and Hendry, 1999), and so lead to the development of a model that dominates them all by drawing on the strengths of each. The encompassing principle, that requires of preferred models that they can account for the strengths and weaknesses of alternative congruent models, provides an attractive means of model discrimination. An encompassing model is defined by its most appealing feature, namely that it renders each of the alternative congruent models inferentially redundant since it can account for the results obtainable from the alternatives. More detailed discussions of the encompassing principle are contained in *inter alia* Mizon (1984), Mizon and Richard (1986), Hendry and Richard (1989), and Hendry (1995). Hendry (2003), in addition to commenting on the dangers of both extremes of theory-based modelling and data-based modelling, presents the case for adopting procedures that automatically select empirically congruent and encompassing models within a general framework that embraces a rich collection of potentially relevant data and enables a wide range of theories to be compared.

The econometric constructs that correspond to simultaneous and dynamic causal links in the DGP are simultaneity and Granger causality. Of particular relevance for economic policy analysis is the fact that Granger causality in a model does not entail its existence in the DGP, and conversely, Granger causation in the DGP need not be reflected in a model thereof. The fact that economic policy analysis always relies on an econometric model, and that only empirical Granger non-causality (EGNC) as opposed to actual Granger non-causality can be tested, strengthens the argument for using congruent and encompassing models since no difference between the DGP and such an econometric model has been detected. Also, as pointed out by Hendry and Mizon (1999), Granger causality might simply be reflecting a reduction phenomenon (i.e. the presence or absence of feedbacks in a limited data set), irrespective of whether or not they are 'genuine DGP causes'. Clearly this can have serious consequences for the estimation of policy responses from econometric models.

Finally, it is noted that economic policy analysis will not be robust unless the policy change being considered does not alter the econometric model in a self-contradictory way – see Frisch (1938) for an early statement of this and Lucas (1976) for a more recent analysis. Since most economies are subject to numerous changes, including changes in economic policy, it is important for econometric modelling that some of their features are invariant. Without such invariance econometric modelling and economic policy analysis using econometric models would be of limited value. Hence the invariance of ϕ_1 is necessary for the predicted effects of an economic policy using the conditional econometric model $f_{y|z}(\mathbf{y}_t|\mathbf{z}_t, \mathbf{X}_{t-1}, \boldsymbol{\phi}_1)$ to match the out-turn. Since $\boldsymbol{\phi}_1$ is unknown, the weak exogeneity of $\mathbf{z}_t$ for the parameters of interest will be required for efficient estimation from the conditional distribution. The presence of regime shifts introduces non-stationarities into DGPs and models thereof. However, when there exist linear combinations of shifted variables that are constant then these linear combinations are said to be a co-breaking relationships, and as such they are analogous to cointegrating relationships that are of a lower order of integration than that of their constituent variables. Hendry and Mizon (1998) establish co-breaking and weak exogeneity conditions under which conditional models are immune to the critique when the policy change involves a shift in the unconditional mean of $\mathbf{z}_t$.

Hence econometric constructs such as causality, congruence, co-breaking, encompassing, exogeneity, and invariance have important roles in economic policy analysis using econometric models. Fortunately, each of these constructs has testable implications thus rendering an econometric approach to policy analysis feasible.

6.4. A cointegrated VAR model

Many macroeconomic time series variables are non-stationary as a result of integratedness and deterministic non-stationarities, and so the cointegrated VAR with deterministic variables (such as trend, seasonal, and event specific dummies) included is adopted often as the statistical model for econometric modelling of them. If the variables to be modelled cannot be well represented as a multivariate linear process then the VAR will not be congruent (Hendry, 1995; Bontemps and Mizon, 2003), and thus will exhibit signs of misspecification. Were this to be the case reformulation of the model (perhaps by variable transformation or by the inclusion of intervention dummy variables), will often enable the reformulated system to be well characterized by a VAR. Hence, provided that attention is paid to ensuring that it is congruent, the VAR can be expected to be a widely appropriate statistical model to use for modelling macroeconomic time series.

For k lags on a vector of n variables $\mathbf{x}_t$ and with intercepts being the only deterministic variables for simplicity the corresponding VAR is:

$$\mathbf{x}_t = \sum_{j=1}^{k} \mathbf{A}_j \mathbf{x}_{t-j} + \boldsymbol{\delta} + \boldsymbol{\epsilon}_t \quad \text{with} \quad \boldsymbol{\epsilon}_t \sim \text{IN}_n(\mathbf{0}, \boldsymbol{\Sigma}). \tag{6.7}$$

When $\mathbf{A}_j$ is an $n \times n$ matrix of autoregressive coefficients, $\boldsymbol{\delta}$ is an $n \times 1$

vector of intercepts, and $\boldsymbol{\epsilon}_t$ is a vector of n unobserved errors which have a zero mean and constant covariance matrix $\boldsymbol{\Sigma}$. When the variables being modelled $\mathbf{x}_t$ are $I(1)$ but there are $r < N$ long run relationships $\boldsymbol{\beta}'\mathbf{x}_t$ which are $I(0)$, the VAR in Equation (6.7) can be written as a vector equilibrium correction mechanism VEqCM (Johansen, 1988, 1992; Hendry, 1995):

$$\Delta\mathbf{x}_t = \sum_{j=1}^{k-1} \boldsymbol{\Gamma}_j\Delta\mathbf{x}_{t-j} + \boldsymbol{\alpha}(\boldsymbol{\beta}'\mathbf{x}_{t-1}) + \boldsymbol{\delta} + \boldsymbol{\epsilon}_t, \qquad (6.8)$$

where Δ is the first difference operator, $\boldsymbol{\Gamma}_j = -\sum_{i=j+1}^{k}\mathbf{A}_i$, and $\boldsymbol{\alpha}$ and $\boldsymbol{\beta}$ are $n \times r$ matrices of rank r such that $\boldsymbol{\alpha}\boldsymbol{\beta}' = -(\mathbf{I}_N - \sum_{i=1}^{k}\mathbf{A}_i)$, with identification restrictions being required to ensure uniqueness of $\boldsymbol{\alpha}$ and $\boldsymbol{\beta}$. The model in Equation (6.8) is in $I(0)$ space when correctly formulated, thus inference concerning its parameters $\boldsymbol{\Gamma}_1, \boldsymbol{\Gamma}_2,\ldots\boldsymbol{\Gamma}_{s-1}, \boldsymbol{\alpha}, \boldsymbol{\alpha}, \boldsymbol{\delta}$ and $\boldsymbol{\Sigma}$ can be conducted using conventional procedures. Since r is not known a priori its value has to be determined empirically, and a commonly adopted approach is the maximum likelihood procedure developed by Johansen (1988).

The properties of this system are conveniently considered for a second-order system ($k = 2$) in which case (6.8) becomes the VEqCM:

$$\Delta\mathbf{x}_t = \boldsymbol{\delta} + \boldsymbol{\alpha}\boldsymbol{\beta}'\mathbf{x}_{t-1} + \boldsymbol{\Gamma}\Delta\mathbf{x}_{t-1} + \boldsymbol{\epsilon}_t. \qquad (6.9)$$

The possibility that $\mathbf{x}_t$ is $I(2)$ is ruled out when the following condition is satisfied

$$\text{rank}(\boldsymbol{\alpha}'_\perp\boldsymbol{\Phi}\boldsymbol{\beta}_\perp) = n - r \qquad (6.10)$$

when $\boldsymbol{\Phi}$ is the mean-lag matrix:

$$\boldsymbol{\Phi} = (\mathbf{I}_n + \boldsymbol{\alpha}\boldsymbol{\beta}' - \boldsymbol{\Gamma}),$$

with $\boldsymbol{\Gamma}_1 = \boldsymbol{\Gamma}$, and $\boldsymbol{\alpha}_\perp$ and $\boldsymbol{\beta}_\perp$ are $n \times (n - r)$ and satisfy $\boldsymbol{\alpha}'_\perp\boldsymbol{\alpha} = \boldsymbol{\beta}'_\perp\boldsymbol{\beta} = \mathbf{0}$, such that $(\boldsymbol{\alpha} : \boldsymbol{\alpha}_\perp)$ and $(\boldsymbol{\beta} : \boldsymbol{\beta}_\perp)$ are full rank n. Letting $\mathbf{A}(L) = \mathbf{I}_n - (\mathbf{I}_n + \boldsymbol{\alpha}\boldsymbol{\beta}' + \boldsymbol{\Gamma})L + \boldsymbol{\Gamma}L^2$ and $\mathbf{A}(L)^{-1} = \mathbf{C}(L) = \mathbf{C}(1) + \mathbf{C}^*(L)\Delta$ the solution of Equation (6.9) for $\mathbf{x}_t$ is

$$\mathbf{x}_t = \mathbf{K}_{\boldsymbol{\beta}_\perp}\mathbf{x}_0 + \mathbf{C}(1)\sum_{i=1}^{t}(\boldsymbol{\epsilon}_i + \boldsymbol{\delta}) + \mathbf{C}^*(L)(\boldsymbol{\epsilon}_t + \boldsymbol{\delta}) \qquad (6.11)$$

when

$$\mathbf{K}_{\beta_\perp} = \beta_\perp(\beta'_\perp\beta_\perp)^{-1}\beta'_\perp$$

and

$$\mathbf{C}(1) = \boldsymbol{\beta}_\perp (\boldsymbol{\alpha}_\perp' \boldsymbol{\Xi} \boldsymbol{\beta}_\perp)^{-1} \boldsymbol{\alpha}_\perp' \quad \text{with} \quad \boldsymbol{\Xi} = \boldsymbol{\Gamma} - \mathbf{I}_n. \tag{6.12}$$

As pointed out in Hendry and Mizon (1993), when both $\Delta \mathbf{x}_t$ and $\boldsymbol{\beta}' \mathbf{x}_t$ are $I(0)$, the variables grow at the vector rate $E[\Delta \mathbf{x}_t] = \boldsymbol{\gamma}$, and the r dimensional equilibrium of the system is $E[\boldsymbol{\beta}' \mathbf{x}_t] = \boldsymbol{\mu}$, the long-run solution of the system is:

$$\boldsymbol{\alpha} E[\boldsymbol{\beta}' \mathbf{x}_t] = (\mathbf{I}_n - \boldsymbol{\Gamma}) \boldsymbol{\gamma} - \boldsymbol{\delta}, \tag{6.13}$$

so that:

$$\boldsymbol{\delta} = -\boldsymbol{\Xi} \boldsymbol{\gamma} - \boldsymbol{\alpha} \boldsymbol{\mu}, \tag{6.14}$$

and yields:

$$(\Delta \mathbf{x}_t - \boldsymbol{\gamma}) = \boldsymbol{\alpha}(\boldsymbol{\beta}' \mathbf{x}_{t-1} - \boldsymbol{\mu}) + \boldsymbol{\Gamma}(\Delta \mathbf{x}_{t-1} - \boldsymbol{\gamma}) + \boldsymbol{\epsilon}_t. \tag{6.15}$$

When $\mathbf{x}_t$ is $I(1)$ and r is correctly specified all terms in Equation (6.15) have zero means, and since $\Delta(\boldsymbol{\beta}' \mathbf{x}_t)$ is the difference of a stationary variable, $\boldsymbol{\beta}' \boldsymbol{\gamma} = \mathbf{0}$. These latter r restrictions together with Equation (6.14) identify $\boldsymbol{\gamma}$ and $\boldsymbol{\mu}$, although both $\boldsymbol{\delta}$ and $\boldsymbol{\gamma}$ are $n \times 1$ and $\boldsymbol{\mu}$ is $r \times 1$. The solution of Equation (6.15) for $\mathbf{x}_t$ is:

$$\mathbf{x}_t = \mathbf{K}_{\boldsymbol{\beta}_\perp} \mathbf{x}_0 + \mathbf{C}(1) \sum_{i=1}^{t} (\boldsymbol{\epsilon}_i - \boldsymbol{\Xi} \boldsymbol{\gamma}) + \mathbf{C}^*(L)(\boldsymbol{\epsilon}_t - \boldsymbol{\Xi} \boldsymbol{\gamma} - \boldsymbol{\alpha} \boldsymbol{\mu}) \tag{6.16}$$

Equations (6.11) and (6.16) indicate that major determinants of the elements in $\mathbf{x}_t$ are the innovations $\boldsymbol{\epsilon}_i$ for $i = 1, 2, \ldots t$, and the intercepts $\boldsymbol{\delta}$, or equivalently the mean growth rate $\boldsymbol{\gamma}$, and the equilibrium mean $\boldsymbol{\mu}$. Thus in this framework economic policy implemented via changes in $\mathbf{z}_t$ can be achieved by direct control of $\mathbf{z}_t$, or indirectly by changes the mean growth rate $\boldsymbol{\gamma}_z$, of $\mathbf{z}_t$ when $\mathbf{x}_t' = (\mathbf{y}_t', \mathbf{z}_t')$ and $\boldsymbol{\gamma}' = (E[\Delta \mathbf{y}_t'], E[\Delta \mathbf{z}_t']) = (\boldsymbol{\gamma}_y', \boldsymbol{\gamma}_z')$, or alternatively by introducing particular shocks into the $\mathbf{z}_t$ process. Another class of policy can be implemented by changing the desired value of some of the elements of the equilibrium mean vector $\boldsymbol{\mu}$ such as shifting attention from the maintenance of full employment to controlling inflation. Whichever form of policy is being contemplated economic policy analysis will require an estimate of the response in the target variables $\mathbf{y}_t$ to the particular policy change. This is the topic of the next section.

6.5. Response analysis

The early research into the development of macroeconometric models for both policy analysis and forecasting was routed in the simultaneous equations paradigm, and essentially confined to station-ary models (see, e.g. Duesenberry *et al.*, 1965; Johnston, 1963). However, within this framework there was a well-developed theory for the estimation of policy responses via (dynamic) multiplier analysis – see, e.g. the early textbook presentations in Goldberger (1964) and Wallis (1979), and the more recent evaluation in Hendry (1995). The former has ceased to be a dominant paradigm in macroeconometrics largely as a result of: (i) the strictures of Box and Jenkins (1976) and Granger and Newbold (1974) against economists for paying too little attention to the non-stationarity of economic time series, and (ii) the critique, particularly by Sims (1980), of the 'incredible' over-identifying restrictions used in developing simul-taneous equations models. Further, the latter has fallen into neglect following the onslaught of the theory of rational expectations (see, e.g. Lucas and Sargent, 1981), and the Lucas critique (Lucas, 1976), which cast doubt on the possibility that econometric models can provide reliable guides to policy responses when agents react rationally to announced policy regime shifts. Although a commonly adopted framework for modelling today is that of cointegrated vector autoregressions, which does provide an answer to the criticisms (i) and (ii) above, this approach has been criticized for paying insufficient attention to economic theory. That this is not an inherent feature of this class of model was demonstrated by Hendry and Mizon (1993), who on the contrary argued that a congruent and encompassing vector equilibrium correction model (VEqCM) itself can be based on economic fundamentals and provides a good basis for testing more sophisticated economic hypotheses.

Attached as an adjunct to the adoption of VAR models as a dominant class for modelling macroeconomic time series, was the development of impulse response analysis as the primary means of conducting policy analysis. In this approach attention is focused on estimation of the reaction of modelled variables to temporary 'shocks' in innovations, e.g. $\partial \mathbf{x}_{t+h}/\partial \boldsymbol{\epsilon}_t'$, rather than estimating the response of some variables to changes in others as in dynamic multiplier analysis, e.g. $\partial \mathbf{y}_{t+h}/\partial \mathbf{z}_t'$. Hendry and Mizon (1998) argued that many changes in economic policy instruments $\mathbf{z}_t$ are deterministic (e.g. the Bank of England's Monetary Policy Committee might change its interest rate by 1%, leave it unchanged for 6 months, and then change it by 0.5%, and so on), and that in order to assess the effect of these changes on target variables $\mathbf{y}_t$, impulse response analysis is not necessarily appropriate.

6.5.1. Response analysis in closed models

In closed models such as Equation (6.7) contemporaneous partial derivatives, and so contemporaneous partial responses like $\partial \mathbf{y}_t / \partial \mathbf{z}'_t$, are not easily interpreted. In particular, it is not clear what is being held constant when there is simultaneous determination of all variables. Therefore, it is not surprising that the most commonly used form of response analysis in closed models, especially closed VAR models, is impulse response analysis which evaluates dynamic responses to impulses in innovations.

6.5.1.1. I(0) Case

Consider Equation (6.7) for $k = 1$ without substantive loss of generality. Then when $\mathbf{x}_t \sim I(0)$ there is a Wold representation:

$$\mathbf{x}_t = \sum_{i=0}^{\infty} \mathbf{A}^i (\boldsymbol{\delta} + \boldsymbol{\epsilon}_{t-i}) \tag{6.17}$$

when $\mathbf{A} = \mathbf{A}_1$ in the notation of Equation (6.7). In this case Hendry and Mizon (1998) showed that the response in the target variables to a shock in the instrument innovations is given by:

$$
\begin{aligned}
\frac{\partial \mathbf{y}_{t+h}}{\partial \boldsymbol{\epsilon}'_{z,t}} &= (\mathbf{I}_{n_1} : \mathbf{0}) \begin{pmatrix} \mathbf{A}_{yy} & \mathbf{A}_{yz} \\ \mathbf{A}_{zy} & \mathbf{A}_{zz} \end{pmatrix}^h \begin{pmatrix} \mathbf{0} \\ \mathbf{I}_{n_2} \end{pmatrix} \\
&= (\mathbf{I}_{n_1} : \mathbf{0}) \begin{pmatrix} \mathbf{E}_h & \mathbf{F}_h \\ \mathbf{G}_h & \mathbf{H}_h \end{pmatrix} \begin{pmatrix} \mathbf{0} \\ \mathbf{I}_{n_2} \end{pmatrix} = \mathbf{F}_h
\end{aligned} \tag{6.18}
$$

with $\mathbf{F}_0 = \mathbf{0}$. Hence the impulse response in Equation (6.18) depends on the dynamics of the system.

In the context of closed VAR models in $I(0)$ variables Ericsson *et al.* (1998) presented seven critical comments on the use of impulse response analysis such as that represented in Equation (6.18). The points made included: impulse responses are an alternative way to present information about the dynamic properties of the system which is contained in the roots of the companion matrix; impulse responses describe the dynamics of the estimated model regardless of the estimators' properties or the model specification; estimated closed VAR's often have non-constant parameters as a result of regime shifts and structural breaks and impulse responses being sensitive to parameter change have problematic interpretations for policy analysis. The problems associated with the last point are compounded when it is noted that it is rare for estimated VARs to be checked for parameter constancy, and that many changes in parameters (especially those that are the coefficients of zero mean variables) are difficult to detect using conventional tests (Hendry, 2000). Hence there are many problems associated with impulse response analysis per se and particularly with respect to the assessment of the responses to policy changes. Further these problems are not resolved in general by orthogonalization and identification schemes.

Also in the context of closed VARs, Hendry and Mizon (1998) demonstrated the importance of the policy instruments being weakly exogenous for the parameters linking $\mathbf{y}_t$ to $\mathbf{z}_t$, as well as the requirement of co-breaking between $\mathbf{y}_t$ and $\mathbf{z}_t$ (so that deterministic changes in $\mathbf{z}_t$ are mirrored by deterministic changes in $\mathbf{y}_{t+h}$ $h \geq 0$) for policy to be effective, and the policy response reliably estimated. In contrast to the impulse response which reflects dynamics only, the response to a deterministic shift in the mean of $\mathbf{z}_t$ reflects the relationship between the unconditional means of $\mathbf{y}_t$ and $\mathbf{z}_t$ which might be a structural relationship.

6.5.1.2. *I(1) Case*

When economic policy is considered in the context of a cointegrated VAR as in Equation (6.15), the target variables $\mathbf{y}_t$ being $I(1)$ will have unconditional means that depend on initial conditions and deterministic trend when there is drift. Hence targeting the unconditional mean of $\mathbf{y}_t$ or $\mathbf{y}_t$ itself, in these circumstances might be difficult. However, Johansen and Juselius (2001) analyse the problem of controlling $I(1)$ target variables by manipulation of $I(1)$ instruments, and show that if the policy is successful then the target process becomes stationary around the target value. Also it is relevant to note that although many macroeconomic time series exhibit $I(1)$ characteristics in particular samples, some of these variables, such as inflation rates, exchange rates, and unemployment rates, might be intrinsically $I(0)$ and hence potentially valid target variables. The results in Johansen and Juselius (2001) suggests that there is little point in targeting variables that are intrinsically $I(1)$ such as nominal money supply or nominal GDP, whereas targeting variables such as inflation, unemployment or exchange rates might be feasible even though these variables can exhibit $I(1)$ behaviour in particular periods.

More natural target variables though are growth rates ($\Delta\mathbf{y}_t$) and equilibria ($\boldsymbol{\beta}'\mathbf{x}_t$) which are both $I(0)$, as well as their means $\boldsymbol{\gamma}_y$ and $\boldsymbol{\mu}$. Candidates for permanent shifts are changes in the equilibrium means $\boldsymbol{\mu}$ resulting (e.g.) from shifts in the attitude of policy makers to acceptable levels of disequilibria $\boldsymbol{\beta}'\mathbf{x}_t$, or shifts in the instrument variables' growth rates $\boldsymbol{\gamma}_z$, whereas transitory shocks are still possible via $\boldsymbol{\epsilon}_{z,t}$.

Consider now the cointegrated VAR in VEqCM form as in Equation (6.15) which since $\boldsymbol{\beta}'\mathbf{x}_t$ and $\Delta\mathbf{x}_t$ are $I(0)$ has a Wold representation:

$$\Delta\mathbf{x}_t = \mathbf{C}(L)(\boldsymbol{\epsilon}_t - \boldsymbol{\Xi}\boldsymbol{\gamma} - \boldsymbol{\alpha}\boldsymbol{\mu})$$

$$= [\mathbf{C}(1) + \Delta\mathbf{C}^*(L)](\boldsymbol{\epsilon}_t - \boldsymbol{\Xi}\boldsymbol{\gamma} - \boldsymbol{\alpha}\boldsymbol{\mu})$$

$$= \mathbf{C}(1)(\boldsymbol{\epsilon}_t - \boldsymbol{\Xi}\boldsymbol{\gamma}) + \mathbf{C}^*(L)\Delta(\boldsymbol{\epsilon}_t - \boldsymbol{\Xi}\boldsymbol{\gamma} - \boldsymbol{\alpha}\boldsymbol{\mu}) \quad (6.19)$$

The corresponding moving-average representation for the cointegrating vectors is:

$$\boldsymbol{\beta}'\mathbf{x}_t = \boldsymbol{\beta}'\mathbf{C}^*(L)\boldsymbol{\epsilon}_t - \boldsymbol{\beta}'\mathbf{C}^*(1)(\boldsymbol{\Xi}\boldsymbol{\gamma} + \boldsymbol{\alpha}\boldsymbol{\mu}). \quad (6.20)$$

Partitioning Equation (6.19) yields:

$$\begin{pmatrix} \Delta\mathbf{y}_t \\ \Delta\mathbf{z}_t \end{pmatrix} = \begin{pmatrix} \mathbf{C}_{yy}(1) & \mathbf{C}_{yz}(1) \\ \mathbf{C}_{zy}(1) & \mathbf{C}_{zz}(1) \end{pmatrix} \left[\begin{pmatrix} \boldsymbol{\epsilon}_{y,t} \\ \boldsymbol{\epsilon}_{z,t} \end{pmatrix} - \begin{pmatrix} \boldsymbol{\Xi}_{yy} & \boldsymbol{\Xi}_{yz} \\ \boldsymbol{\Xi}_{zy} & \boldsymbol{\Xi}_{zz} \end{pmatrix} \begin{pmatrix} \boldsymbol{\gamma}_y \\ \boldsymbol{\gamma}_z \end{pmatrix} \right]$$

$$+ \begin{pmatrix} \mathbf{C}_{yy}^*(L) & \mathbf{C}_{yz}^*(L) \\ \mathbf{C}_{zy}^*(L) & \mathbf{C}_{zz}^*(L) \end{pmatrix} \Delta \left(\begin{pmatrix} \boldsymbol{\epsilon}_{y,t} - \boldsymbol{\alpha}_y\boldsymbol{\mu} \\ \boldsymbol{\epsilon}_{z,t} - \boldsymbol{\alpha}_z\boldsymbol{\mu} \end{pmatrix} \right.$$

$$\left. - \begin{pmatrix} \boldsymbol{\Xi}_{yy} & \boldsymbol{\Xi}_{yz} \\ \boldsymbol{\Xi}_{zy} & \boldsymbol{\Xi}_{zz} \end{pmatrix} \begin{pmatrix} \boldsymbol{\gamma}_y \\ \boldsymbol{\gamma}_z \end{pmatrix} \right) \quad (6.21)$$

With this notation Hendry and Mizon (1998) show that the responses to impulses in the instrument innovations are given by:

$$\frac{\partial\Delta\mathbf{y}_{t+h}}{\partial\boldsymbol{\epsilon}_{z,t}'} = (\mathbf{C}_{yz,h}^* - \mathbf{C}_{yz,h-1}^*) \qquad \forall h > 0, \quad (6.22)$$

$$\frac{\partial\Delta\mathbf{y}_t}{\partial\boldsymbol{\epsilon}_{z,t}'} = (\mathbf{C}_{yz}(1) + \mathbf{C}_{yz,0}^*) = \mathbf{0} \quad (6.23)$$

and

$$\frac{\partial\boldsymbol{\beta}'\mathbf{x}_{t+h}}{\partial\boldsymbol{\epsilon}_{z,t}'} = \boldsymbol{\beta}_z'(\mathbf{C}_{zy,h}^* + \mathbf{C}_{zz,h}^*) \qquad \forall h \geq 0. \quad (6.24)$$

Noting that $\det \mathbf{C}^*(L) = 0$ has all its roots outside the unit circle:

$$\frac{\partial\Delta\mathbf{y}_{t+h}}{\partial\boldsymbol{\epsilon}_{z,t}'} \to \mathbf{0} \quad \text{and} \quad \frac{\partial\mathbf{y}_{t+h}}{\partial\boldsymbol{\epsilon}_{z,t}'} \to \mathbf{C}_{yz}(1) \quad \text{as } h \to \infty$$

and

$$\frac{\partial \boldsymbol{\beta}' \mathbf{x}_{t+h}}{\partial \boldsymbol{\epsilon}'_{z,t}} \to \mathbf{0} \quad \text{as} \quad h \to \infty.$$

Hence, as to be expected, shocks to $\boldsymbol{\epsilon}_{z,t}$ do not have persistent effects on $\Delta \mathbf{y}_{t+h}$ and $\boldsymbol{\beta}' \mathbf{x}_{t+h}$, though they do have for $\mathbf{y}_t$.

Turning to deterministic shifts in $\boldsymbol{\mu}$ and $\boldsymbol{\gamma}_z$, the growth rate $(\Delta \mathbf{y}_t)$ responses are given by:

$$\frac{\partial \Delta \mathbf{y}_{t+h}}{\partial \boldsymbol{\mu}'} = -(\mathbf{C}^*_{yy,h}\boldsymbol{\alpha}_y + \mathbf{C}^*_{yz,h}\boldsymbol{\alpha}_z) = -\mathbf{C}^*_{y,h}\boldsymbol{\alpha} \tag{6.25}$$

and

$$\frac{\partial \Delta \mathbf{y}_{t+h}}{\partial \boldsymbol{\gamma}'_z} = -((\mathbf{C}_{yy}(1) + \mathbf{C}^*_{yy,h})\boldsymbol{\Xi}_{yz} + (\mathbf{C}_{yz}(1) + \mathbf{C}^*_{yz,h})\boldsymbol{\Xi}_{zz}), \tag{6.26}$$

and the responses of the equilibria $(\boldsymbol{\beta}' \mathbf{x}_{t+h})$ by:

$$\frac{\partial \boldsymbol{\beta}' \mathbf{x}_{t+h}}{\partial \boldsymbol{\mu}'} = -\boldsymbol{\beta}' \mathbf{C}^*(1)\boldsymbol{\alpha} \qquad \forall h \geq 0$$

and

$$\frac{\partial \boldsymbol{\beta}' \mathbf{x}_{t+h}}{\partial \boldsymbol{\gamma}'_z} = -\left[(\boldsymbol{\beta}'_y \mathbf{C}^*_{yy}(1) + \boldsymbol{\beta}'_z \mathbf{C}^*_{zy}(1))\boldsymbol{\Xi}_{yz} + (\boldsymbol{\beta}'_y \mathbf{C}^*_{yz}(1) + \boldsymbol{\beta}'_z \mathbf{C}^*_{zz}(1))\boldsymbol{\Xi}_{zz} \right].$$

Noting that $det\ \mathbf{C} * (L) = 0$ has all its roots outside the unit circle:

$$\frac{\partial \Delta \mathbf{y}_{t+h}}{\partial \boldsymbol{\mu}'} \to \mathbf{0} \quad \text{as} \quad h \to \infty$$

$$\frac{\partial \Delta \mathbf{y}_{t+h}}{\partial \boldsymbol{\gamma}'_z} \to \mathbf{C}_{yy}(1)\boldsymbol{\Xi}_{yz} + \mathbf{C}_{yz}(1)\boldsymbol{\Xi}_{zz} \quad \text{as} \quad h \to \infty$$

so that there are no long-run effects in the growth rate of $\mathbf{y}_t$ of shifts in the equilibrium mean $\boldsymbol{\mu}$, but shifts in the mean growth rate of $\mathbf{y}_t$ do have long run effects on $\Delta \mathbf{y}_t$.

It has been argued in this section that response analysis in closed models is fraught with many problems of implementation, interpretation and relevance. The most promising lines of research in this area are those concerning interpretation of cointegrating relationships in Johansen (2002), and the conduct of economic policy analysis in closed cointegrated VARs in Johansen and Juselius (2001). The alternative of conducting such analysis in open models is considered in the next section.

6.5.2. *Response analysis in open models*

Many of the problems in analysing the responses of targets to changes in instruments noted above are absent when the modelling is done conditionally on the instruments. In addition, it is often difficult to model the instruments well, whereas modelling conditionally on them is much easier. Equally, when the modelling of high dimensional systems is difficult or infeasible, it is often preferable to model conditionally on a subset of the variables rather than omit them from the analysis. For economic policy analysis another advantage of modelling target variables conditionally on instrument variables, is that the required policy responses $\partial \mathbf{y}_{t+h}/\partial \mathbf{z}_t'$ are directly estimable and interpretable in open models. Though formally the weak exogeneity of $\mathbf{z}_t$ is required for there to be no loss of information in making inferences on the parameters of interest, in practice it is likely that reliable estimates of policy responses will be obtained without $\mathbf{z}_t$ being weakly exogenous. A major reason for this being the case is the fact that for cointegrated systems the cointegrating vectors $\boldsymbol{\beta}'\mathbf{x}_t$ are usually estimated in the closed system, and so it is only the short run coefficients $\boldsymbol{\Gamma}$, $\boldsymbol{\Psi}_0$, $\boldsymbol{\Psi}_1$ and $\boldsymbol{\alpha}_y$ that are estimated in the open system (6.33) below prior to conducting economic policy analysis. Despite this, it is relevant to note that the fact that the $\{\mathbf{z}_t\}$ process is under the control of a policy agency does not imply, and certainly not ensure, that it is valid to condition on $\mathbf{z}_t$. Whether the policy involves a regime shift or a shock the instruments must be super exogenous for the parameters of interest if modelling with an open econometric model is to result in no loss of information. For example, if there is a policy regime shift then co-breaking between the targets and instruments ensures that the policy is effective, and that the response of $\mathbf{y}_t$ can be efficiently and reliably estimated when $\mathbf{z}_t$ is weakly exogenous for the response parameters (see, e.g. Hendry and Mizon, 1998).

6.5.2.1. *I(0) Case*

This section draws on some results in Ericsson *et al.* (1998) and is presented for completeness, and as a preliminary for considering the $I(1)$ case in the next section.

Consider the following conditional/marginal factorization of Equation (6.17):

$$
\begin{pmatrix} \mathbf{y}_t \\ \mathbf{z}_t \end{pmatrix} = \begin{pmatrix} \mathbf{\Pi} & (\mathbf{A}_{yy} - \mathbf{\Pi}\mathbf{A}_{zy}) & (\mathbf{A}_{yz} - \mathbf{\Pi}\mathbf{A}_{zz}) \\ \mathbf{0} & \mathbf{A}_{yz} & \mathbf{A}_{zz} \end{pmatrix} \begin{pmatrix} \mathbf{z}_t \\ \mathbf{y}_{t-1} \\ \mathbf{z}_{t-1} \end{pmatrix}
$$
$$
+ \begin{pmatrix} \boldsymbol{\nu} \\ \boldsymbol{\eta}_z \end{pmatrix} + \begin{pmatrix} \boldsymbol{\varepsilon}_t \\ \boldsymbol{\epsilon}_{z,t} \end{pmatrix} \tag{6.27}
$$

with

$$
\begin{pmatrix} \boldsymbol{\varepsilon}_t \\ \boldsymbol{\epsilon}_{z,t} \end{pmatrix} \sim \text{IN}\left(\begin{pmatrix} \mathbf{0} \\ \mathbf{0} \end{pmatrix}, \begin{pmatrix} \boldsymbol{\Omega}_{yy} & \mathbf{0} \\ \mathbf{0} & \boldsymbol{\Sigma}_{zz} \end{pmatrix} \right) \tag{6.28}
$$

when

$$
\begin{pmatrix} \boldsymbol{\eta}_y \boldsymbol{\eta}_z \end{pmatrix} = \begin{pmatrix} (\mathbf{I} - \mathbf{A}_{yy}) & -\mathbf{A}_{yz} \\ -\mathbf{A}_{zy} & (\mathbf{I} - \mathbf{A}_{zz}) \end{pmatrix}^{-1} \begin{pmatrix} \boldsymbol{\delta}_y \\ \boldsymbol{\delta}_z \end{pmatrix} \quad \text{and} \quad \boldsymbol{\nu} = (\boldsymbol{\eta}_y - \mathbf{\Pi}\boldsymbol{\eta}_z) \tag{6.29}
$$

$$
\mathbf{\Pi} = \boldsymbol{\Sigma}_{yz}\boldsymbol{\Sigma}_{zz}^{-1} \quad \text{and} \quad \boldsymbol{\Omega}_{yy} = (\boldsymbol{\Sigma}_{yy} - \mathbf{\Pi}\boldsymbol{\Sigma}_{zz}\mathbf{\Pi}'). \tag{6.30}
$$

Modelling the conditional distribution for $\mathbf{y}_t$ given $\mathbf{z}_t$ and $\mathbf{x}_{t-1}$ will yield efficient inference on the parameters of interest if $\mathbf{z}_t$ is weakly exogenous for those parameters. In addition, the conditional model will provide reliable estimates of the response in $\mathbf{y}_t$ to policy changes in $\mathbf{z}_t$ when its parameters are invariant to the policy change. When these conditions are satisfied it is relevant to use the conditional model to derive impulse responses and dynamic multipliers for assessing the effects of policy. However, Ericsson et $al.$ (1998) showed that orthogonalized impulse responses generally will be inappropriate since the resulting transformed variables $\mathbf{z}_t^+$ will not be weakly exogenous for the parameters of interest, and the latter might fail to be invariant with respect to policy regime shifts in the marginal process $f_z(\mathbf{z}_t|\mathbf{X}_{t-1}, \boldsymbol{\phi}_{2,t})$.

Irrespective of the exogeneity status of $\mathbf{z}_t$, inspection of the first equation of (6.27) reveals that modelling the conditional distribution alone will result in the following impulse response matrix:

$$
\frac{\partial \mathbf{y}_{t+h}}{\partial \boldsymbol{\varepsilon}_t'} = (\mathbf{A}_{yy} - \mathbf{\Pi}\mathbf{A}_{zy})^h. \tag{6.31}
$$

It follows from Equations (6.30) and (6.31) that $\mathbf{A}_{zy} = 0$ (i.e. $\mathbf{y}$ is EGNC for $\mathbf{z}$) provides a sufficient condition for the raw impulse responses for $\mathbf{y}_t$ derived from the system and from the conditional model to be equivalent:

$$\frac{\partial \mathbf{y}_{t+h}}{\partial \boldsymbol{\epsilon}'_{y,t}} = \frac{\partial \mathbf{y}_{t+h}}{\partial \boldsymbol{\epsilon}'_t} = \mathbf{A}^h_{yy}.$$

However, $\mathbf{A}_{zy} = \mathbf{0}$ is most unlikely to hold in practice since feedback from past values of target variables is often a major determinant of policy decisions. Further, it is not clear why response of $\mathbf{y}_t$ to an impulse in the innovation $\boldsymbol{\epsilon}_t$ of the conditional model is the relevant response for assessing the effects of policy changes in the $\{\mathbf{z}_t\}$ process. A direct estimate of this effect can be obtained from the dynamic multipliers, which for this model are given by:

$$\frac{\partial \mathbf{y}_{t+h}}{\partial \mathbf{z}'_t} = (\mathbf{A}_{yy} - \mathbf{\Pi}\mathbf{A}_{zy})^{h-1}\Big[(\mathbf{A}_{yy} - \mathbf{\Pi}\mathbf{A}_{zy})\mathbf{\Pi} + (\mathbf{A}_{yz} - \mathbf{\Pi}\mathbf{A}_{zz})\Big]. \quad (6.32)$$

This is a much richer response than the impulse response in Equation (6.31), and than that given in Equation (21) of Hendry and Mizon (1998) as a result of conditioning on $\mathbf{z}_t$ taking into account the effect from lagged $\mathbf{z}_t$. The dynamic multipliers in Equation (6.32) are relevant for assessing the effects of changes in $\mathbf{z}_t$ directly. Therefore, in the next sub-section only dynamic multipliers are considered.

6.5.2.2. I(1) Case

The class of open model considered in the $I(1)$ case is given by:

$$(\Delta \mathbf{y}_t - \boldsymbol{\lambda}) = \boldsymbol{\Gamma}(\Delta \mathbf{y}_{t-1} - \boldsymbol{\lambda}) + \boldsymbol{\alpha}_y(\boldsymbol{\beta}'\mathbf{x}_{t-1} - \boldsymbol{\mu}) + \boldsymbol{\Psi}_0(\Delta \mathbf{z}_t - \boldsymbol{\pi}_z)$$

$$+ \boldsymbol{\Psi}_1(\Delta \mathbf{z}_{t-1} - \boldsymbol{\pi}_z) + \boldsymbol{\epsilon}_t. \quad (6.33)$$

An advantage of using an open model in this context is that it is possible to consider cases in which $\mathbf{z}_t \sim I(1)$, which were more problematic for the closed models considered in Section 6.5.1.2 for which the analysis in Johansen and Juselius (2001) is relevant. It is assumed that the variables considered as policy instruments, $\mathbf{z}_t$, are $I(1)$, and that modelling is conditional on $\mathbf{z}_t$. This analysis requires that $\mathbf{z}_t$ is weakly exogenous for the long run parameters $\boldsymbol{\beta}$ and the short run response parameters $\boldsymbol{\alpha}$, $\boldsymbol{\Gamma}$ and $\boldsymbol{\Psi}_i$ each of which is invariant to the policy change, if there is to be no loss of information. Under these conditions it is possible to model situations in which the policy instruments are $I(1)$, by estimating the responses in the target growth rates $\Delta \mathbf{y}_t$ and the equilibria $\boldsymbol{\beta}'\mathbf{x}_t$ to particular choices of the instruments $\mathbf{z}_t$. Note that $\mathbf{z}_t$ is weakly exogenous for $\boldsymbol{\beta}$ if and only if $\boldsymbol{\alpha}_z = \mathbf{0}$, and so any drift in $\mathbf{z}_t$ can be factored into a component lying in the cointegrating space and that which is orthogonal to α_y. The former is implicitly captured in the equilibrium mean $E[\beta'x_t] = \mu$, provided that the cointegration properties (the cointegration rank r and coefficient matrix β) of the system are invariant to any policy changes in this component of drift. The latter component of drift is represented by π_z. Similarly, λ is the component of the conditional mean of Δy_t that does not lie in the cointegration space. Hence $\beta'_y y_t$ are feasible target variables in this context despite y_t being $I(1)$. In general, this implies that the particular linear combinations, $\beta'_y y_t$, which form part of the equilibria of the system, are potential targets in the present framework. An implication of the analysis is that very special conditions are required for it to be appropriate for policy to target a single variable when that variable is $I(1)$. More particularly, it will be difficult to achieve a particular value for a single target variable y_i (e.g. inflation) by controlling some of the instruments z_t (e.g. an interest rate) when there is more than one variable in y_t. Conversely, Johansen and Juselius (2001) show that if a policy targeting an $I(1)$ variable is successful, then that policy will render the target variable $I(0)$.

The dynamic multipliers for this case are given by:

$$\frac{\partial \Delta y_{t+h}}{\partial \Delta z'_t} = \Gamma^{h-1}(\Gamma \Psi_0 + \Psi_1) \tag{6.34}$$

which approach zero as $h \to \infty$ since Γ has its roots less than unity. However, if there is co-breaking between Δy_t and Δz_t so that $\partial \lambda / \partial \pi'_z = 0$, then a change in π_z will result in a change in the unconditional mean of Δy_t. Hence, just as in Hendry and Mizon (1998), Hendry and Mizon (2000), linkages between deterministic terms are critical for policy to be effective when it is implemented via shifts in deterministic terms in the instrument process.

6.6. Forecasting in open models

In addition to estimating policy responses it is often desired to forecast target variables for different policy scenarios. This section considers forecasting using open systems which condition on the policy variables z_t (now assumed to be $I(0)$) in the context of structural breaks which are usually induced by unknown autonomous factors, and in the presence of regime shifts to implement economic policy changes that are known or under consideration.

Not only are deterministic shifts important for characterizing policy regime changes in econometric models, but they have been shown by Clements and Hendry (1995) and Hendry and Doornik (1997) to be the primary source of systematic forecast failure in econometric models. Nevertheless, there exist devices (e.g. differencing and intercept adjusting) that can robustify forecasting models against structural breaks, provided they have occurred prior to forecasting (see, e.g. Clements and Hendry, 1996; Hendry and Clements, 2000). Such 'tricks' can help mitigate forecast failures, but the resulting models need not have useful policy implications. However, no methods are robust to unanticipated breaks that occur after forecasting, and Clements and Hendry (1999) show that those same 'robustifying' devices do not offset post-forecasting breaks. Moreover, post-forecasting policy changes induce breaks in models that do not embody policy variables or links, so such models lose their robustness in that setting. Conversely, despite having experienced forecast failures from pre-forecasting breaks, econometric models that do embody the relevant policy effects need not experience a post-forecasting structural break induced by the policy-regime shift – invariance to the class of policy regime shifts ensures this. Consequently, when both structural breaks and regime shifts occur, neither class of model alone is likely to be adequate. Hendry and Mizon (2000) investigated in the context of closed models whether, and if so how, information from robust forecasting devices can be combined with information from econometric models incorporating the relevant policy responses, to yield improved estimates of the effects of known policy changes. This analysis was extended in Hendry and Mizon (2004) to open models in which the effects of structural breaks in cointegrating vectors were also analysed. The results show that when forecast failure results from an in-sample structural break, forecasts from a robust statistical device may be improved by combining them with the predicted response from an econometric model of a *known* out-of-sample policy change even though the econometric model is not robust to the in-sample structural break. In addition, it is shown that as well as being an improvement over either forecast alone the combined forecast is potentially better than intercept correction and an improvement on pooling the two forecasts by averaging.

This analysis has implications for the empirical relevance of the Lucas (1976) critique. Indeed, the converse of this critique turns out to be more empirically relevant. Namely, since forecast failure often results from extraneous factors such as the OPEC oil price hikes in 1973 and 1979, or the Soros funds attacking the Italian lira and sterling in 1992, rather than from the policy changes typically considered in policy analysis (e.g. changes in income tax or interest rates), econometric models may continue to characterize the response of the economy to the policy change, despite their forecast inaccuracy.

6.7. Conclusions

The role of econometric models in the evaluation of alternative economic policies has been considered, and necessary conditions for them to provide relevant, reliable and robust inferences about policy experiments presented. In summary the conditions required of models are that they involve both the targets y_t and the instruments z_t, together with other relevant variables; be congruent and encompassing; there be empirical causality between y_t and z_t via contemporaneous causality, empirical Granger causality, or co-breaking; and they have constant and invariant parameters. These conditions are demanding, but they are all testable and thus provide a viable route and challenge to the development of econometric models appropriate for economic policy analysis.

The relative merits of impulse response analysis and dynamic multiplier analysis were discussed. In closed $I(0)$ and $I(1)$ systems dynamic multiplier analysis is not available without identification schemes that in general have dubious interpretations. Although impulse response analysis is available in closed $I(0)$ and $I(1)$ systems there are many well known problems attendant, and orthogonalization and identification schemes in general do not resolve them. Further, many economic policies involve changes other than shocks to system innovations, and so impulse response analysis does not provide information relevant for these policies. In particular, important policy changes, for example those affecting base or repo interest rates are well characterized as shifts in deterministic terms such as unconditional means. In addition, in an $I(1)$ system it may not be appropriate to regard y_t as targets and z_t as instruments when both are $I(1)$ variables. For example, if nominal money supply is intrinsically $I(1)$ then it is likely to be inappropriate to have it as a target of economic policy. Whereas, if inflation is genuinely $I(0)$ it could be an appropriate target, even though it appears to be $I(1)$ in particular samples. Growth rates and disequilibria together with their means appear to be the relevant variables for targets and instruments in closed $I(1)$ systems.

Alternatively, economic policy analysis can be done using open systems, conditioning on the target variables, thus allowing the possibility of using dynamic multiplier analysis. Indeed, it has been argued that this form of response analysis is the most relevant for most economic policy analyses. Conditions were presented under which it will be appropriate to model conditionally on the policy instruments even when they are $I(1)$. In this framework it was noted that very special conditions are required for it to be appropriate for policy to target a single variable when that variable is $I(1)$. Related results on using open $I(1)$ systems which condition on policy instruments z_t for forecasting were summarized. In particular, it is pointed out that in the presence of within-sample structural breaks and known but out-of-sample policy regime shifts, the best forecasting device using in-sample information may be uninformative about the effects of out-of-sample policy regime shifts. Hence there is a case for using a combination of time series forecasts that are robust to structural breaks but uninformative about the effects of policy changes, with open econometric model forecasts that provide valuable information about the effects of policy changes despite suffering predictive failure.

Acknowledgements

This is a revised version of a paper presented to an International ADRES Conference on the "Econometrics of Policy Evaluation", Paris, January 2000. Financial support from the UK Economic and Social Research Council under grant L148351009 is gratefully acknowledged, as are the valuable comments of David Hendry, Katarina Juselius, Francoise Maurel, and Anders Vredin.

References

Bontemps, C. and G.E. Mizon (2003), "Congruence and encompassing", pp. 354–378 in: B. Stigum, editor, *Econometrics and the Philosophy of Economics*, Princeton: Princeton University Press.

Box, G.E.P. and G.M. Jenkins (1976), *Time Series Analysis, Forecasting and Control*, San Francisco: Holden-Day, First published, 1970.

Clements, M.P. and D.F. Hendry (1995), "Forecasting in macroeconomics", pp. 99–138 in: D. Cox, D. Hinkley and O. Barndorff-Nielsen, editors, *Time Series Models in Econometrics, Finance and Other Fields*, London: Chapman & Hall.

Clements, M.P. and D.F. Hendry (1996), "Intercept corrections and structural change", *Journal of Applied Econometrics*, Vol. 11, pp. 475–494.

Clements, M.P. and D.F. Hendry (1999), "On winning forecasting competitions in economics", *Spanish Economic Review*, Vol. 1, pp. 123–160.

Duesenberry, J.S., L.R. Klein, G. Fromm and E. Kuh (eds.) (1965), *Brookings Quarterly Econometric Model of the United States*, Amsterdam: North-Holland.

Engle, R.F., D.F. Hendry and J.-F. Richard (1983), "Exogeneity", *Econometrica*, Vol. 51, pp. 277–304, Reprinted in Hendry, D.F. (1993), *Econometrics: Alchemy or Science?* Oxford: Blackwell Publishers/Oxford University Press, 2000, and in: N.R. Ericsson and J.S. Irons, editors. *Testing Exogeneity*, Oxford: Oxford University Press, 1994.

Ericsson, N.R. and D.F. Hendry (1999), "Encompassing and rational expectations: how sequential corroboration can imply refutation", *Empirical Economics*, Vol. 24, pp. 1–21.

Ericsson, N.R., D.F. Hendry and G.E. Mizon (1998), "Exogeneity, cointegration and economic policy analysis", *Journal of Business and Economic Statistics*, Vol. 16, pp. 370–387.

Frisch, R. (1938), Statistical versus theoretical relations in economic macrodynamics. Mimeograph dated 17 July 1938, League of Nations Memorandum. Reproduced by

University of Oslo in 1948 with Tinbergen's comments. Contained in Memorandum 'Autonomy of Economic Relations', 6 November 1948, Oslo, Universitets Økonomiske Institutt. Reprinted in Hendry D.F. and M.S. Morgan (1995), *The Foundations of Econometric Analysis*, Cambridge: Cambridge University Press.

Goldberger, A.S. (1964), *Econometric Theory*, New York: Wiley.

Granger, C.W.J. (1969), "Investigating causal relations by econometric models and cross-spectral methods", *Econometrica*, Vol. 37, pp. 424–438.

Granger, C.W.J. and M. Deutsch (1992), "Comments on the evaluation of policy models", *Journal of Policy Modeling*, Vol. 14, pp. 497–516.

Granger, C.W.J. and P. Newbold (1974), "Spurious regressions in econometrics", *Journal of Econometrics*, Vol. 2, pp. 111–120.

Harvey, A.C. (1993), *Time Series Models*, 2nd edition, Hemel Hempstead: Harvester Wheatsheaf.

Hendry, D.F. (1995), *Dynamic Econometrics*, Oxford: Oxford University Press.

Hendry, D.F. (2000), "On detectable and non-detectable structural change", *Structural Change and Economic Dynamics*, Vol. 11, pp. 45–65, Reprinted in *The Economics of Structural Change*, H. Hagemann, M. Landesman and Scazzieri, editors (2002), Cheltenham: Edward Elgar.

Hendry, D.F. (2003), *Econometric Modelling in a Policy Context*, Economics Department, Oxford University, mimeo.

Hendry, D.F. and M.P. Clements (2000), "Economic forecasting in the face of structural breaks", pp. 3–37 in: S. Holly and M. Weale, editors, *Econometric Modelling: Techniques and Applications*, Cambridge: Cambridge University Press.

Hendry, D.F. and J.A. Doornik (1997), "The implications for econometric modelling of forecast failure", *Scottish Journal of Political Economy*, Vol. 44, pp. 437–461, Special Issue.

Hendry, D.F. and G.E. Mizon (1993), "Evaluating dynamic econometric models by encompassing the VAR", pp. 272–300 in: P.C.B. Phillips, editor, *Models, Methods and Applications of Econometrics*, Oxford: Basil Blackwell.

Hendry, D.F. and G.E. Mizon (1998), "Exogeneity, causality, and co-breaking in economic policy analysis of a small econometric model of money in the UK", *Empirical Economics*, Vol. 23, pp. 267–294.

Hendry, D.F. and G.E. Mizon (1999), "The pervasiveness of Granger causality in econometrics", pp. 104–134 in: R.F. Engle and H. White, editors, *Cointegration, Causality, and Forecasting*, Oxford: Oxford University Press.

Hendry, D.F. and G.E. Mizon (2000), "On selecting policy analysis models by forecast accuracy", pp. 71–119 in: A.B. Atkinson, H. Glennester and N.H. Stern, editors, *Putting Economics to Work. Volume in Honour of Michio Morishima*, London: London School of Economics, STICERD Occasional Paper No. 22 ISBN 0 7530 1399 1.

Hendry, D.F. and G.E. Mizon (2004), "Forecasting in the presence of structural breaks and policy regime shifts", in: D.W. Andrews and J. Stock, editors, *Identification and Inference for Econometric Models: Festschrift in Honor of Tom Rothenberg*, Cambridge: Cambridge University Press.

Hendry, D.F. and J.-F. Richard (1989), "Recent developments in the theory of encompassing", pp. 393–440 in: B. Cornet and H. Tulkens, editors, *Contributions to Operations Research and Economics, The XXth Anniversary of CORE*, Cambridge, MA: MIT Press.

Johansen, S. (1988), "Statistical analysis of cointegration vectors", *Journal of Economic Dynamics and Control*, Vol. 12, pp. 231–254, Reprinted in R.F. Engle and

C.W.J. Granger, editors (1991), *Long-Run Economic Relationships*, pp. 131–52, Oxford: Oxford University Press.

Johansen, S. (1992), "Determination of cointegration rank in the presence of a linear trend", *Oxford Bulletin of Economics and Statistics*, Vol. 54, pp. 383–398.

Johansen, S. (2002), "The interpretation of cointegrating coefficients in the cointegrated vector autoregressive model". Preprint no.14, Department of Theoretical Statistics.

Johansen, S. and K. Juselius (2001), "Controlling inflation in a vector autoregressive model with an application to US data". Discussion paper no. ECO 2001/2, European University Institute.

Johnston, J. (1963), *Econometric Methods*, 1st edition, New York: McGraw-Hill.

Lucas, R.E. (1976), "Econometric policy evaluation: a critique", pp. 19–46 in: K. Brunner and A. Meltzer, editors, *The Phillips Curve and Labor Markets, Vol. 1 of Carnegie-Rochester Conferences on Public Policy*, Amsterdam: North-Holland Publishing Company.

Lucas, R.E. and T. Sargent (eds.) (1981), *Rational Expectations and Econometric Practice*, London: Allen and Unwin.

Mizon, G.E. (1984), "The encompassing approach in econometrics", pp. 135–172 in: D.F. Hendry and K.F. Wallis, editors, *Econometrics and Quantitative Economics*, Oxford: Basil Blackwell.

Mizon, G.E. (1989), "The role of econometric modelling in economic analysis", *Revista Espanola de Economia*, Vol. 6, pp. 167–191.

Mizon, G.E. (1995), "Progressive modelling of macroeconomic time series: the LSE methodology", pp. 107–169 in: K.D. Hoover, editor, *Macroeconometrics: Developments, Tensions and Prospects*, Dordrecht: Kluwer Academic Press.

Mizon, G.E. and J.-F. Richard (1986), "The encompassing principle and its application to non-nested hypothesis tests", *Econometrica*, Vol. 54, pp. 657–678.

Sims, C.A. (1980), "Macroeconomics and reality", *Econometrica*, Vol. 48, pp. 1–48, Reprinted in Granger, C.W.J., editor (1990), *Modelling Economic Series*, Oxford: Clarendon Press.

Wallis, K.F. (1979), *Topics in Applied Econometrics*, 2nd edition, Oxford: Basil Blackwell.

New Directions in Macromodelling
A. Welfe (Editor)
© 2004 Elsevier B.V. All rights reserved.
DOI: 10.1016/S0573-8555(04)69007-9

CHAPTER 7

Bayesian Comparison of Bivariate GARCH Processes. The Role of the Conditional Mean Specification

Jacek Osiewalski and Mateusz Pipień

Department of Econometrics, Cracow University of Economics, ul. Rakowicka 27, 31-510 Kraków, Poland

Abstract

We use the official daily PLN/USD and PLN/DEM exchange rates to compare various bivariate ARCH-type models through their Bayes factors, similarly to Osiewalski and Pipień (2004). In the previous paper a pure VAR(1)-VechGARCH(1,1) framework (with no exogenous variable) was assumed. In this chapter we introduce the DEM/USD rate from the FOREX market; it is assumed exogenous. Using the relation (PLN/USD)/(PLN/DEM) ≈ DEM/USD, treated as the cointegration equation, we build a conditional ECM model with competing bivariate GARCH structures for the error process. We also use much longer time series than in the previous work. Bayesian comparison of different GARCH specifications indicates that a simple t-BEKK(1,1) is clearly the best, no matter whether our exogenous variable and the ECM term are included or not. The presence of these important variables in the conditional mean of the bivariate process enormously helps in improving the model fit, but has only small effect on our inference on the conditional covariance matrix.

Keywords: Bayes factors, multivariate GARCH, BEKK models, error correction mechanism, exchange rates

JEL classifications: C11, C32, C52

7.1. Introduction

In order to illustrate a formal Bayesian comparison of various bivariate ARCH-type models through their Bayes factors, Osiewalski and Pipień (2004) use two foreign exchange rates that were most important for the Polish economy till the end of 2001, namely the zloty (PLN) values of the US dollar and German mark. Their data consist of the official daily exchange rates of the National Bank of Poland (NBP fixing rates), covering the relatively short period from February 1, 1996 till December 31, 1997 (less than 500 observations).

By considering such a short series and restricting to only bivariate VAR(1) models with GARCH(1,1) or ARCH(1) disturbances, it was possible to estimate unparsimoniously parameterized specifications, such as general multivariate GARCH models presented by Engle and Kroner (1995) and Gourieroux (1997). These models have much more parameters than univariate ARCH and GARCH models, proposed originally by Engle (1982) and Bollerslev (1986), and analyzed using the Bayesian approach by Geweke (1989), Kleibergen and Van Dijk (1993), Bauwens and Lubrano (1998), Bauwens *et al.* (1999), Osiewalski and Pipień (1999, 2000), Bos *et al.* (2000) and Vrontos *et al.* (2000). The number of free parameters of multivariate ARCH-type models can increase very fast as the dimension k of the vector time series grows. In the general version of the k-variate VechGARCH(p,q) (or VECH(p,q)) model, this number is a fourth order polynomial of k, making even VECH(1,1) impractical for $k > 2$. Thus, within ARCH-type models, interest focuses on restricted ARCH and GARCH specifications or on factor ARCH models; see, e.g. Diebold and Nerlove (1989), King *et al.* (1994) and Gourieroux (1997). Obviously, not only the dimension of the parameter space but also other aspects of empirical ARCH-type specifications are very important: free conditional covariances vs. constant conditional covariances or correlations, direct ARCH vs. latent factor ARCH models, conditional Normality vs. Student t tails, and the ARCH(1) structure vs. GARCH(1,1).

Our previous study focused only on pure time-series models for daily data, without introducing any extra variables that would be motivated by economic or financial considerations. In particular, Osiewalski and Pipień (2004) ignored the relationship: (PLN/USD)/(PLN/DEM) $\approx$ DEM/USD, linking the two Polish official exchange rates to the international FOREX market. In this chapter, we assume that this approximate relation (in log terms) is a cointegration equation in the sense of Engle and Granger (1987). We also assume that the DEM/USD rate is weakly exogenous (for inferences on the parameters describing two Polish exchange rates) in the Bayesian sense of Florens and Mouchart (1985) and Osiewalski and Steel (1996).

Under these assumptions we build a two-equation conditional model with the error correction mechanism (ECM) and the disturbances following one of the competing bivariate GARCH specifications. Thus, our main goal is to check the sensitivity of the results of Bayesian model comparison with respect to the form of the conditional mean specification, i.e. the presence of the third (exogenous) exchange rate and the ECM term. The other aim of the chapter is to investigate the effect of extending the series till the very end of 2001, i.e. until the common European currency (euro) replaced some national currencies, including German mark. Using our computational experience from the previous work (and a faster computer) we were able to estimate bivariate GARCH structures with about 1500 daily data.

For the sake of comparison, the class of models considered in this chapter consists of bivariate GARCH specifications prior to 2001, which were assumed by Osiewalski and Pipień (2004). Thus, our class does not contain more recent models proposed by Engle (2002), Tse and Tsui (2002) and van der Weide (2002).

In view of the high dimensionality of the parameter spaces in many of our models and in view of non-standard forms of the posterior densities as well as their full conditionals, we use the Metropolis–Hastings (M–H) algorithm to simulate and explore the posterior distributions. The values of the marginal data densities for each model, which are the main quantities for Bayesian model comparison, are approximated by means of the Newton and Raftery's (1994) estimator, based on the harmonic mean of the likelihood values calculated at M–H draws from the posterior.

The structure of the chapter is as follows. The next section shows the data and the ECM-type model framework for daily growth rates of two exchange rates. The computational aspects are discussed in Section 7.3. Section 7.4 presents all the models used for the bivariate error term of the basic specification, ranks the models using Bayes factors and discusses sensitivity issues. Section 7.5 shows main posterior results for the best model and tries to explain the failure of many other specifications. Section 7.6 provides concluding remarks.

7.2. The data and model framework

In order to compare competing bivariate ARCH-type specifications we use the growth rates of PLN/USD and PLN/DEM. Our original data set consists of 1485 daily observations on the exchange rates themselves, PLN/USD (x_{1t}), PLN/DEM (x_{2t}) and DEM/USD (w_t). It covers the period from February 1, 1996 till December 28, 2001. The first three observations from 1996 (February 1, 2, 5) are used to construct initial conditions.

Thus T, the length of the modelled vector time series of daily growth rates of x_{1t} and x_{2t} is equal to 1482.

We denote our modelled bivariate observations as $y_t = (y_{1t}, y_{2t})'$, where y_{1t} is the daily growth (or return) rate of the PLN value of US dollar and y_{2t} is the daily growth (or return) rate of the PLN value of German mark, both expressed in percentage points and obtained from the daily exchange rates $x_{it}(i = 1, 2)$ by the formula $y_{it} = 100 \ln(x_{it}/x_{it-1})$. We also define $\text{ECM}_t = \ln x_{1t} - \ln x_{2t} - \ln w_t$ and $z_t = 100 \ln(w_t/w_{t-1})$, and model our data using the conditional ECM-type VAR(1) framework:

$$y_t - \delta = R(y_{t-1} - \delta) + \alpha z_t + \lambda \, \text{ECM}_{t-1} + \varepsilon_t$$

with the error term described by competing bivariate ARCH specifications. More specifically,

$$\begin{pmatrix} y_{1t} \\ y_{2t} \end{pmatrix} - \begin{pmatrix} \delta_1 \\ \delta_2 \end{pmatrix} = \begin{pmatrix} R_{11} & R_{12} \\ R_{21} & R_{22} \end{pmatrix} \left\{ \begin{pmatrix} y_{1t-1} \\ y_{2t-1} \end{pmatrix} - \begin{pmatrix} \delta_1 \\ \delta_2 \end{pmatrix} \right\} + \begin{pmatrix} \alpha_1 \\ \alpha_2 \end{pmatrix} z_t$$

$$+ \begin{pmatrix} \lambda_1 \\ \lambda_2 \end{pmatrix} \text{ECM}_{t-1} + \begin{pmatrix} \varepsilon_{1t} \\ \varepsilon_{2t} \end{pmatrix}, \quad t = 1, ..., T. \qquad (7.1)$$

Our assumption that $\ln x_{1t}, \ln x_{2t}$ and $\ln w_t$ are cointegrated has been informally checked using simple non-Bayesian tools, namely the Dickey-Fuller (DF) test and the Durbin-Watson (DW) statistic applied to the series ECM_t. Although the DW statistic applied to ECM_t itself gives 1.32, indicating autocorrelation in this series, the DF value (-27.05) together with the DW value (2.16) for the DF regression $(\Delta \text{ECM}_t = \varphi \times \text{ECM}_{t-1} + u_t)$ supports stationarity.

The elements of δ, R, α and λ in Equation (7.1) are common parameters, which we treat as a priori independent of model-specific parameters and assume for them the multivariate standardized Normal prior $N(0, I_{10})$, truncated by the restriction that all eigenvalues of R lie inside the unit circle.

The data on daily growth rates y_{1t}, y_{2t} and z_t are plotted in Figures 7.1, 7.2 and 7.3, respectively. Note that y_{1t} and y_{2t} are more volatile than z_t and have more outliers. Osiewalski and Pipień (2004) use only the data on y_{1t} and y_{2t} till the end of 1997 (475 data points), and their model formally corresponds to $\alpha = \lambda = 0_{[2 \times 1]}$ in Equation (7.1). Now we focus on the effects of relaxing these zero restrictions and of using all $T = 1482$ observations.

7.3. Computing Bayes factors for competing models

In the next section we present and compare 10 different GARCH specifications for the disturbances of the bivariate VAR(1) model in

Figure 7.1. Daily growth rates of PLN/USD (February 2, 1996–December 31, 2001)

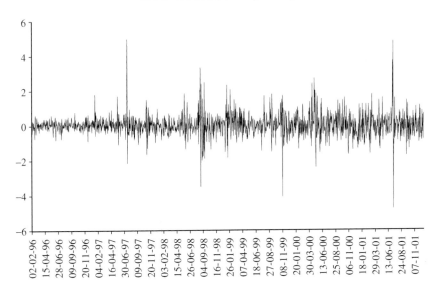

Equation (7.1). Our class of models does not include the latent factor GARCH model, considered originally by Osiewalski and Pipień (2004); that model is computationally very demanding (especially when $T = 1482$) and was completely improbable a posteriori when $T = 475$.

Figure 7.2. Daily growth rates of PLN/DEM (February 2, 1996–December 31, 2001)

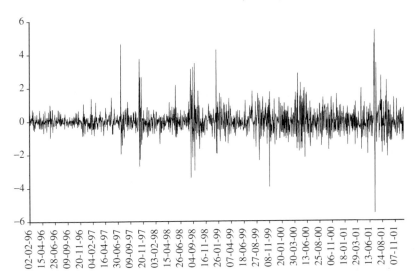

Figure 7.3.   Daily growth rates of DEM/USD (February 2, 1996–December 31, 2001)

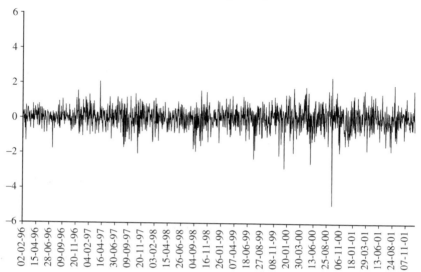

Within the Bayesian posterior odds approach, the explanatory power of the ith model is summarized by the marginal density of the $T \times 2$ observation matrix $y = (y_1 ... y_T)$ (given the initial conditions $y_{(0)}$), evaluated at the actual data. This density value is calculated by integrating (averaging) the likelihood function with respect to the proper prior measure of the parameter vector $\theta_{(i)} \in \Theta_i$:

$$p(y|M_i, y_{(0)}) = \int_{\Theta_i} p(y|M_i, \theta_{(i)}, y_{(0)}) p(\theta_{(i)}) \mathrm{d}\theta_{(i)}. \tag{7.2}$$

Note that a model with a high maximum likelihood value can lead to a low average likelihood, Equation (7.2), when the areas in the parameter space, which are very likely a priori, are characterized by small likelihood values. Competing models are compared pair-wise through the Bayes factor $B_{ij} = p(y|M_i, y_{(0)})/p(y|M_j, y_{(0)})$, which, together with the prior odds ratio $P(M_i)/P(M_j)$, determines the posterior odds of M_i against M_j:

$$\frac{P(M_i|y, y_{(0)})}{P(M_j|y, y_{(0)})} = \frac{P(M_i)}{P(M_j)} B_{ij},$$

where $P(M_h)$ and $P(M_h|y, y_{(0)})$ are, respectively, the prior and posterior probability of M_h; see, e.g. O'Hagan (1994). Direct evaluation of the integral in Equation (7.2) (through either numerical quadratures or

Monte Carlo sampling from the prior density) is not efficient or even not feasible when the dimension of the parameter space is as high as in the models considered in this chapter. Thus, we have to resort to other numerical tools, based on good exploration of the parameter space through sampling from the posterior. Here, we use Metropolis–Hastings Markov chains; see, e.g. O'Hagan (1994) and Gamerman (1997).

Using simple identities, we can write the marginal data density in the form

$$p(y|M_i, y_{(0)}) = \left\{ \int_{\Theta_i} [p(y|M_i, \theta_{(i)}, y_{(0)})]^{-1} dP(\theta_{(i)}|M_i, y, y_{(0)}) \right\}^{-1}, \quad (7.3)$$

where $P(\theta_{(i)}|M_i, y, y_{(0)})$ denotes the posterior cumulative distribution function. Formula (7.3) is the basis of the method by Newton and Raftery (1994), which approximates the marginal data density by the harmonic mean of the values $p(y|M_i, \theta_{(i)}, y_{(0)})$, calculated for the observed y and for $\theta_{(i)}$ drawn from the posterior distribution. The N–R harmonic mean estimator is consistent, but without finite asymptotic variance. Despite this serious theoretical weakness, the N–R estimator (very easy to compute) was quite stable for all our models; see Osiewalski and Pipień (2004) for more discussion of computational aspects.

In order to sample from the posterior distribution in a model with the parameter vector θ, we rely on a sequential version of the Metropolis–Hastings algorithm, where the proposal density $q(\theta|\theta^{(m-1)})$ for the next value of θ given the previous draw $\theta^{(m-1)}$ is proportional to $f_S(\theta|3, \theta^{(m-1)}, C)$, a Student t density with 3 degrees of freedom, mean $\theta^{(m-1)}$ and a fixed covariance matrix C (approximating the posterior covariance matrix). This Student t density (symmetric in θ and $\theta^{(m-1)}$) is truncated by the inequality restrictions described in Section 7.4, i.e.

$$q(\theta|\theta^{(m-1)}) = a_q(\theta^{(m-1)})f_S(\theta|3, \theta^{(m-1)}, C)I(\theta \in \Theta),$$

$$a_q(\theta^{(m-1)}) = \left[\int_{\Theta} f_S(\theta|3, \theta^{(m-1)}, C)d\theta \right]^{-1}.$$

This leads to the M–H Markov chain with the following acceptance probability:

$$\alpha(\theta; \theta^{(m-1)}) = \min\left\{ (g_y(\theta)a_q(\theta))/(g_y(\theta^{(m-1)})a_q(\theta^{(m-1)})), \ 1 \right\},$$

where $g_y(\cdot)$ denotes the kernel of the posterior density.

Applications of Markov Chain Monte Carlo (MCMC) methods require monitoring convergence of the transition distribution of the chain to its limiting stationary distribution; for a review of convergence criteria see Cowles and Carlin (1996). In our research we use a simple tool that was proposed by Yu and Mykland (1994), namely the CUMSUM statistics for the Monte Carlo estimates (after the burn-in period) of the posterior means of individual parameters; see also Bauwens *et al.* (1999). Our results, presented in next sections, are usually based on 500,000 states of the Markov chain, generated after 10,000 burnt-in states.

7.4. Competing specifications

In this section, we present and compare 10 different ARCH-type specifications for the disturbances of the bivariate VAR(1) model (Equation (7.1)). We start with two non-nested, conditionally t distributed multivariate GARCH(1,1)-type processes: the Vech-GARCH specification and Bollerslev's (1990) constant conditional correlation (CCC) model. We then consider five simplifications of t-VECH(1,1), including a simple BEKK formulation, which explains our data surprisingly well. Hence, we also examine special cases of our favourite t-BEKK(1,1) specification in search of a good and even more parsimonious model.

7.4.1. Two basic Bayesian models

In the t-VECH(1,1) model (M_1), the conditional distribution of ε_t (given its past, ψ_{t-1}) is Student t with zero location vector, inverse precision matrix H_t and unknown degrees of freedom $\nu > 2$, i.e.

$$\varepsilon_t | \psi_{t-1} \sim t(0_{[2\times1]}, H_t, \nu), \qquad H_t = \begin{bmatrix} h_{11,t} & h_{12,t} \\ h_{12,t} & h_{22,t} \end{bmatrix},$$

where the vectorization of the lower part of H_t is parameterized as

$$\text{Vech}(H_t) = \begin{pmatrix} h_{11,t} \\ h_{12,t} \\ h_{22,t} \end{pmatrix} = \begin{pmatrix} a_{10} \\ a_{20} \\ a_{30} \end{pmatrix} + \begin{pmatrix} a_{11} & a_{12} & a_{13} \\ a_{21} & a_{22} & a_{23} \\ a_{31} & a_{32} & a_{33} \end{pmatrix} \begin{pmatrix} \varepsilon_{1,t-1}^2 \\ \varepsilon_{1,t-1}\varepsilon_{2,t-1} \\ \varepsilon_{2,t-1}^2 \end{pmatrix}$$

$$+ \begin{pmatrix} b_{11} & b_{12} & b_{13} \\ b_{21} & b_{22} & b_{23} \\ b_{31} & b_{32} & b_{33} \end{pmatrix} \begin{pmatrix} h_{11,t-1} \\ h_{12,t-1} \\ h_{22,t-1} \end{pmatrix}, \tag{7.4}$$

with $H_0 = h_0 I_2$ and h_0 treated as an additional free parameter. Thus, the conditional covariance matrix of ε_t given ψ_{t-1} is $(\nu - 2)^{-1} \nu H_t$. In the k-variate version of this model the number of free parameters of the error process ε_t is $2 + [1 + k(k+1)]k(k+1)/2$, a fourth order polynomial of k; this gives 23 parameters when $k = 2$. We assume prior independence for ν, h_0 and the three groups of parameters in Equation (7.4). The degrees of freedom parameter follows the Exponential distribution with mean 10, $\text{Exp}(10)$, truncated by the condition $\nu > 2$. The initial value h_0 has the Exponential prior with mean 1, $\text{Exp}(1)$. For a'_{j0}s we assume the product of the densities of the following distributions: $\text{Exp}(1)$ for a_{10} and a_{30}, and $N(0,1)$ for a_{20}, truncated by the restriction that $a_{10}a_{30} - a_{20}^2 > 0$. The prior densities of the other parameters are the products of the densities of the following Normal distributions:

$$a_{11} \sim N(0.5; 1), a_{33} \sim N(0.5; 1), b_{11} \sim N(0.5; 1), b_{33} \sim N(0.5; 1),$$
$$a_{ij} \sim N(0,1) \text{ and } b_{ij} \sim N(0,1) \text{ for all other pairs } (i,j);$$

these densities are truncated by the restrictions that the matrices

$$A_1 = \begin{pmatrix} a_{11} & a_{12}/2 & a_{21} & a_{22}/2 \\ a_{12}/2 & a_{13} & a_{22}/2 & a_{23} \\ a_{21} & a_{22}/2 & a_{31} & a_{32}/2 \\ a_{22}/2 & a_{23} & a_{32}/2 & a_{33} \end{pmatrix},$$

$$B_1 = \begin{pmatrix} b_{11} & b_{12}/2 & b_{21} & b_{22}/2 \\ b_{12}/2 & b_{13} & b_{22}/2 & b_{23} \\ b_{21} & b_{22}/2 & b_{31} & b_{32}/2 \\ b_{22}/2 & b_{23} & b_{32}/2 & b_{33} \end{pmatrix}$$

be non-negative definite (Gourieroux, 1997) and the eigenvalues of B_1 lie inside the unit circle.

Bollerslev (1990) argues that, for exchange rates, the assumption of CCC may be appropriate. Thus, we also consider the following model (M_2):

$$\varepsilon_t | \psi_{t-1} \sim t(0_{[2 \times 1]}, H_t, \nu), \qquad H_t = \begin{bmatrix} h_{11,t} & h_{12,t} \\ h_{12,t} & h_{22,t} \end{bmatrix},$$

$$h_{11,t} = a_{10} + a_{11}\varepsilon_{1,t-1}^2 + b_{11}h_{11,t-1},$$

$$h_{22,t} = a_{20} + a_{22}\varepsilon_{2,t-1}^2 + b_{22}h_{22,t-1}, \qquad h_{12,t} = \rho_{12}\sqrt{h_{11,t}h_{22,t}},$$

where ρ_{12} is the time-invariant conditional correlation coefficient. In M_2, as in $M_1, H_0 = h_0 I_2$, where h_0 has the Exponential prior with mean 1. For the remaining parameters we take the following priors:

$$a_{10} \sim \text{Exp}(1), \; a_{20} \sim \text{Exp}(1), \; (a_{11}, a_{22}, b_{11}, b_{22}) \sim U([0,1]^4),$$

$$\rho_{12} \sim U([-1,1]),$$

where $U(A)$ denotes the uniform distribution over A. In its k-variate version, M_2 describes ε_t using only $2 + 3k + k(k-1)/2$ free parameters; so we have 9 parameters when $k = 2$.

Table 7.1 summarizes model assumptions and presents the decimal logarithms of the Bayes factors in favour of $M_1, \log_{10}(B_{1j})$ for $j = 1, 2$. The decimal logarithm of the Bayes factor of M_1 against M_2, $\log_{10}(B_{12}) = 73.71$, indicates that – under equal prior probabilities – M_1 is more than 70 orders of magnitude more probable a posteriori than M_2. This means that the CCC assumption is simply improbable a posteriori (relative to the VECH model with no restrictions on its conditional correlations). M_2 seems too restrictive, so its simplifications and special cases will not be considered. However, the VECH model is unparsimoniously parameterized, and thus impractical for $k > 2$. Hence, we consider some of its special cases in search of even better models. As one more possibility, not exploited here, we could consider the dynamic conditional correlation (DCC) structures of Engle (2002), which nest the CCC specification of Bollerslev (1990). Then we could compare them to the VECH(1,1) model and its best special cases. Such Bayesian comparison is a subject of our ongoing research.

Table 7.1.   *Two basic models and logs of Bayes factors in favour of M_1*

Model	Description	$\log_{10}(B_{1j})$
M_1 t-VECH(1,1)	$\varepsilon_t \| H_t, \nu \sim t(0, \nu, H_t)$ with vech H_t in Equation (7.4)	0
M_2 t-constant conditional correlations	$\varepsilon_t \| H_t, \nu \sim t(0, \nu, H_t)$ $h_{ii,t} = a_{i0} + a_{ii}\varepsilon_{i,t-1}^2 + b_{ii}h_{ii,t-1}$ $(i = 1, 2)$ $h_{12,t} = \rho_{12}\sqrt{h_{11,t}h_{22,t}}$	73.71

Priors: $a_{10}, a_{30}, h_0 \sim \text{Exp}(1)$, $\nu \sim \text{Exp}(10)$, $a_{11}, a_{22}, a_{33} \sim N(0.5, 1)$, $\rho_{12} \sim U(-1, 1)$, other $\sim N(0, 1)$. Restrictions: see the main text.

7.4.2. Models nested in t-VECH(1,1)

The models considered in this section can be obtained from t-VECH(1,1) by imposing certain restrictions on its parameters; the restrictions are linear and very simple for four specifications, but non-linear in the fifth case. The prior distributions for the four simpler models (M_3, M_4, M_5, M_6) are defined as the appropriate conditional distributions from the prior distribution in M_1. Only for the last model, M_7, the prior distribution is elicited separately, without any use of conditioning. The five models (M_3-M_7) as well as the decimal logarithms of the Bayes factors in favour of M_1, $\log_{10}(B_{1j})$ for $j = 3, ..., 7$, are shown in Table 7.2.

First, we mention the t-VECH(1,1) specification with zero restrictions on α and λ, i.e. the most richly parameterized model considered by Osiewalski and Pipień (2004). Since in M_1 zero values of α and λ are completely improbable a posteriori, it is not surprising that the Bayes factor of M_1 against M_3 is so extremely high. The next specification is the conditionally normal VECH(1,1) model, N-VECH(1,1) or M_4, obtained from M_1 through conditioning on $\nu = +\infty$ (and thus losing only one free parameter). Another simplification amounts to setting $a_{2j} = b_{2j} = 0$, $j = 1, 2, 3$, in Equation (7.4). This leads to M_5, the t-VECH(1,1) model with constant conditional covariance, equal to $\nu(\nu - 2)^{-1}a_{20}$ for all t. In its k-variate version this model describes ε_t with $2 + (1 + 2k)k(k + 1)/2$ (i.e. $O(k^3)$) unknown parameters (17 free parameters when $k = 2$). Of course, such a specification induces variable conditional correlations (except for $a_{20} = 0$) and thus is very different from M_2, the model with CCCs. M_4 and especially M_5 fit the data much worse than M_1, but not as poorly as M_3.

The fourth simplification, defining M_6, assumes $b_{ij} = 0, i, j = 1, 2, 3$, in Equation (7.4). This leads to the t-VechARCH(1) or t-VECH(1,0) specification with $1 + [1 + k(k + 1)/2]k(k + 1)/2(13$ for $k = 2)$ free parameters describing ε_t. The ARCH(1) structure does not seem enough for our bivariate series, which requires the dependence of conditional covariance matrix on the more distant past of the series, which is assured by the GARCH(1,1) structure. It is quite interesting that M_6 has the same explanatory power as M_4. For our series, the ARCH(1) structure with Student t conditional distribution fits as good as the GARCH(1,1) model with conditional Normality.

All four simplifications described above have (in their k-variate versions) too many parameters to be of practical use for $k > 2$; the number of parameters in M_3, M_4 and M_6 is $O(k^4)$, similarly as in M_1, and in M_5 it is a third order polynomial of k. Now, we consider a much more sophisticated simplification, where this number is only $O(k^2)$. This parsimonious model, M_7, is a simple special case of the elegant multivariate GARCH

Table 7.2.   *Simplifications of the t-VECH(1,1) specification (M_1)*

Model	Description	$\log_{10}(B_{1j})$
M_3	t-VECH(1,1) with $\alpha = \lambda = 0_{[0 \times 2]}$ (no exogenous variable)	240.41
M_4 N-VECH(1,1)	t-VECH(1,1) with $\nu \rightarrow +\infty$	69.67
M_5 t-VECH with constant conditional covariances	t-VECH(1,1) with the following restrictions in Equation (7.4): $$\begin{pmatrix} h_{11,t} \\ h_{12,t} \\ h_{22,t} \end{pmatrix} = \begin{pmatrix} a_{10} \\ a_{20} \\ a_{30} \end{pmatrix} + \begin{pmatrix} a_{11} & a_{12} & a_{13} \\ 0 & 0 & 0 \\ a_{31} & a_{32} & a_{33} \end{pmatrix} \begin{pmatrix} \varepsilon_{1,t-1}^2 \\ \varepsilon_{1,t-1}\varepsilon_{2,t-1} \\ \varepsilon_{2,t-1}^2 \end{pmatrix} + \begin{pmatrix} b_{11} & b_{12} & b_{13} \\ 0 & 0 & 0 \\ b_{31} & b_{32} & b_{33} \end{pmatrix} \begin{pmatrix} h_{11,t-1} \\ h_{12,t-1} \\ h_{22,t-1} \end{pmatrix}$$	117.15
M_6 t-VECH(1,0)	t-VECH(1,1) with restrictions $b_{ij} = 0$, $i,j = 1,2,3$	70.74
M_7 t-BEKK(1,1)	For restrictions in Equation (7.4) see Osiewalski and Pipień (2002); assumed vech H_t is presented in Equation (7.5)	−4.37

Priors specified through conditioning (in M_3–M_6) or independently (in M_7).

specification proposed by Baba *et al.* (1989), and thus called BEKK in the literature. Engle and Kroner (1995) discuss general BEKK formulations and their equivalence to VechGARCH models. We consider a simple *t*-BEKK(1,1) specification where the conditional distribution of ε_t (given its past, ψ_{t-1}) is Student *t* with zero location vector, BEKK-type inverse precision matrix H_t and unknown degrees of freedom $\nu > 2$, i.e.

$$\varepsilon_t | \psi_{t-1} \sim t(0_{[2\times1]}, H_t, \nu),$$

$$H_t = \begin{bmatrix} a_{11} & a_{12} \\ a_{12} & a_{22} \end{bmatrix} + \begin{bmatrix} b_{11} & b_{12} \\ b_{21} & b_{22} \end{bmatrix}' (\varepsilon_{t-1}\varepsilon_{t-1}') \begin{bmatrix} b_{11} & b_{12} \\ b_{21} & b_{22} \end{bmatrix}$$
$$+ \begin{bmatrix} c_{11} & c_{12} \\ c_{21} & c_{22} \end{bmatrix}' H_{t-1} \begin{bmatrix} c_{11} & c_{12} \\ c_{21} & c_{22} \end{bmatrix}, \tag{7.5}$$

with $H_0 = h_0 I_2$ and h_0 treated as an additional parameter. Both the degrees of freedom parameter and h_0 are a priori independent of the other parameters and follow the same prior distributions as in the previous models. The other parameters are all independent a priori and with the following prior distributions:

$$a_{11} \sim \text{Exp}(1), \quad a_{22} \sim \text{Exp}(1), \quad a_{12} \sim N(0,1),$$

$$b_{11} \sim N(0.5;1), \quad b_{12} \sim N(0,1), \quad b_{21} \sim N(0,1), b_{22} \sim N(0.5;1),$$

$$c_{11} \sim N(0.5;1), \quad c_{12} \sim N(0,1), \quad c_{21} \sim N(0,1), c_{22} \sim N(0.5;1),$$

truncated by the restrictions of positive semi-definiteness of the symmetric (2×2) matrix A consisting of a_{ij} and stability of the general (2×2) matrix C consisting of c_{ij} (all eigenvalues of C lie inside the unit circle). Some identifiability restrictions should be imposed on C and on the general (2×2) matrix B (consisting of b_{ij}), since B and $-B$ as well as C and $-C$ lead to the same H_t in Equation (7.5), and thus are observationally equivalent. The condition: $b_{11} > 0$ and $c_{11} > 0$ guarantees identifiability. In the *k*-variate version, this *t*-BEKK(1,1) specification describes ε_t using $2 + k(k+1)/2 + 2k^2$ free parameters (13 parameters for $k = 2$).

Since M_7 is much, much better than $M_2 - M_6$, and even about 4–5 orders of magnitude better than M_1, let us comment on the relation between M_7 and M_1. In spite of formal incompatibility of their prior specifications, both models lead to almost the same posterior distributions of quantities of interest (common parameters or conditional covariances and correlations) and to the same predictive results. Osiewalski and Pipień (2002) show that the simple BEKK(1,1) error process can be obtained from Vech-GARCH(1,1) in 64 alternative ways, each time by imposing 10 non-linear restrictions on $a_{ij}s$ and $b_{ij}s$ in Equation (7.4). In order to verify these restrictions, they suggest to use a Lindley type test based on approximate Normality of certain non-linear functions of basic parameters in the t-VECH(1,1) model. Here, we follow a more fundamental Bayesian testing principle based on the posterior odds ratio, which favours parsimony. Because of similar posterior results in M_7 and M_1, parsimony considerations point at M_7, leaving no doubt about the superiority of the t-BEKK(1,1) error structure. Our data favour the t-BEKK(1,1) model over all the alternatives considered so far. It appears as flexible as the t-VECH(1,1) specification, leading to virtually the same posterior inference on quantities of interest, but it has much less free parameters. In the next subsection we show consequences of further simplifications of M_7. The main question is whether reducing the number of free parameters in M_7 can increase the marginal data density value.

7.4.3. Simplifications of t-BEKK(1,1)

There are two natural reductions of M_7. One is the t-BEKK(1,0) specification, M_8, which is the result of imposing zero restrictions on all $c_{ij}s$ in Equation (7.5), the other is the N-BEKK(1,1) model, M_9, obtained by taking the limit $\nu = +\infty$ for the degrees of freedom parameter. The third model, N-BEKK(1,0) or M_{10}, results from jointly imposing all these restrictions. The prior distributions for all three simpler models (M_8, M_9, M_{10}) are defined as the appropriate conditional distributions from the prior distribution in M_7. Table 7.3 presents the three models and the decimal logarithms of the Bayes factors in favour of M_7, $\log_{10}(B_{7i})$ $(i = 8, 9, 10)$, calculated using the N–R method. Clearly, M_8, M_9 and especially M_{10} are very strongly rejected by the data; M_8 and M_9 are 20–25 orders of magnitude worse than their restricted VECH counterparts, M_6 and M_4, respectively.

The overall qualitative conclusion (based on the N–R estimates of the marginal data density values) is that M_7, i.e. the t-BEKK(1,1) specification (with free a and λ), is the best model among all 10 models

Table 7.3.   Simplifications of the t-BEKK(1,1) specification (M_7)

Model	Description	$\log_{10}(B_{7j})$
M_8 t-BEKK(1,0)	t-BEKK(1,1) with $c_{ij} = 0$ $(i,j = 1,2)$ in Equation (7.5)	100.25
M_9 N-BEKK(1,1)	t-BEKK(1,1) $\nu \rightarrow +\infty$	94.35
M_{10} N-BEKK(1,0)	N-BEKK(1,1) with $c_{ij} = 0$ $(i,j = 1,2)$ in Equation (7.5)	181.13

Priors obtained through conditioning.

under consideration. The Bayes factors in favour of M_7 are so high that this particular specification would receive practically all the posterior probability mass under any reasonable prior model probabilities.

7.4.4. The role of the conditional mean specification and the length of the series

In this subsection, we briefly discuss stability of Bayes factors and model ranks with respect to the assumption $\alpha = \lambda = 0$, i.e. the lack of the exogenous variable and the ECM term, as well as with respect to the length of our multivariate series ($T = 1482$ or only 475). Table 7.4 presents the decimal logarithms of the Bayes factors in favour of the t-BEKK(1,1) model (M_7), i.e. the values of $\log_{10}(B_{7i})$. Table 7.4 also shows the total number of free parameters of each model, including common δ, α, λ and R from Equation (7.1). While the Bayes factors can be very different, they always indicate the leading position of the t-BEKK(1,1) specification. The unparsimonious t-VECH(1,1) specification is the only other model that is worth mentioning; it is always the second best. When $T = 1482$, the lack of z_t and ECM$_t$ in the conditional mean of the process makes the full VECH(1,1) covariance structure almost as good (in terms of the marginal data density value) as the elegant BEKK(1,1) specification. This suggests that volatility of the long series is so large that the greater flexibility of VECH can outweigh the parsimony of BEKK. This is no longer the case when we extend the conditional mean specification by introducing z_t and ECM$_t$.

When we use the short series, the t-BEKK(1,0) model (a pure ARCH(1) specification) is the third best and not so much worse as in the case of the long series. When the latter is used for estimation and model comparison, the simple ARCH(1) structure is strongly rejected and the full GARCH(1,1) process seems necessary to describe the observed volatility. The long series makes the Bayes factors for all remaining specifications (all except the two leading models) extremely high: they are 20–140 orders of magnitude higher than when $T = 475$. In terms of the posterior model probabilities, the longer series very clearly confirms adequacy of the two leading specifications – more data lead to stronger (more conclusive) results. Table 7.4 also shows that the appropriate specification of the conditional mean of our bivariate stochastic process is crucial for obtaining good model fit, especially for the long series. In the latter case, the best model with no exogenous variable and the ECM term is more than 60 orders of magnitude worse than the worst model with free α and λ, and about 240 (!) orders of magnitude worse than the best model with free α and λ.

Table 7.4. Logs of Bayes factors in favour of t-BEKK(1,1)

Model	With Exogenous Variable			No Exogenous Variable		
	Number of parameters	Rank	$\log_{10}(B_{7i})$	Number of parameters	Rank	$\log_{10}(B_{7ii})$
$T = 1482$						
M_7, t-BEKK(1,1)	23	1	0	19	1	0
M_1, t-VECH(1,1)	33	2	4.37	29	2	1.38
M_4, N-VECH(1,1)	32	3	74.03	28	5	71.13
M_6, t-VECH(1,0)	23	4	75.11	19	6	81.50
M_2, t-ConstCor(1,1)	19	5	78.08	15	3	64.29
M_9, N-BEKK(1,1)	22	6	94.35	18	8	88.72
M_8, t-BEKK(1,0)	18	7	100.25	14	7	87.84
M_5, t-VECH(1,1) ConstCovar.	27	8	121.51	23	4	68.88
M_{10}, N-BEKK(1,0)	17	9	181.13	13	9	162.39
t-VECH(1,1) no exo	29	10	244.77	see M_1	–	–
$T = 475$						
M_7, t-BEKK(1,1)	23	1	0	19	1	0
M_1, t-VECH(1,1)	33	2	2.52	29	2	4.50
M_4, N-VECH(1,1)	32	5	10.16	28	9	48.10
M_6, t-VECH(1,0)	23	4	6.94	19	4	10.74
M_2, t-ConstCor(1,1)	19	7	32.15	15	6	27.84
M_9, N-BEKK(1,1)	22	8	36.82	18	7	44.53
M_8, t-BEKK(1,0)	18	3	6.05	14	3	6.22
M_5, t-VECH(1,1) ConstCovar.	27	6	25.25	23	5	11.53
M_{10}, N-BEKK(1,0)	17	9	39.35	13	8	47.42
t-VECH(1,1) no exo	29	10	84.49	see M_1	–	–

7.5. *Main posterior results for the best model*

In this section, we present main characteristics of the posterior distribution (based on $T = 1482$ observations) in the t-BEKK(1,1) model, which receives virtually all the posterior probability mass under any reasonable prior model probabilities. We focus on the posterior results that explain why many other competing specifications did so poorly in our model competition. We also discuss similarity of posterior results based on the simpler specification (with $\alpha = \lambda = 0$).

First, let us look at the plots of the sampling conditional covariances $(\nu - 2)^{-1} \nu h_{12,t}$ and corresponding correlations for each $t = 1, ..., T; T = 1482$. They are presented in Figures 7.4 and 7.5, where we draw two lines: the upper one representing the posterior mean plus two posterior standard deviations and the lower one – the posterior mean minus two posterior standard deviations. It is clear that constancy of conditional correlations is not supported by our data; the same holds for conditional covariances, which seem to be concentrated even more tightly around their abruptly changing posterior means. Thus, the models assuming constant correlations (M_2) or constant covariances (M_5) receive negligible posterior probability when compared to BEKK specifications with the same tail behaviour.

Figure 7.4. *Conditional covariances (posterior mean ± 2 standard deviations) in $M_7(T = 1482)$*

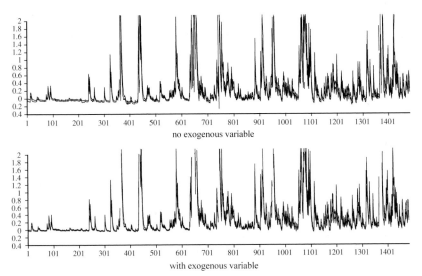

no exogenous variable

with exogenous variable

J. Osiewalski and M. Pipień

Figure 7.5.   Conditional correlations (posterior mean ± 2 standard deviations) in M_7 ($T = 1482$)

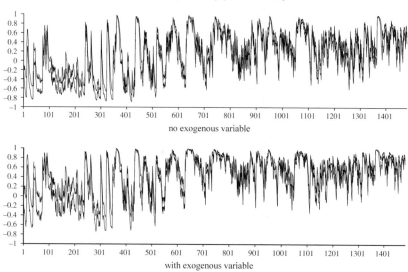

In Table 7.5 we present the posterior means and standard deviations of all basic parameters of M_7. Our results confirm that the tails of the conditional distribution are crucial in good statistical modelling with the use of GARCH processes. The Student t specification (with degrees of freedom treated as a free parameter) helps enormously in explaining observed volatility and outliers. High posterior density for low values of $\nu(4.5-6)$ explains inadequacy of models assuming conditional Normality. Incidentally, the truncation at $\nu = 2$ is not binding, confirming our assumption that the sampling conditional variances and covariances exist. Also, the stability conditions imposed on R and the matrices extending ARCH to GARCH were not binding. As regards the necessity of the extension of ARCH(1) to GARCH(1,1), at least two parameters c_{ij}, namely c_{12} and c_{21}, are concentrated very far from zero.

The results of model comparison indicate that model parsimony is almost as important as flexibility of the covariance structure and thick tails of the conditional sampling distribution. Our very simple t-BEKK(1,1) specification M_7 is almost as flexible as heavily parameterized t-VechGARCH models, so the BEKK model wins the competition due to its relative simplicity. However, when parsimonious parameterization is achieved at the cost of too strong assumptions about the covariance structure, the resulting models have little explanatory power.

Table 7.5. *The posterior means and standard deviations of the parameters of M_7 (free α and λ, T = 1482)*

h_0	ν	δ_1	δ_2	R_{11}	R_{12}	R_{21}	R_{22}
0.0302 (0.0113)	5.15 (0.37)	0.030 (0.0051)	0.015 (0.0083)	−0.005 (0.020)	0.027 (0.018)	0.034 (0.019)	−0.026 (0.022)
a_{11}	a_{12}	a_{22}	b_{11}	b_{12}	b_{21}	b_{22}	c_{11}
0.0015 (0.00066)	0.0014 (0.00036)	0.0019 (0.00063)	0.3440 (0.0325)	0.2584 (0.0337)	0.1500 (0.0268)	0.2639 (0.0279)	0.1049 (0.0430)
c_{12}	c_{21}	c_{22}	α_1	α_2	λ_1	λ_2	
−0.9537 (0.0337))	−0.8651 (0.0328)	0.0554 (0.0465)	0.3452 (0.0126)	−0.3760 (0.0186)	−7.23 (0.64)	7.84 (0.86)	

Table 7.6. The posterior means and standard deviations of the parameters of t-BEKK(1,1) with no exogenous variables (T = 1482)

h_0	ν	δ_1	δ_2	R_{11}	R_{12}	R_{21}	R_{22}
0.0579 (0.0257)	5.01 (0.45)	0.045 (0.0085)	0.002 (0.0097)	−0.020 (0.022)	0.017 (0.020)	0.010 (0.025)	−0.042 (0.024)
a_{11}	a_{12}	a_{22}	b_{11}	b_{12}	b_{21}	b_{22}	c_{11}
0.0021 (0.0011)	0.0013 (0.0006)	0.0024 (0.0014)	0.3157 (0.0248)	0.2128 (0.0257)	0.1728 (0.0199)	0.2752 (0.0232)	0.0992 (0.0409)
c_{12}	c_{21}	c_{22}					
−1.0163 (0.0303)	−0.8145 (0.0236)	0.0532 (0.0430)					

Figure 7.6. Point estimates of the conditional standard deviations in $M_7 (T = 1482)$

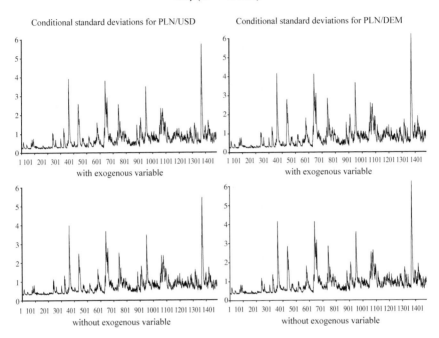

It is also important to note that the posterior means of α and λ are far enough from zero to strongly reject the simplifying assumption $\alpha = \lambda = 0$. Incidentally, these posterior means have correct signs and reasonable interpretation in terms of the ECM.

In Table 7.6 we present the basic posterior results obtained for the t-BEKK(1,1) model with no exogenous variable ($\alpha = \lambda = 0$). These results should be compared to the ones in Table 7.5. Although we can see some differences in the location and scale of the marginal posterior distributions of individual parameters, the main conclusions based on the simpler model remain valid when the exogenous variable and the ECM term are introduced. In particular, our point estimates of the conditional sampling standard deviation (measuring volatility of the series) exhibit the same dynamic pattern in both cases. This is presented in Figure 7.6 where we show the plots of $\sqrt{(\nu - 2)^{-1} \nu h_{ii,t}}$ ($i = 1, 2$) evaluated at the posterior means of the parameters. The correlation coefficient between two series of 1482 point estimates is 0.9957 for $i = 1$ and 0.9960 for $i = 2$. Of course, when we introduce the important exogenous variable, the unexplained volatility of the series is reduced. The average estimated conditional standard deviation decreases from 0.79 to 0.74 for $i = 1$ and from 0.88 to

0.78 for $i = 2$; see also the posterior results for a_{11} and a_{22}, the constants in the conditional variance equations. It is worth noting that the dynamic patterns of the sampling conditional covariances and correlations are basically the same, no matter whether the exogenous variable is introduced into the model. The correlation coefficient between the posterior means of the consecutive 1482 conditional covariances in these two cases is as high as 0.9995; for the conditional correlations the corresponding number is 0.9706. However, the magnitudes of the sampling conditional covariances and correlations are somewhat sensitive to the presence of z_t and ECM_t. The full specification leads to the average of the estimated correlations equal to 0.44, while the restricted model gives only 0.16. Thus, we can conclude that the appropriate specification of the conditional mean of the bivariate process is crucial for improving model fit, and not that crucial (but still somewhat important) for the inference on changing conditional variances and correlation coefficients.

7.6. Concluding remarks

Introducing the exogenous DEM/USD exchange rate (through our conditional ECM model) has only marginal effect on the results of Bayesian comparison of competing bivariate GARCH error processes for the pair of growth rates of the official PLN/USD and PLN/DEM exchange rates. The simple t-BEKK(1,1) structure is always the best, receiving practically all the posterior model probability mass. Obviously, the presence of the DEM/USD exchange rate (through its growth rate and the ECM) is of enormous importance for explaining the modelled growth rates and thus it reduces the unexplained volatility of the modelled bivariate series. This does not mean, however, that we suggest using such relevant exogenous variables (and conditional models) in predictive analyses like option pricing or building dynamic hedging strategies. Exogenous variables are very useful in explaining volatility ex post, but are uncertain ex ante. Hence, it seems reasonable to base predictive analyses on good models of marginal processes for the forecasted financial instruments. For our data set and class of models, the simple VAR(1)-t-BEKK(1,1) specification considered by Osiewalski and Pipień (2004) seems a reasonable approximation of the marginal bivariate process generating PLN/USD and PLN/DEM.

Our model comparison focused on older multivariate GARCH structures, proposed prior to 2001. However, some preliminary results (based on the same data set) show that the promising, parsimoniously parameterized DCC models of Engle (2002) are not as good (using Bayesian criteria) as the BEKK(1,1) structure.

References

Baba, Y., R.F. Engle, D. Kraft and K. Kroner (1989), *Multivariate Simultaneous Generalised ARCH*. Manuscript, Department of Economics, University of California at San Diego.

Bauwens, L. and M. Lubrano (1998), "Bayesian inference on GARCH models using the Gibbs sampler", *Econometrics Journal*, Vol. 1, pp. C23–C46.

Bauwens, L., M. Lubrano and J.-F. Richard (1999), *Bayesian Inference in Dynamic Econometric Models*, Oxford: Oxford University Press.

Bollerslev, T. (1986), "Generalised autoregressive conditional heteroskedasticity", *Journal of Econometrics*, Vol. 31, pp. 307–327.

Bollerslev, T. (1990), "Modelling the coherence in short-run nominal exchange rates: a multivariate generalised ARCH model", *Review of Economics and Statistics*, Vol. 72, pp. 498–505.

Bos, Ch.S., R.J. Mahieu and H.K. Van Dijk (2000), "Daily exchange rate behaviour and hedging of currency risk", *Journal of Applied Econometrics*, Vol. 15, pp. 671–696.

Cowles, M.K. and B.P. Carlin (1996), "Markov Chain Monte Carlo convergence diagnostics: a comparative review", *Journal of the American Statistical Association*, Vol. 91, pp. 883–904.

Diebold, F. and M. Nerlove (1989), "The dynamic of exchange rate volatility: a multivariate latent factor ARCH model", *Journal of Applied Econometrics*, Vol. 4, pp. 1–22.

Engle, R.F. (1982), "Autoregressive conditional heteroskedasticity with estimates of the variance of United Kingdom inflation", *Econometrica*, Vol. 50, pp. 987–1007.

Engle, R. (2002), "Dynamic conditional correlation: a simple class of multivariate generalized autoregressive conditional heteroskedasticity models", *Journal of Business and Economic Statistics*, Vol. 20, pp. 339–350.

Engle, R.F. and C.W.J. Granger (1987), "Co-integration and error correction: representation, estimation and testing", *Econometrica*, Vol. 55, pp. 251–276.

Engle, R.F. and K.F. Kroner (1995), "Multivariate simultaneous generalised ARCH", *Econometric Theory*, Vol. 11, pp. 122–150.

Florens, J.-P. and M. Mouchart (1985), "Conditioning in dynamic models", *Journal of Time Series Analysis*, Vol. 6, pp. 15–34.

Gamerman, D. (1997), *Markov Chain Monte Carlo. Stochastic Simulation for Bayesian Inference*, London: Chapman and Hall.

Geweke, J. (1989), "Exact predictive densities for linear models with ARCH disturbances", *Journal of Econometrics*, Vol. 40, pp. 63–86.

Gourieroux, C. (1997), *ARCH Models and Financial Applications*, New York: Springer.

King, M., E. Sentana and S. Wadhwani (1994), "Volatility and links between national stock markets", *Econometrica*, Vol. 62, pp. 901–934.

Kleibergen, F. and H.K. Van Dijk (1993), "Non-stationarity in GARCH models: a Bayesian analysis". *Journal of Applied Econometrics*, Vol. 8, pp. 41–61.

Newton, M.A. and A.E. Raftery (1994), "Approximate Bayesian inference by the weighted likelihood bootstrap (with discussion)", *Journal of the Royal Statistical Society B*, Vol. 56, pp. 3–48.

O'Hagan, A. (1994), *Bayesian Inference*, London: Edward Arnold.

Osiewalski, J. and M. Pipień (1999), "Bayesian forecasting of foreign exchange rates using GARCH models with skewed *t* conditional distributions", pp. 195–218 in: W. Welfe, editor, *MACROMODELS '98 – Conference Proceedings*, Vol. 2, Łódź: Absolwent.

Osiewalski, J. and M. Pipień (2000), "GARCH-In-Mean through skewed t conditional distributions: Bayesian inference for exchange rates", pp. 354–369 in: W. Welfe and P. Wdowiński, editors, *MACROMODELS '99 – Conference Proceedings*, Łódź: Absolwent.

Osiewalski, J. and M. Pipień (2002), "Multivariate t-GARCH models – Bayesian analysis for exchange rates", pp. 151–167 in: W. Welfe, editor, *Modelling Economies in Transition – Proceedings of the Sixth AMFET Conference*, Łódź: Absolwent.

Osiewalski, J. and M. Pipień (2004), "Bayesian comparison of bivariate ARCH-type models for the main exchange rates in Poland", *Journal of Econometrics*, in press.

Osiewalski, J. and M.F.J. Steel (1996), "A Bayesian analysis of exogeneity in models pooling time-series and cross-sectional data", *Journal of Statistical Planning and Inference*, Vol. 50, pp. 187–206.

Tse, Y.K. and A.K.C. Tsui (2002), "A multivariate generalized autoregressive conditional heteroskedasticity model with time-varying correlations", *Journal of Business and Economic Statistics*, Vol. 20, pp. 351–362.

van der Weide, R. (2002), "GO-GARCH: a multivariate generalized orthogonal GARCH model", *Journal of Applied Econometrics*, Vol. 17, pp. 549–564.

Vrontos, I.D., P. Dellaportas and D.N. Politis (2000), "Full Bayesian inference for GARCH and EGARCH models", *Journal of Business and Economic Statistics*, Vol. 18, pp. 187–198.

Yu, B. and P. Mykland (1994), "Looking at Markov samplers through CUMSUM paths plots: a simple diagnostic idea", Technical Report 413, Department of Statistics, University of California at Berkeley.

New Directions in Macromodelling
A. Welfe (Editor)
© 2004 Published by Elsevier B.V.
DOI: 10.1016/S0573-8555(04)69008-0

CHAPTER 8

Modelling Polish Economy: An Application of SVEqCM

Aleksander Welfe, Piotr Karp and Piotr Kębłowski

Chair of Econometric Models and Forecasts, University of Lodz, 41 Rewolucji 1905r. Str., 90-214 Lodz, Poland

Abstract

The aim of the chapter is to investigate the long-run relationships between wages, prices, labour productivity and other variables in the Polish economy in the period of transition by applying a multivariate cointegration analysis. In particular, the chapter draws heavily on results obtained by Greenslade et al. (2000) and follows similar modelling strategy. We present succeeding stages of the analysis that lead to a fully economically identified system representing long-run relationships.

The investigation is based on the monthly data covering the period from January 1993 to December 2002. The empirical results allow to conclude that costs and unemployment were the main forces driving inflation in Poland during the transition years. On the other hand, the data confirmed that foreign direct investments and privatization were significantly influencing GDP.

Keywords: cointegration, modelling economies in transition

JEL classification: C32

8.1. Introduction

Successful applications of multivariate cointegration analysis to modelling economies in transition (recently called EU New Member States) are still rare for several reasons (see Hall *et al.*, 2000). First, most investigations concentrated on systems comprising 2–3 variables, more rarely 4, among which only one cointegration relationship was typically identified. As a consequence, multivariate analysis turned out to be unnecessary. Besides, authors often assumed the exogeneity of variables that was not evidenced by tests, or the exogeneity hypothesis was left untested at all. This indirectly reveals the deficiencies of the models' specifications. Secondly, in most cases vector equilibrium correction models (VEqCM) were the limit and results without economic interpretation were considered satisfactory; at the same time dynamic interactions between variables were tested by means of impulse response analysis only exceptionally. Thirdly, many analyses attempt to mechanically use models designed for the developed countries to describe economies in transition without any effort to modify and to extend the models in order to include specific aspects of such economies' behaviour. Besides, authors frequently forget that specifications of particular functions of models they are copying are based on assumptions that are not met by economies in transition.

One of the major problems affecting investigations into economies in transition is (very) short statistical series. The reason is that the process of transition started in 1990. Additionally, as we are going to show using the example of Poland, not all the period of 15 years can be used in research. In this context it becomes crucial to reduce the size of the problem in question at a relatively early stage by employing an adequate strategy. The approach we used had been proposed by Greenslade et al. (2000). We do not present a discussion of the specification and estimation of the VEqCM models with restrictions for the cointegrating relations, as this material can be found in remarkable texts of other authors in this book.

8.2. Economic development. The data

The Polish economy started to evolve from a centrally planned one towards a market economy following the change of the political system, i.e. in the second half of 1989. January 1, 1990, when a scheme frequently called the 'stabilization programme' was launched, has gone down in history. The programme's implementation resulted in: (nearly full) liberalization of prices and removal of subsidies, removal of red tape restricting the private sector, liberalization of foreign trade and introduction of active monetary policy, as well as rigid borrowing ceilings (see also Hoen, 1998). Owing to price adjustments over 2 years (1990–1991) the cost of living index increased 12 times. Later, as a result of several anchors such as wage indexation and the fixing of the exchange rate against the US dollar (after a draconian devaluation of the

Polish zloty) the rate of inflation was successfully reduced to slightly over 10% in the middle of the 1990 s (broader historical background in Welfe, 1998). Because of the dramatic pace of economic processes in the first years of transition attempts to account for the period turned out very difficult (see results of earlier research: Welfe, 2000; Welfe and Majsterek, 2002). In our opinion, the reason was the changing speed of adjustments, but we failed to build an appropriate model with parameters varying in time. Another important reason for skipping the first transition years was the unavailability of monthly data; some pieces of information describing major macrocategories started to be published only from 1993.

As a result of the economic reform, equilibrium was restored in most consumer goods' markets in Poland within 6–8 quarters (for the estimates of excess demand see Welfe, 1989). The economic system started to be increasingly demand-constrained in contrast to the supply-driven shortage economy in the previous years (see classical work of Kornai, 1980). It should be added that adjustments in the economy were followed by changes in human mentality that influenced job-taking decisions and workers' expectations for their wages.

Restrictive fiscal and monetary policies made industrial output decline by 30% in 1990. This triggered an outbreak of unemployment rate from practically zero to almost 15% at the beginning of the 1990s. At the same time a process was initiated to liquidate labour hoarding in state owned enterprises, and those that had already been privatized. As a result GDP growth in the next years was primarily fuelled by higher and higher productivity of labour. It was accompanied by a steadily increasing unemployment rate that went up to almost 20% at the end of the sample period. This dramatic change influenced the formation of wages which became sensitive to unemployment (in the years preceding transition wages were found to be sensitive to excess demand for labour; see Welfe, 1991).

In the next years the inflation rate systematically declined, followed by falling interest rates. However, the developments in Poland show that its economy still suffers from cost-push inflation. Wage costs and costs of imported goods, especially of raw materials (including oil), play the most significant role in this process. Another important effect of the transformation was rapidly growing foreign trade deficit caused by the escalating import of both final goods, raw materials and intermediate goods. Consequently, the imports–output ratio went up vis-à-vis the previous period, which made domestic prices more sensitive to variations in imported goods' prices (see more in Gomułka, 1998; Welfe, 1999).

Also the structure of ownership was profoundly adjusted in the Polish economy – in 1993 less than 20% of GDP was generated by the private sector, but in 2004 it was as much as 75%. Naturally, management methods in enterprises were radically revised, resulting in an autonomous growth in production. In those years Poland became an attractive country for foreign investors. The inflow of FDIs was accompanied by a stream of modern and very productive capital whose share keeps growing. Consequently, both the effects – one related to privatisation and another to the restructuring of capital – should be expected to be adequately reflected in the production function.

In this study we restricted our interest mainly to the supply side of the Polish economy. The model is built around three relationships explaining wages, w_t, consumer price index, p_t, and productivity, z_t. The set of potentially weak exogenous variables consists of unemployment rate, U_t, import prices, pm_t, capital–labour ratio, kl_t, cumulated foreign direct investments (FDIs) per employee, fd_t, and a share of GDP generated in the private sector in total GDP measuring privatization, V_t. Small letters denote natural logarithms. For the above reasons the sample covers the period January 1993 to December 2002. Monthly, seasonally unadjusted data is used. The series are plotted in Figure 8.1.

Results presented in Table 8.1 prove that all variables are $I(1)$, even though the joint ADF–KPSS test (for small sample critical values see Kębłowski and Welfe, 2004) suggests that wages, consumer price index and cumulated foreign direct investments per employee could be considered as $I(2)$. A number of lags in ADF was chosen for every variable at a minimum level (varying from 3 to 12) to get rid of serial correlation and to ensure normal distribution of the residuals, which was verified by the cumulated periodogram test (Durbin, 1969), for which the small sample's 5% critical value equals 0.17.

8.3. The model

We argue that real wages depend on both productivity and pressures in the labour market measured by the rate of unemployment:

$$E[w_t - \delta_0^w - \delta_1^w z - \delta_2^w U_t - \delta_3^w p_t] = 0. \qquad (8.1a)$$

The wage indexation mechanism is generally considered to be one of the main determinants of inflation. In the short run its impact is related to the power of the labour unions and the effectiveness of their bargaining with employers, or to the existing indexation clauses. However, in the long run price elasticity of wages is expected to be one, $\delta_3^w = 1$. The equation

Figure 8.1.   Seasonally unadjusted monthly data, 1993.01–2002.12

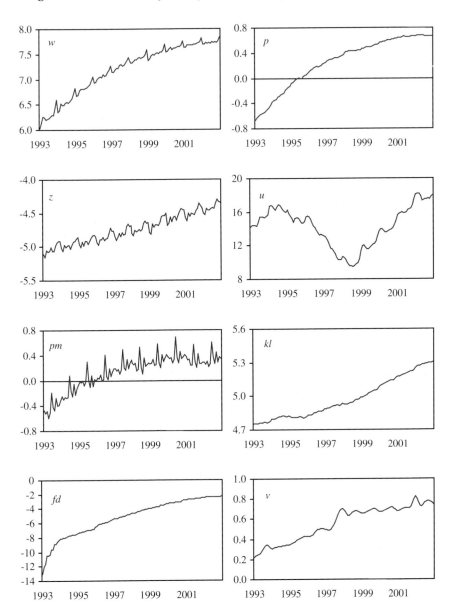

above is a standard wage function (Tobin, 1995), which can be also derived from the analysis of the pay system in Poland and from other institutional solutions (Welfe, 1991). Analogous function results from the acceptance of the bargaining model of wages and prices (Nickell, 1984; Layard *et al.*, 1991).

Table 8.1. Inference on the order of integration

Variable	Hypotheses	t statistic of the ADF test	LM statistic of the KPSS test	ADF test conclusion (limit distribution) size, 5%	ADF–KPSS joint test conclusion (exact distribution)		K-S statistics of the cumulated periodogram test	Order of deterministic polynomial
					Order of integration	Probability of joint confirmation		
w_t	$I(2)$ vs. $I(1)$	-4.023	0.740	$I(1)$	$I(2)$	0.95	0.1261	2
p_t		-5.413	0.120	$I(1)$	$I(2)$	0.95	0.0900	2
z_t		-4.153	0.039	$I(1)$	$I(1)$	0.95	0.1320	1
U_t		-3.150	0.189	$I(1)$	$I(1)$	0.95	0.0745	0
pm_t		-5.880	0.053	$I(1)$	$I(1)$	0.95	0.1109	2
kl_t		-3.761	0.085	$I(1)$	$I(1)$	0.85	0.0739	2
fd_t		-4.307	0.166	$I(1)$	$I(2)$	0.95	0.0482	2
V_t		-3.807	0.048	$I(1)$	$I(1)$	0.90	0.0954	2
w_t	$I(1)$ vs. $I(0)$	1.197	0.357	$I(1)$	$I(1)$	0.95	0.1378	2
p_t		-3.154	0.347	$I(1)$	$I(1)$	0.95	0.0627	2
z_t		2.123	1.442	$I(1)$	$I(1)$	0.95	0.1446	1
U_t		0.115	4.364	$I(1)$	$I(1)$	0.95	0.0979	0
pm_t		-1.851	0.330	$I(1)$	$I(1)$	0.95	0.1099	2
kl_t		-1.329	0.347	$I(1)$	$I(1)$	0.95	0.0953	2
fd_t		0.768	0.292	$I(1)$	$I(1)$	0.95	0.0581	2
V_t		-0.940	0.268	$I(1)$	$I(1)$	0.95	0.1013	2

Wages can affect inflation if their increases are not compensated for by productivity growth. In addition, inflation reacts positively to increases in import prices as it changes costs of imported materials, intermediate products, and final goods:

$$E[p_t - \delta_0^p - \delta_1^p w - \delta_2^p z - \delta_3^p \text{pm}] = 0. \tag{8.1b}$$

This equation originates from the cost-push inflation theory and follows the hypothesis that prices are influenced by the output costs enlarged by a constant mark-up assumed to be proportional to the costs (see classic work of Tobin, 1972). Function (8.1b) is based on the maximizing condition for an individual firm. The price mark-up equation can be obtained by aggregating an individual firm's product demand function across the firms. Naturally, Equation (8.1b) must satisfy the homogeneity condition $\delta_1^p + \delta_3^p = 1$.

The labour productivity equation can be derived from the elementary Cobb–Douglas production function with no returns to scale and endogenised technical progress:

$$E[z_t - \delta_0^z - \delta_1^z \text{kl} - \delta_2^z \text{fd} - \delta_3^z V] = 0 \tag{8.1c}$$

In the above equation technical progress was decomposed into two effects: embodied technical progress resulting from a much higher quality of capital installed in the recent years and directly linked to FDIs and organizational changes being the consequence of improved management. The latter were forced by market competition closely connected to the privatization of the Polish economy.

8.4. Structural VAR

The structural vector equilibrium correction model (SVEqCM) can be written as follows:

$$\Delta \mathbf{y}_t \mathbf{A}_0 = \tilde{\mathbf{y}}_{t-1} \tilde{\mathbf{\Pi}} + \sum_{s=1}^{S-1} \Delta \mathbf{y}_{t-s} \mathbf{A}_s + \mathbf{d}_t^z \tilde{\mathbf{C}} + \varepsilon_t \tag{8.2}$$

where $\tilde{\mathbf{\Pi}} = \mathbf{\Pi} \mathbf{A}_0$, $\mathbf{A}_s = \mathbf{\Gamma}_s \mathbf{A}_0$, $\tilde{\mathbf{C}} = \mathbf{C} \mathbf{A}_0$, $\varepsilon_t = \xi_t \mathbf{A}_0$, and

$\mathbf{A}_0$ is the contemporaneous coefficients matrix,
$\tilde{\mathbf{y}}_t = [\mathbf{y}_t \mathbf{d}_t^x]$,
$\mathbf{y}_t = [y_{1t} \ldots y_{Mt}]$ the vector of M stochastic variables,
$\mathbf{d}_t^x = [d_{1t} \ldots d_{Nt}]$ the vector of N deterministic variables restricted to the cointegrating space,
$\mathbf{d}_t^z = [d_{1t} \ldots d_{Pt}]$ the vector of P deterministic variables,

$\mathbf{\Pi}$ the total impact multipliers matrix,

$\mathbf{\Gamma}_s$ the short-run parameter matrices,

$\xi_t = [\xi_{1t}...\xi_{Mt}]$ is the vector of white noise disturbances.

$\mathbf{\Pi}$ matrix can be decomposed as $\mathbf{\Pi} = \mathbf{BA}^T$, provided the cointegrating rank of the system is $R(0 \leq R < M)$, which implies that matrices $\mathbf{\Pi}$ and $\mathbf{B}$ are of rank R. If $\mathbf{y}_t \sim I(1)$ then $\Delta\mathbf{y}_t \sim I(0)$ and $\mathbf{y}_{t-1}\mathbf{B} \sim \mathbf{I}(0)$, thus Equation (8.2) includes exclusively stationary variables. Columns of matrix $\mathbf{B}$ represent cointegrating vectors while rows of matrix $\mathbf{A}$ – loading weights related to the cointegrating vectors. Zero weight proves an insignificant role of the cointegrating vector in explaining the long-run behaviour of the particular variable. The above equation represents the DGP process on which the inference was based.

Identification of the above system includes identification of contemporaneous coefficients $\mathbf{A}_0$ and the short-run dynamic coefficients $\mathbf{A}_s$. Since $\mathbf{\Pi} = \mathbf{BA}^T$ and $\tilde{\mathbf{\Pi}} = \mathbf{BA}^T\mathbf{A}_0$, cointegrating matrix $\mathbf{B}$ does not depend on the short-run specification. Consequently, identification of the short-run structure is not directly connected with identification of the long-run structure of the model (Greenslade et al., 2000). For any non-singular R-dimensional matrix $\mathbf{U}$, $\mathbf{\Pi} = \mathbf{BUU}^{-1}\mathbf{A}^T = \mathbf{B}^*\mathbf{A}^{*T}$ where $\mathbf{B}^* = \mathbf{BU}$ and $\mathbf{A}^* = \mathbf{AU}^{-1}$, so at least R^2 restrictions are necessary to identify cointegrating matrix $\mathbf{B}$. The estimation of the VEqCM gives total impact multipliers included in matrix $\mathbf{\Pi}$. The problem of its decomposition into adjustments and cointegrating matrix is analogous to the classic problem of identification of simultaneous models.

Exact identification of the long-run structure requires R^2 independent restrictions $((R-1)R$ non-normalizing restrictions) in the whole system. An order condition for exact identification is the same, thus if the number of restrictions $k < R^2$ or if $k > R^2$ the system is underidentified or overidentified, respectively (Pesaran and Shin, 2002).

Greenslade et al. (2000) showed that it is asymptotically irrelevant whether the overidentifying restrictions are tested before or after the model has been marginalized and its dynamic structure determined. In limited samples of typical sizes, however, the power of the tests is low, if the dynamics is not restricted. On the other hand, the distribution of the test statistic for cointegration rank is not known when the dynamics is restricted, thus the cointegrating rank should be tested before the dynamics is restricted. Moreover, results of the Monte Carlo experiments indicate that the cointegration test works better after marginalization has been determined; this speaks for fixing exogeneity early in the nesting procedure. All the above arguments considered, the following iterative procedure was employed in this study:

First, the cointegrating rank is found by the standard Johansen procedure.

Secondly, weak exogeneity hypotheses are tested. The exogeneity tests are sensitive to the cointegrating rank. Therefore, the procedure is an iterative one. After R in the unrestricted system is found, the exogeneity of a particular variable is tested. Then, under the assumption that this variable is weakly exogenous, the testing of cointegrating rank is repeated.

Thirdly, the short-run structure is found. If estimates of gammas do not significantly differ from zero, then the order of the lag is reduced.

Fourthly, at least R^2 restrictions are imposed, which defines the long-run structural model.

In the last step, the overidentifying restrictions are tested. The test is based on the likelihood ratio between restricted and unrestricted models.

8.5. *Cointegrating rank, weak exogeneity and specification of the model*

The Johansen (1988) procedure was employed to determine the cointegrating rank. Two tests based on the maximum eigenvalue and the trace statistic were used and their outcomes were juxtaposed with Pesaran *et al.* (2000) asymptotical critical values (for 5% size of both tests) which hold, when the conditional inference is conducted. A top-down approach was applied, i.e. inference on the cointegrating rank starting with zero cointegrating relationships under the null. It should be noted that the test based on the asymptotical critical values tends to overestimate the number of cointegrating vectors (Doornik, 1998), nevertheless preliminary results based on Bartlett correction (Johansen, 2002) suggest that the bias towards more cointegrating relationships is relatively small. Besides, Johansen (1988) argues that consequences of underestimated cointegrating rank are much more serious than of overestimated.

The cointegrating rank and exogeneity restrictions were tested alternately for a set of eight variables (see Tables 8.2 and 8.3, respectively). In the first step λ_{max} suggests that six cointegrating relations exist while λ_{trace} implies four. Then exogeneity restrictions were tested under the assumption of four common trends. The test indicates that the unemployment rate, import prices, capital–labour ratio and shares of GDP produced in the private sector in total GDP are most probably weakly exogenous. In the second iteration the cointegrating rank was tested in a system conditional on these four variables. Now, both tests cannot reject the null hypothesis of cointegration rank three. LR test for weak exogeneity suggests in turn that foreign direct investments can be treated as weakly exogenous. In the last stage the

Table 8.2.   Inference on the cointegration rank

Number of common trends	λ_{max}	λ_{trace}
8	93.93	351.80
7	86.73	257.87
6	57.06	171.14
5	49.85	114.08
4	26.71	64.23
3	18.03	37.52
2	15.79	19.49
1	3.70	3.70
Exogenous variables: U_t, V_t, pm_t, kl_t		
4	82.84	204.96
3	65.68	122.12
2	38.00	56.43
1	18.43	18.43
Exogenous variables: U_t, V_t, pm_t, fd_t, kl_t		
3	75.50	171.13
2	63.80	95.62
1	31.83	31.83

Model with restricted intercepts.

cointegrating rank was tested for the marginalized system and no more common stochastic trends were found. This let us accept the share of GDP produced in the private sector in total GDP, unemployment rate, import prices, foreign direct investments and capital labour ratio as long-run factors forcing wages, the price index and productivity.

Table 8.3.   Inference on weak-exogeneity

Variable	$\chi^2(4)$
w_t	32.47
p_t	39.70
z_t	31.82
U_t	19.43
pm_t	19.05
kl_t	20.49
fd_t	24.80
V_t	18.18
Exogenous variables: U_t, pm_t, kl_t, V_t	
Variable	$\chi^2(3)$
w_t	28.14
p_t	46.70
z_t	34.98
fd_t	15.40

Table 8.4a. Misspecification tests

Multivariate tests		
Residual autocorrelation LM_1	$\chi^2(64) = 76.758$	p-value $= 0.13$
Residual autocorrelation LM_4	$\chi^2(64) = 73.664$	p-value $= 0.19$
Normality: LM	$\chi^2(16) = 78.577$	p-value $= 0.00$

Multivariate and univariate misspecification tests presented in Tables 8.4a and b confirm that the model is acceptable, except for capital–labour ratio and the share of GDP produced in the private sector in total GDP equations which show signs of non-normal distribution of residuals. ARCH effect was detected in the equation explaining foreign direct investments and in the afore-mentioned equations. However, none of them entered into the marginalized system.

Restrictions imposed on the model's parameters were not rejected by the data at standard significance level ($\alpha = 0.01$), because the value of the LR statistic is 24.842 for 13 overidentifying restrictions.

8.6. Empirical results

Since Equation (8.2) is based entirely on stationary variables the standard t-ratios as well as other classical tests keep their properties and can be used to find loading coefficients and short-run parameters that significantly differ from zero. To get the dynamic structure of the model as parsimonious as possible, lags with the smallest absolute values of t-ratios were sequentially eliminated together with the cointegrating vectors that were unimportant for explaining variation of the modelled variables.

Table 8.4b. Misspecification tests

		Univariate tests			
Variable	K-S statistics of Durbin test	Normality, $\chi^2(2) =$	ARCH(3), $\chi^2(3) =$	ARCH(12), $\chi^2(12) =$	R^2
w_t	0.0709	0.052	0.806363	9.457840	0.962
p_t	0.1083	3.413	3.287529	9.419137	0.918
z_t	0.0858	1.079	3.354847	8.067576	0.944
U_t	0.0977	1.217	4.265223	15.595788	0.851
pm_t	0.1012	2.098	5.178503	13.423459	0.985
kl_t	0.0746	24.476	2.512048	33.697334	0.818
fd_t	0.1661	7.041	26.630728	15.819733	0.739
V_t	0.2196	25.818	8.526650	15.781820	0.963

This led to the following (*t* statistics are in parentheses):

$[\Delta w_t \; \Delta p_t \; \Delta z_t]$

$$= [\mathbf{ec}_1 \; \mathbf{ec}_2 \; \mathbf{ec}_3] \begin{bmatrix} \underset{(-3.76)}{-0.428} & 0 & \underset{(-3.81)}{-0.251} \\ 0 & \underset{(-5.90)}{-0.101} & 0 \\ 0 & 0 & \underset{(-14.43)}{-0.649} \end{bmatrix}$$

$$+ [\Delta w_{t-1} \; \Delta p_{t-1} \; \Delta z_{t-1} \; \Delta pm_{t-1}] \begin{bmatrix} \underset{(4.71)}{0.249} & 0 & \underset{(2.35)}{0.202} \\ 0 & \underset{(8.35)}{0.586} & 0 \\ 0 & \underset{(5.10)}{0.059} & 0 \\ 0 & \underset{(-3.87)}{-0.032} & \underset{(6.04)}{0.238} \end{bmatrix}$$

$$+ [\Delta pm_{t-2}]\begin{bmatrix} 0 & \underset{(6.04)}{-0.014} & \underset{(4.50)}{0.157} \end{bmatrix} + [\Delta z_{t-3}]\begin{bmatrix} \underset{(3.69)}{0.168} & 0 & 0 \end{bmatrix}$$

$$+ [\Delta z_{t-4}]\begin{bmatrix} \underset{(3.55)}{0.166} & 0 & 0 \end{bmatrix} + [u_{1t} \; u_{2t} \; u_{3t}] \tag{8.3}$$

where $\mathbf{ec}_1$, $\mathbf{ec}_2$ and $\mathbf{ec}_3$ are cointegrating vectors as specified by Equations (8.1a–c), respectively. Interestingly enough, in the equation explaining wages and prices only cointegrating vectors identified as the long-run wage and price functions were significant. In the productivity equation two cointegrating vectors defining wages and productivity are present.

The maximum likelihood estimator of the long-run relationships is (deterministic terms are abandoned):

$$w - p = \underset{(51.401)}{9.214} + \underset{(11.067)}{0.425z} - \underset{(-4.075)}{0.014U} \tag{8.4a}$$

$$p = - \underset{(-6.203)}{6.376} + \underset{(8.500)}{0.681w} - \underset{(-3.381)}{0.362z} + 0.319pm \tag{8.4b}$$

$$z = \underset{(-33.078)}{-8.663} + \underset{(16.523)}{0.795kl} + \underset{(3.117)}{0.022fd} + \underset{(1.978)}{0.178V} \tag{8.4c}$$

The elasticity of wages with respect to productivity of labour (0.425) is slightly less than the estimate obtained in the previous study based on the quarterly data (Welfe and Majsterek, 2002). Unemployment proved to be a significant determinant of real wages which is worth stressing, as the previous attempts to account for the effects of unemployment were unsuccessful.

The elasticity of prices with respect to wages equals 0.681, but 0.319 for import prices. If the elasticity of prices were equal with respect to labour productivity and wages, the W/Z ratio would define wage costs exactly. The condition of the equality of parameters was, however, rejected by the data. This means that labour productivity growth only partly contributed to declining inflation. This effect is due to the fact that in Poland labour productivity improvements were stimulated not only by increasing intensity of labour but also technical progress as well. In consequence, the productivity growth made costs drop, while improving the quality of products which gave producers arguments to rise their prices. As a result the elasticity of prices with respect to labour productivity is roughly half of that with respect to wages (similar results in Welfe, 2002).

The estimate of the elasticity of production (GDP) as regards capital is 0.795 and may be considered high, which should not be surprising, as the variability of employment was very limited throughout the sample period during which production and capital grew swiftly. Changes in the quality of capital are approximated by cumulated FDIs and this effect turns out significant. Estimates show that the elasticity of production with respect to capital quality (represented by FDIs) is ca. 0.02. The results prove also that privatization was an important pro-growth factor in the period in question.

8.7. Conclusions

Economies in transition are not an easy modelling target: time series are relatively short and noisy about the long run. However, if the model is appropriately based on theory and correctly captures the specific features of such economies, then it is able to exploit all data variability and allows us to arrive at fully interpretable, sensible and sound results. Also the strategy employed is important here for enabling successful estimation of a fully dynamic SVEqCM by maximum likelihood, despite the limited sample. The approach that marginalizes the model at the initial stage of the analysis proved to be very effective.

By employing a multivariate cointegration analysis it became possible to identify three crucial long-term relationships in the Polish economy. The influence of unemployment on the evolution of average wages and FDIs and of privatization processes on Polish GDP has been confirmed.

Acknowledgements

We are indebted to Stephen Hall and Katarina Juselius for valuable discussions concerning the modelling strategy. Financial support under KBN grant No. 2 H02B 00725 is gratefully acknowledged. All remaining shortcomings lie solely with the authors.

References

Doornik, J.A. (1998), "Approximations to the asymptotic distribution of cointegration tests", *Journal of Economic Surveys*, Vol. 12, pp. 573–593.

Durbin, J. (1969), "Tests for serial correlation in regression analysis based on the periodogram of least squares residuals", *Biometrika*, Vol. 56, pp. 1–16.

Gomułka, S. (1998), "Output: causes of the decline and the recovery", in: P. Boone, S. Gomułka and R. Layard, editors, *Emerging from Communism: Lessons from Russia, China and Eastern Europe*, Cambridge: MIT Press.

Greenslade, J.V., S.G. Hall and S.G.B. Henry (2000), "On the identification of cointegrated systems in small samples: practical procedures with an application to UK wages and prices", *Journal of Economic Dynamics and Control*, Vol. 26, pp. 1517–1537.

Hall, S., G. Mizon and A. Welfe (2000), "Modelling economies in transition: an introduction", *Economic Modelling*, Vol. 17, pp. 339–357.

Hoen, H.W. (1998), *The Transformation of Economic Systems in Central Europe*, Cheltenham: E. Elgar.

Johansen, S. (1988), "Statistical analysis of cointegration vectors", *Journal of Economic Dynamics and Control*, Vol. 12, pp. 231–254.

Johansen, S. (2002), "A small sample correction of the test for cointegrating rank in the vector autoregressive model", *Econometrica*, Vol. 70, pp. 192–1961.

Kębłowski, P. and A. Welfe (2004), "The ADF-KPSS test of the joint confirmation hypothesis of unit autoregressive root", *Economics Letters*, Vol. 85, pp. 257–263.

Kornai, J. (1980), *Economics of Shortage*, Amsterdam: North Holland.

Layard, R., S.J. Nickell and R. Jackman (1991), *Unemployment: Macroeconomic Performance and the Labor Market*, Oxford: Oxford University Press.

Nickell, S.J. (1984), "The modelling of wages and employment", in: D.F. Hendry and K.F. Wallis, editors, *Econometrics and Quantitative Economics*, Oxford: Basil Blackwell.

Pesaran, M.H. and Y. Shin (2002), "Long run structural modelling", *Econometrics Reviews*, Vol. 21, pp. 49–87.

Pesaran, M.H., Y. Shin and R.J. Smith (2000), "Structural analysis of vector error correction models with exogenous $I(1)$ variables", *Journal of Econometrics*, Vol. 97, pp. 293–343.

Tobin, J. (1972), The Wage-Price Mechanism: Overview of the Conference, The Econometrics of Price Determination Conference, Washington, DC: Federal Reserve System.

Tobin, J. (1995), "The natural rate as new classical macroeconomics", in: R. Cross, editor, *The Natural Rate of Unemployment*, Cambridge: Cambridge University Press.

Welfe, A. (1989), "Savings and consumption in the centrally planned economy: a disequilibrium approach", in: C.M. Davis and W. Charemza, editors, *Models of Disequilibrium and Shortage in Centrally Planned Economies*, London: Chapman & Hall.

Welfe, A. (1991), "Modelling wages in centrally planned economies: the case of poland", *Economics of Planning*, Vol. 24, pp. 47–58.

Welfe, W. (1998), "Modeling inflation in Poland", *Przeglad Statystyczny*, Vol. 45, pp. 309–329.

Welfe, W. (1999), "Economic past, market reforms in Poland and the prospects for growth in the '90s", in: R. Courbis and W. Welfe, editors, *Central and Eastern Europe on Its Way to European Union*, Frankfurt am Main: P. Lang.

Welfe, A. (2000), "Modelling inflation in Poland", *Economic Modelling*, Vol. 17, pp. 375–385.

Welfe, A. (2002), "Long-run relationships in the transition economy of Poland: an application of SVEqCM", in: I. Klein and S. Mittnik, editors, *Contributions to Modern Econometrics*, Dordrecht: Kluwer.

Welfe, A. and M. Majsterek (2002), "Wage and price inflation in Poland in the period of transition: the cointegration analysis", *Economics of Planning*, Vol. 35, pp. 205–219.

New Directions in Macromodelling
A. Welfe (Editor)
DOI: 10.1016/S0573-8555(04)69009-2

CHAPTER 9

Optimal Lag Structure Selection in VEC-Models

Peter Winker and Dietmar Maringer

Chair of Econometrics, Faculty of Economics, Law and Social Sciences, University of Erfurt,
Nordhaeuser Strasse 63, D-99089 Erfurt, Germany

Abstract

For the modelling of time series, multivariate linear and non-linear systems of equations became a standard tool. These models are also applied for non-stationary processes. However, estimation results in finite samples might depend on the specification of the model dynamics.

We propose a method for automatic identification of the dynamic part of VEC-models. Model selection is based on a modified information criterion. The lag structure of the model is selected according to this objective function allowing for 'holes'. The resulting complex discrete optimization problem is tackled using a hybrid heuristic combining ideas from threshold accepting (TA) and memetic algorithms. We present the algorithm and results of a simulation study indicating the performance both with regard to the dynamic structure and the rank selection in the VEC-model.

Keywords: model selection, cointegration rank, order selection, reduced rank regression, VECM

JEL classifications: C32, C61

9.1. Introduction

For the modelling of economic and financial time series, multivariate linear (VAR, SVAR, VECM) and non-linear systems of equations (MS-VAR) became a standard tool over the last few years. As compared to univariate approaches, these models exhibit interesting features, e.g. dealing with non-stationary processes and cointegration. However, the issue of finite sample performance becomes even more relevant for these models which typically require the simultaneous estimation of a large set of parameters.[1] While economic theory might provide a guideline for long-run or equilibrium relationships,[2] the modelling of the dynamic part has to rely on different inputs.[3]

In order to avoid a simple ad hoc specification of the dynamic part, several statistical procedures have been proposed. For example, the lag structure in VAR-models is based on tests on residual autocorrelation (Jacobson, 1995) or information criteria like AIC and BIC (Winker, 2000).[4] However, these approaches did not take into account potential non-stationarity of the time series and the restrictions imposed by the rank conditions in a cointegration framework. In several contributions,[5] the effect of lag length selection on the outcomes of tests for cointegration,[6] in particular on the cointegration rank, has been demonstrated. Bewley and Yang (1998) compare the performance of different system tests for cointegration when the lag length is selected by means of a standard information criterion (AIC or BIC, respectively). Both under- and overspecification of the lag length appear to have a negative impact.[7] While the effect on size is small for tests for rank equal to zero, the effect on power is more substantial for certain parameter combinations. This effect becomes even more pronounced for tests of the null of a cointegration rank of one.

---

[1] For example, a small sample correction of Johansen's test is proposed by Johansen (2002).

[2] The issue of identification and restriction of long-run relationships based on statistical tests and prior information is discussed by Omtzigt (2002).

[3] In this chapter, we neglect the specification of deterministic trend terms, which might have similar implications on the outcomes (Ahking, 2002).

[4] A different approach focusing on general-to-specific reductions, which eliminates statistically insignificant variables and uses diagnostic tests to check the validity of reductions is presented by Hoover and Perez (1999), Hendry and Krolzig (2001) and Krolzig and Hendry (2001). Brüggemann et al. (2003) provide a comparison of different methods.

[5] See also the references provided by Ho and Sørensen (1996) in their introduction and by Pötscher (1991).

[6] In general, the analysis is conducted in the framework of Johansen's testing procedure (Johansen, 1988, 1991, 1992, 1995).

[7] Gonzalo and Pitarakis (1999) analyse the performance of model selection criteria in large dimensional VARs. They find that underfitting might become as important as overfitting when the dimension of the process increases even for the AIC. Furthermore, the performance of information criteria depends critically on the specific DGP under consideration.

Ho and Sørensen (1996) considered higher dimensional systems and found that the negative impact of overspecification increases with the dimension. In particular, application of Johansen's test tends to underestimate the number of unit roots in the system, and, in due course, to overestimate the cointegration rank in this case.

The model selection procedure analysed in this chapter differs in two aspects from the methods mentioned above. First, we employ a modified information criterion discussed by Chao and Phillips (1999) for the case of partially non-stationary VAR-models.[8] Consequently, the dynamic model selection is performed taking the restrictions of reduced rank regressions into account. Second, we allow for 'holes' in the lag structures, i.e. lag structures are not constrained to sequences of lags up to lag k, but might consist, e.g. of the first and fourth lag only in an application to quarterly data. Using this approach, different lag structures can be used for different variables and in different equations of the system. This feature has to be taken into account in the estimation procedure for a given dynamic structure.[9] For this purpose, we use a SURE-like modification of the two-step reduced rank estimator proposed by Ahn and Reinsel (1990).[10]

Using this approach, the problem of model specification becomes an integer optimization problem on the huge set of all possible lag structures. In the context of VAR-models several methods have been proposed to tackle this problem of high computational complexity. Exact algorithms are based on an intelligent enumeration of possible models avoiding the evaluation of all cases (Gatu and Kontoghiorghes, 2003). Nevertheless, this approach is still of high computational complexity and appears to be limited in the current stage to linear models without further restrictions. In contrast, heuristic optimization techniques which have already been applied to the linear VAR (Winker, 2000) can be extended to structural VAR- and VEC-models. However, the numerical methods used in estimating the model for a given dynamic structure, i.e. the two-step reduced rank estimator used in this chapter or an ML estimator, become more involved in a VEC setting.

---

[8] Analyzing the effects of choosing alternative criteria, e.g. along the lines suggested by Campos *et al.* (2003), is left for future research. The same applies to the combination with a pre-selecting step also discussed by Campos *et al.* (2003).

[9] As pointed out by Gredenhoff and Karlsson (1999), in the literature on model selection in VAR-models, the possibility that the true model may have unequal lag-length or even holes in the lag structure has received little attention. Although they use the Hsiao procedure which does not investigate all combinations of lag-lengths for the different variables and does not allow for holes at all, their simulation results indicate that, in particular for more complex lag structures, their unequal lag length procedure appears to improve results.

[10] An application in the ML setting of Johansen's procedure is left for future research.

In due course, the overall computational complexity increases. This high computational load sets a limit to the number of different data generating processes (DGPs) and parameter settings which can be used for our MC simulation analysis. Nevertheless, our first results indicate that the method works well in practice and might be superior to the standard 'take all up to the kth lag' approach in specific settings.

The chapter is organized as follows. Section 9.2 introduces the model selection problem in the context of VEC-models. We present the model, the information criteria and the resulting integer optimization problem. Section 9.3 describes the implementation of the heuristic used to solve this optimization problem. In Section 9.4 we present some Monte Carlo evidence on the performance of the method applied to different DGPs. The results are compared to the standard method of choosing all lags up to a certain order. Section 9.5 summarizes the findings and provides an outlook to further steps of our analysis.

9.2. The model selection procedure

The standard procedure for model selection in a VEC-model setting consists of a sequential procedure. First, information criteria like AIC or BIC are used to choose a lag length for the unrestricted VAR-model.[11] For the next steps of the analysis, it is assumed that the correct specification of the lag structure is given.[12] Then, for the determination of the cointegration rank, a sequence of cointegration tests is performed. The statistical properties of this sequential procedure are difficult to assess. Consequently, it cannot be guaranteed that the final estimation of the cointegration rank obtained by this procedure is a consistent estimate (Johansen, 1992; Jacobson, 1995; Chao and Phillips, 1999).

In order to circumvent these shortcomings of the traditional approach, Chao and Phillips (1999) propose to reconsider the problem from the viewpoint of model selection.[13] They propose a modification of the BIC and a posterior information criterion (PIC) for the

---

[11] Ho and Sørensen (1996) find evidence in favour of using BIC when a cointegration analysis is intended. Winker (1995, 2000) generalizes this model selection step to allow for different lag structures across equations including 'holes'.

[12] However, several simulation studies have demonstrated that lag misspecification adversely affects the outcome of the cointegration tests conducted in the second step (Ho and Sørensen, 1996; Bewley and Yang, 1998).

[13] Bahmani-Oskooee and Brooks (2003) also propose a global criterion based on the goodness of fit of the resulting long-run relationships. However, they do not provide MC evidence on the relative performance of this approach.

application to VAR processes with reduced rank cointegration structure. Using these criteria for model selection exhibits three advantages: First, lag structure and the cointegration rank can be selected in a single step. Second, the penalty function of both criteria reacts to under- and over-parameterization, which both might have a detrimental effect on the estimation of the cointegration rank (Bewley and Yang, 1998). Application of this criterion provides a consistent estimation of lag structure and cointegration rank (Chao and Phillips, 1999). Third, the method can easily be extended to cover the case of different lag structures across equations including 'holes'.

For the MC simulations presented in this chapter, we consider both the modified BIC (BICm) and the modified posterior information criterion (PICm) presented in Chao and Phillips (1999, p. 236). However, the PICm is considered solely for a comparison of different criteria applied to models containing all lags up to a certain order. Our goal is to assess the advantage of allowing for holes in the lag structure for the determination of the cointegration rank of a VECM as compared to the standard 'take all up to the kth lag' approach. For the optimization of lag structures allowing for holes, we restrict the analysis to the BICm for computational reasons. Inclusion of the PICm is part of our future research agenda.

We consider the d-dimensional VAR-model of order $k + 1$

$$Y_t = \sum_{i=1}^{k+1} \Pi_i Y_{t-i} + \varepsilon_t \tag{9.1}$$

with initial values $\{Y_0, Y_{-1}, ..., Y_{-k}\}$. Thereby, the error terms ε_t are assumed to be iid $N(0, \Omega)$. Furthermore, it is assumed that the characteristic polynomial of the VAR may have unit roots on the unit circle, but no explosive components. The VAR-model (9.1) can also be expressed in vector error-correction notation as[14]

$$\Delta Y_t = \sum_{i=1}^{k} \Gamma_i \Delta Y_{t-i} + \Pi Y_{t-k-1} + \varepsilon_t. \tag{9.2}$$

The matrix Π represents the parameters of the error correction term of the model. Consequently, the cointegration rank of the system is given by the rank of Π. For each $0 \leq r \leq d$, there exist $d \cdot r$ matrices α and β of full rank

---

[14] For the empirical application, we employ the asymptotically equivalent representation from, e.g. Ahn and Reinsel (1990, p. 817), of $\Delta Y_t = \sum_{i=1}^{k} \Gamma_i \Delta Y_{t-i} + \Pi Y_{t-1} + \varepsilon_t$.

such that $\Pi = \alpha\beta'$.[15] Finally, we require that ΔY_t is a stationary process allowing for a Wold representation (Chao and Phillips, 1999, p. 229).

In the standard approach, i.e. taking all lags up to a specified order in all equations, the model selection problem consists in determining values for k and r. If a maximum lag length k_{max} is assumed to be given, the number of models to be considered amounts to $d \cdot k_{max}$. A complete enumeration of these models is feasible and will serve as a benchmark in our simulation analysis. However, a priori there is no reason to expect that the dynamic structure is of this standard type. Therefore, we extend this approach to allow for different lag structures across equations and for 'holes' in the lag structure of any equation. Consequently, we have to choose a lag structure out of $2^{d^2 \cdot k_{max}}$ possible sets. Obviously, a simple enumeration approach will fail in this case except for very small instances. As in Winker (1995, 2000), we employ a heuristic optimization technique to tackle this problem. The method will be described in Section 9.3.

Before turning to the optimal selection of the dynamic lag structure, we have to provide more details on the calculation of the information criterion BICm for given lag structure and cointegration rank. We use a modification of the iterative estimation procedure proposed by Ahn and Reinsel (1990) for the reduced rank case. However, we have to modify this method to allow for different lag structures across equations. The parameter estimates are obtained iteratively by

$$\hat{b}^{\iota+1} = \hat{b}^{\iota} + \left(\sum_{t=1}^{T} U_t^* \hat{\Omega}_\varepsilon^{-1} U_t^{*\prime}\right)^{(-1)} \left(\sum_{t=1}^{T} U_t^* \hat{\Omega}_\varepsilon^{-1} \hat{\varepsilon}_t\right) \tag{9.3}$$

where ι is the current iteration, $\hat{\Omega}_\varepsilon$ the covariance matrix of the residuals, $\hat{\varepsilon}$, under the current parameter estimates $\hat{\beta}^{\iota}$ and

$$U_t^* = [(\alpha' \otimes [0, I_{d-r}] Y_{t-1})', I_d \otimes [(\beta Y_{t-1})', \Delta Y_{t-1}, ..., \Delta Y_{t-k}]']' \tag{9.4}$$

where β is normalized so that $\beta = [I_r, \beta_0]$. The matrices Π and Γ_i can then be determined by decomposing the parameter vector b with

$$b = [\text{vec}(\beta_0')', \text{vec}((\alpha, \Gamma_1, ..., \Gamma_k)')']'. \tag{9.5}$$

The initial solution for b^0, can be found from a full rank SUR estimate which decreases the number of necessary iterations significantly and, therefore, increases the convergence speed.

To introduce the 'holes' into the lag structure, i.e. setting some of the elements of the Γ_is equal to 0, the respective columns in $U_t^{*\prime}$ are eliminated

---

[15] For $r = 0$, we choose $\alpha = \beta = 0$, for $r = d$, $\alpha = \Pi$ and $\beta = I$ is a solution.

and the (de-)composition of b has to be adapted. The information criterion BICm can then be calculated according to

$$\text{BICm} = \ln|\hat{\Omega}_{Y,r}| + \frac{\nu + r(d - r) + dr}{T}\ln(T) \tag{9.6}$$

where Y denotes the set of elements of the Γ_is, and $\nu = \sharp Y$, i.e. is the number of elements of the Γ_is that are not equal to zero. $\hat{\Omega}_{Y,r}$ is computed following Chao and Phillips (1999) in two steps: first, the parameters α, β and Γ_i are estimated iteratively as described previously for given rank r and lag structure Y. Next, the corrected values $\Delta Y_t^* = \Delta Y_t - \alpha\beta' Y_{t-1}$ are computed. Finally, the Γ_is are re-estimated by running an SUR estimation of ΔY_t^* on the ΔY_{t-1}s included in the given lag structure Y. $\hat{\Omega}_{Y,r}$ denotes the covariance matrix of the residuals of this last regression.

9.3. The algorithm

The algorithm for finding the optimal lag structure allowing for holes is a hybrid heuristic combining ideas of the Threshold Accepting (TA) algorithm as described in Winker (2001) and of 'Memetic Algorithms'.[16] For a given cointegration rank r, a random initial lag structure is chosen, the parameters are estimated and the value for the information criterion BICm is computed along the lines described in the previous section. During the following iteration steps, a local search strategy is employed where the structure is modified by either including one additional or excluding one hitherto included lagged variable in one of the equations. If the information criterion is improved or if the impairment is acceptable in the sense that it does not exceed a given threshold, i.e. if $\Delta\text{BICm} \leq T_i$, the modified lag structure is accepted. If, however, the modified lag structure degrades the information criterion more than tolerated by the current value of the threshold sequence (T_i), this modification is undone and the previous lag structure is restored. During the early iteration steps, the threshold is chosen rather generously and most of the modifications are actually accepted. In the course of the iterations, the threshold is persistently lowered, so that hardly any impairment is accepted in the last iterations. Consequently, the algorithm is well apt to overcome local optima and to fine-tune the solution once the 'core structure' has been identified.

Whereas in TA a single agent is representing one solution per iteration, we enhanced the original TA concept much in the sense of Memetic Algorithms by replacing the single agent by a population of agents each of

---

[16] Cf. Moscato (1999) and Maringer and Winker (2003).

which follows the TA search strategy. In addition to their independent local search, the agents 'compete' with each other on a regular basis where one agent challenges another and passes his (current) structure on to the challenged agent if the change in the challenged agent's information criterion does not violate the threshold criterion. Also, agents can combine parts of their solutions using a cross-over operator (Fogel, 2001) where an offspring will replace a parent if, again, the impairment in the information criterion does not exceed the threshold.

The heuristic optimization is repeated for all possible values of the rank r, i.e. $0 \le r \le d - 1$.[17] Let BICm_r denote the minimum value of the information criterion obtained by the optimization heuristic for a rank of r. Let $r^{\text{opt}} = \text{argmin}_{0 \le r \le d-1} \text{BICm}_r$, then the finally selected model is the one with rank r^{opt} and the corresponding dynamic lag structure. The selection of rank and lag length for the standard 'take all up to the kth lag' approach is performed in a similar way. For all possible values of the rank r and all $k, 0 \le k \le k_{\text{max}}$, the value of the criterion BICm is calculated. The pair (r, k) resulting in the minimum value of BICm describes the model identified by the 'take all up to the kth lag' approach.[18]

9.4. Monte Carlo simulation

9.4.1. Motivation

The evaluation of the information criterion BICm used for model selection in this chapter requires the estimation of the parameters of the reduced rank models. For this purpose, we employ the iterative algorithm proposed by Ahn and Reinsel (1990). This procedure is quite time consuming even if good starting values are provided. Consequently, the number of iterations of our hybrid heuristic has to be limited in order to allow for at least some replications in an MC setting. Finally, this high overall computational complexity of automatic lag order selection in the VEC-models limits the number of different settings which can be analysed by means of MC simulation. Consequently, we tried to assess the relative performance of the method by considering a few typical cases. Besides using artificial DGPs, we follow Ho and Sørensen (1996) for some of our simulations by

---

[17] The case $r = d$ is not considered as it corresponds to a stationary VAR-model. A method for model selection in VAR-models by means of optimization heuristics is presented in Winker (2000).

[18] Depending on the assumed rank r, the complexity of the lag structure and the length of the data series, the CPU time ranged from 3 to 7 min per independent optimization run on a Pentium 4 with 2.8 GHz using Matlab R13.

using parameter values obtained from an estimation using actual data. Given that our simulations can only pick a small number of parameter settings out of a huge parameter space, this approach ascertains that we might select empirically relevant parameter settings.

9.4.2. Simulation setup

The results presented in this section are based on the simulation of three different DGPs with different rank and lag structure. The details of these DGPs are introduced below. The first DGP (DGP_1) is taken from Chao and Phillips (1999, pp. 242f, Experiment 5). The second DGP (DGP_2) is based on this example, but adds a second cointegration vector and extends the dynamic structure. Finally, the third DGP (DGP_3) is based on the estimation of a simple money demand system.

For each replication of the first two DGPs 300 observations have been generated from which the first 145 are eliminated, leaving a sample length of $T = 155$. For DGP_3, the process was initialized with the historical values of the variables and samples of length $T = 200$ have been simulated for each replication. We ran 100 and 200 replications, respectively, and for each replication the rank was estimated by the methods 'all up to the kth lag' (labelled 'all') and our optimization heuristic allowing for structures with 'holes' in the k_{max} lags (labelled 'holes') with $k_{max} = 5$ for both methods.

9.4.2.1. DGP_1

Experiment 5 in Chao and Phillips (1999) is a three-dimensional VECM with one cointegration vector entering a single equation of the system and a lag length of one. Thereby, lagged differences of the endogenous variables enter only the equation for the respective variables. The error correction term is described by the matrix Π, Γ_1 provides the coefficients of the dynamic part and Ω_ε the variance–covariance matrix of the normally distributed error terms:

$$\Pi = \begin{pmatrix} 0 \\ -0.01 \\ 0 \end{pmatrix} \begin{pmatrix} 1 & 0.25 & 0.8 \end{pmatrix}$$

$$\Gamma_1 = \begin{pmatrix} 0.99 & 0 & 0 \\ 0 & 0.9025 & 0 \\ 0 & 0 & 0.99 \end{pmatrix}$$

$$\Omega_\varepsilon = \begin{pmatrix} 2.25 & 2.55 & 1.95 \\ 2.55 & 3.25 & 2.81 \\ 1.95 & 2.81 & 2.78 \end{pmatrix}.$$

The moduli of non-zero reverse characteristic roots of the process[19] are
1, 1, 0.99, 0.99, 0.95, 0.95.

9.4.2.2. DGP_2

Modifying the above DGP by adding a second cointegration vector and
lags of order 2 and 3 in the dynamic part, we obtain DGP_2 with an actual
rank of 2 and the following parameters:

$$\Pi = \begin{pmatrix} 0 & -0.005 \\ -0.005 & 0 \\ -0.002 & 0.003 \end{pmatrix} \begin{pmatrix} 0.8 & 0.25 & 0.5 \\ 0.4 & 0.10 & -0.3 \end{pmatrix}$$

$$\Gamma_1 = \begin{pmatrix} 0.59 & 0 & 0 \\ 0 & 0.725 & 0 \\ 0 & 0 & 0.84 \end{pmatrix} \quad \Gamma_2 = \begin{pmatrix} 0.25 & 0 & 0 \\ 0.02 & 0.10 & 0 \\ -0.05 & 0 & 0.05 \end{pmatrix}$$

$$\Gamma_3 = \begin{pmatrix} 0 & 0.05 & -0.1 \\ 0 & 0 & 0 \\ 0.1 & -0.1 & 0.05 \end{pmatrix}$$

$$\Omega_\varepsilon = \begin{pmatrix} 4.5 & 5.1 & 3.9 \\ 5.1 & 6.5 & 5.62 \\ 3.9 & 5.62 & 5.56 \end{pmatrix}.$$

The moduli of non-zero reverse characteristic roots of the process are 1,
0.99755, 0.96160, 0.96160, 0.88443, 0.88443, 0.35230, 0.35230, 0.30986,
0.30986, 0.13375. Obviously, the second root is very close to one which
would correspond to a cointegration rank of two. This finding should be
taken into account when analysing the results obtained for this process.

---

[19] See Lütkepohl (1993) for a description. The roots are calculated using a Maple
implementation with 100 digit precision.

9.4.2.3. DGP₃

Finally, DGP_3 has been obtained by fitting a VECM to the logarithms of M3 (lm), the nominal GDP (ly) and the GDP-Deflator (lp) for the period 1973.1–1989.4, i.e. restricted to West German data. All series have been detrended and seasonally adjusted by regressing them on a constant, a linear trend and seasonal dummies.[20] The cointegration space is spanned by the two vectors corresponding to long-run neutrality of money $(0, 1, -1)$ and no money illusion in the long-run $(1, -1, 0)$. Imposing these restrictions and reducing the model dynamics by a general-to-specific approach, the following parameters resulted:

$$\Pi Y_{t-1} = \begin{pmatrix} 0 & 0 \\ 0.20237 & -0.20453 \\ -0.069713 & 0.16597 \end{pmatrix} \begin{pmatrix} 1 & -1 & 0 \\ 1 & 0 & -1 \end{pmatrix} \begin{pmatrix} \text{lm}_{t-1} \\ \text{ly}_{t-1} \\ \text{lp}_{t-1} \end{pmatrix}$$

$$\Gamma_1 = \begin{pmatrix} 0 & 0 & 0 \\ 0 & -0.35885 & -0.55845 \\ 0 & 0 & 0.29401 \end{pmatrix}$$

$$\Gamma_2 = \begin{pmatrix} 0 & 0 & 0.28511 \\ 0.42088 & -0.24879 & -0.28601 \\ 0 & 0 & 0 \end{pmatrix}$$

$$\Gamma_3 = \begin{pmatrix} 0.15953 & 0 & 0 \\ 0.38674 & 0 & -0.32608 \\ 0.026677 & 0 & 0 \end{pmatrix}$$

$$\Gamma_4 = \begin{pmatrix} 0.13814 & -0.087458 & -0.20802 \\ 0.19475 & 0.24129 & 0 \\ 0 & -0.090326 & 0.062985 \end{pmatrix}$$

[20] From an economic point of view, it appears reasonable to include an indicator of the cost of holding money, too. However, extending the analysis to a four-dimensional system is left for future analysis.

$$\Gamma_5 = \begin{pmatrix} 0 & 0 & 0.20721 \\ 0 & 0 & -0.46694 \\ 0 & -0.082374 & 0 \end{pmatrix}$$

$$\Omega_\varepsilon = \begin{pmatrix} 0.0075836 & 0 & 0 \\ 0 & 0.011097 & 0 \\ 0 & 0 & 0.0056604 \end{pmatrix}.$$

The moduli of non-zero reverse characteristic roots for this pseudo empirical process are 1.08749, 0.87625, 0.87625, 0.85554, 0.85554, 0.81311, 0.81311, 0.68282, 0.68282, 0.65016, 0.65016, 0.61613, 0.61613, 0.57064, 0.25089. Since the largest root is greater than 1, this DGP might not be stable.[21]

9.4.3. Results

The evaluation of the Monte Carlo results could be based on different properties. However, given that our main interest is on the effects of model selection on rank estimation, we focus on the estimated cointegration rank. For the models allowing for 'holes', we also present information on the average size, i.e. the average relative frequency of including a zero coefficient, and the average power, i.e. the probability of including the non-zero coefficients. Alternative criteria comprise, e.g. the relative frequency of finding exactly the true DGP, which is considered to be an uninteresting statistic for real applications, the accuracy of impulse response analysis based on the selected model as compared to the true model or the relative forecasting performance.[22] As a measure of possible overfitting, which might be relevant in a forecasting setting, we also report mean values for the quotient q_{Σ} of the determinant of the residual covariance matrix for the selected models and for the true DGP. Hendry and Krolzig (2003) suggest that values of this quotient close to or above 1 indicate that overfitting does not occur.

---

[21] See Lütkepohl (1993).

[22] Brüggemann et al. (2003) use these characteristics for a comparison of model selection procedures for stationary VAR processes. They find that 'model selection is especially useful in models with larger dimensions.' See also Hansen (1999) for a critical discussion of model selection procedures.

Table 9.1.   Results for the 'take all up to the kth lag' approach (DGP₁)

Rank	Lags 0	1	2	3	4	5	Rank	Lags 0	1	2	3	4	5
	Modified BIC							*Modified PIC*					
0	0	0	0	0	0	0	0	0	0	0	0	0	0
1	0	805	0	0	0	0	1	0	999	0	0	0	0
2	0	160	0	0	0	0	2	0	1	0	0	0	0
3	0	35	0	0	0	0	3	0	0	0	0	0	0
	Johansen (1%)							*Johansen (5%)*					
0	0	0	0	0	0	0	0	0	0	0	0	0	0
1	0	750	0	0	0	0	1	0	509	0	0	0	0
2	0	210	0	0	0	0	2	0	343	0	0	0	0
3	0	40	0	0	0	0	3	0	148	0	0	0	0

9.4.3.1. Results of the 'take all up to the kth lag' approach

Before turning to the results of our optimization algorithm, we first present findings for the 'take all up to the kth lag' approach comparing different methods. Table 9.1 summarizes the findings for 1000 replications of DGP₁. For the modified BIC and PIC criterion, the table entries indicate the number of times the corresponding rank and lag length has been selected by the criteria. For the Johansen testing procedure, a two-step approach is used. First, the lag length of the unrestricted VAR is selected according to the BIC. Then, the trace test for the cointegration rank is conducted using this lag length. The table entries indicate the number of times the corresponding rank and lag length is found by this two-step approach using a 1%- and a 5%-critical value for the trace test, respectively.[23]

Obviously, for DGP₁ all four methods identify the actual lag length of one for all replications. Although the lag structure of DGP₁ is sparse since only the diagonal elements are different from zero, the high numerical values of these diagonal elements force all methods to choose a lag length of one. Nevertheless, the four methods differ markedly in their ability to identify the actual cointegration rank of the model. While the modified PIC points to the correct rank of one in 999 out of 1000 replications,[24] the share of correct identifications of the cointegration rank shrinks to 80.5% for the modified BIC and to 75% and 50.9%, respectively, when using Johansen's procedure with a nominal significance level of 1% and 5%, respectively.

---

[23] It should be noted that for the trace test, standard critical values have been used. Of course, by taking into account the known structure of the DGPs, exact critical values could be obtained by means of simulation.

[24] This corresponds to the findings presented by Chao and Phillips (1999, p. 248).

Table 9.2.   ***Results for the 'take all up to the kth lag' approach (DGP$_2$)***

	Lags							Lags					
Rank	0	1	2	3	4	5	Rank	0	1	2	3	4	5
	Modified BIC							*Modified PIC*					
0	0	81	376	1	0	0	0	0	18	879	4	0	0
1	0	60	357	17	0	0	1	0	7	65	27	0	0
2	0	14	78	1	0	0	2	0	0	0	0	0	0
3	0	35	15	0	0	0	3	0	0	0	0	0	0
	Johansen (1%)							*Johansen (5%)*					
0	0	41	23	0	0	0	0	0	11	3	0	0	0
1	0	95	623	25	0	0	1	0	89	451	18	0	0
2	0	19	149	4	0	0	2	0	44	249	9	0	0
3	0	3	17	1	0	0	3	0	14	109	3	0	0

Table 9.2 exhibits the corresponding results for DGP$_2$. In contrast to the simpler dynamic structure of DGP$_1$, all four methods fail to identify the correct lag length for most replications. However, given that our main interest is in the long-run structure of the model, we might concentrate on the identification of the cointegration rank. Obviously, both the absolute and the relative performance of the methods change drastically. The actual rank of two is found in 17.2% and 30.2% of the replications when using Johansen's procedure with level 1% and 5%, respectively. The modified BIC results in 9.3% correct estimates of the cointegration rank, while the modified PIC never results in a cointegration rank of two. These results confirm the findings by Gonzalo and Pitarakis (1999) that the relative performance of different methods might depend strongly on the DGP under consideration. In particular, our results do not support results of other simulation studies where simpler lag structures allowed for the tentative conclusion that overfitting might be less distorting than underfitting in a cointegration context.[25] Obviously, the second near unit root leads to the high rejection rates of the models with rank 2.

For our third DGP (DGP$_3$), the comparison of the different criteria is based on only 100 replications, which all have been initialized with the historical values of the detrended series. The results are summarized in Table 9.3.

Again, the modified BIC and Johansen's procedure appear more suitable for selecting the actual cointegration rank of two. However, both methods do so while missing the high order dynamic dependencies embedded in the sparse lag structure of the DGP. By contrast, using the

---

[25] See, e.g. Cheung and Lai (1993) and Jacobson (1995).

Table 9.3. Results for DGP₃ and all up to the kth lag approach

Rank	Lags						Rank	Lags					
	0	1	2	3	4	5		0	1	2	3	4	5
Modified BIC								*Modified PIC*					
0	0	0	4	5	0	0	0	0	0	5	11	5	0
1	0	3	10	0	1	0	1	0	0	21	3	13	0
2	33	21	16	0	1	1	2	2	10	20	3	3	4
3	0	2	3	0	0	0	3	0	0	0	0	0	0
Johansen (1%)								*Johansen (5%)*					
0	0	0	0	0	0	0	0	0	0	0	0	0	0
1	0	12	8	0	0	0	1	0	4	2	0	0	0
2	36	18	17	0	1	1	2	34	21	21	0	1	1
3	3	2	2	0	0	0	3	5	7	4	0	0	0

modified PIC points more often to higher lag orders. However, the actual lag order of five is identified only in 4% of all cases as compared to 1% for the other criteria. This deficit might be attributed to the sparse lag structure which implies that in order to capture the actual high order dynamics, the 'take all up to the kth lag' approach has to provide estimates for all entries in the matrices $\Gamma_1, ..., \Gamma_5$. As demonstrated for stationary VAR-processes in Winker (2000) allowing for holes in the lag structure might sensibly reduce this effect and improve the model identification of the dynamic part.

Summarizing the findings for the different criteria, at least for the three DGPs under consideration, the modified BIC criterion appears to be a sensible choice. Thus, the following results of the optimization approach concentrate on this criterion. Nevertheless, it is left to future research to also provide results for the PICm and Johansen's procedure.

9.4.3.2. Results of the optimization heuristic

In the following, we present results of the implementation of the optimization heuristic described in Section 9.3. In order to obtain a concise description of the results, we concentrate on the identification of the cointegration rank when using the modified BIC.[26] Furthermore, due to constraints by available computer resources, we restrict our analysis to a cointegration rank between 0 and $d - 1$. This implies the assumption that the case of a stationary VAR could be excluded by a standard unit root pretest. For DGP₁ and DGP₂ we analyse 200 different realizations with 150

---

[26] Detailed results on the identification of the dynamic structure are available on request.

observations, while for DGP_3 only 100 realizations with 200 observations are considered.[27] For each realization, three different methods have been used to obtain an estimate of the cointegration rank:

'known'. The model is estimated for a cointegration rank of $p = 0, ..., d - 1$ assuming that the actual lag structure is known, i.e. only the non-zero elements of the matrices Γ_i are included in the estimation. The cointegration rank identified by this method is defined by the minimum value of BICm obtained for the different rank conditions.

'all'. The model is estimated for a cointegration rank of $p = 0, ..., d - 1$ and using all lags up to a given order $k = 1, ..., k_{max}$. For our application, $d = 3$ and $k_{max} = 5$. Consequently, 15 different model specifications are estimated. The model resulting in the minimum value of BICm provides the rank estimate of this method.

'holes'. For each possible cointegration rank of $p = 0, ..., d - 1$ a heuristic optimization is performed on the lags to be included in the dynamic part of the model. Afterwards, out of the d resulting models the one resulting in the smallest value of the modified BIC is selected.

Obviously, the method 'known' cannot be used in practical applications, as the true lag structure will not be known. Nevertheless, it is used as a benchmark for our optimization approach ('holes') in order to make sure that by employing the optimization heuristic the identified model has a value of the criterion BICm which is smaller than or equal to the value of BICm for the actual lag structure.[28] By contrast, the method 'all' represents the state of the art in criterion-based model selection. Consequently, it is of interest to evaluate the relative performance of the last two methods.

Table 9.4 summarizes the results for the three methods applied to the three DGPs based on 200, 200, and 100 replications, respectively. For all methods and DGPs the maximum lag length k_{max} has been fixed to five. The numbers in the table indicate the percentage share of replications for which the methods identify a cointegration rank of $p = 0, ..., 2$ based on the modified BIC.

For the first DGP with its quite simple dynamic structure, all three methods appear to work reasonably well. Nevertheless, the chance of

---

[27] First additional experiments for realizations with 300 observations for DGP_2 did not lead to substantially different results.

[28] In fact, this goal is achieved for almost all runs of the optimization algorithm despite a small number of iterations used.

Table 9.4. **Cointegration rank estimates (%)**

Rank	Method 'known'	'all'	'holes'
DGP$_1$ (200 replications)			
0	0.0	0.0	0.0
1	95.0	80.5	88.0
2	5.0	19.5	12.0
DGP$_2$ (200 replications)			
0	13.0	50.5	13.4
1	73.8	35.8	74.8
2	13.2	13.7	11.8
DGP$_3$ (100 replications)			
0	0.0	10.0	3.0
1	19.0	23.0	28.0
2	81.0	67.0	69.0

identifying the actual cointegration rank $p = 1$ based on 150 observations is best if the true dynamics are known. For practical applications only a comparison of the standard method of taking all lags up to a certain order ('all') with our optimization procedure is relevant. For DGP$_1$ the optimization procedure increases the frequency of finding the right cointegration rank from 80 to 88%.

For DGP$_2$ with its quite complex lag structure and the second near unit root (0.99755), even when assuming that the true lag structure is known, only in 13% of all replications the actual cointegration rank of 2 is found. Further analysis is required to identify the reasons for this outcome, in particular, we have to check whether increasing the number of observations tends to improve the results. The two methods which can be used in applications, i.e. 'all' and 'holes', report the correct cointegration rank with frequency 13.7% and 11.8%, respectively. Although, 'all' appears to have a slight advantage in finding the correct cointegration rank, it also results in a more than 50% chance of finding no cointegration at all, whereas the 'holes' approach provides results quite similar to the ones obtained when the true DGP was known.

Finally, for DGP$_3$ constructed from a real data example, the assumption of a known lag structure would result in the best chance to find the real cointegration rank, while the difference between 'all' and 'holes' is smallest for this example, but still in favour of the optimization approach. We assume that the relative performance of the optimization approach will improve when a larger number of iterations can be performed in the optimization step. This has been impossible for these first results due to constraints in computational resources.

Although our main interest is in a correct specification of the cointegration part of our models, we finish by a short look on the dynamic structures selected by the three methods. Of course, this choice appears to be crucial for the determination of the cointegration rank. Table 9.5 reports on the dynamic structure for the three DPGs. The rows labelled ν show the mean number of non-zero elements estimated in the dynamic part of the model, i.e. the number of non-zero entries in $\hat{\Gamma}_1, \ldots, \hat{\Gamma}_5$. In the rows with label 'cl' we provide the share of lags present in the DGP which are included in the estimated models ('average power'), while 'wl' provides the share of lags included in the estimated model, but not present in the DGPs ('average size'). Finally, q_Σ indicates the quotient of the determinant of the residual covariance matrices for the model under consideration as compared to the true DGP.

For a simple dynamic structure like DGP_1, the optimization method appears to work extremely well by finding the relevant lags (on the diagonal of $\hat{\Gamma}_1$) for all replications and including only a small number of additional lags. The standard method has to include all nine first order lags in order to capture the relevant lags. Consequently, the share of non-relevant lags increases as the mean number of lags included ($\nu = 9$). Only for this rather simple DGP, q_Σ indicates a slight tendency of

Table 9.5. *Reported lag structure for different selection methods*

	Method		
	'known'	'all'	'holes'
DGP_1 (200 replications)			
ν	3	9	4.47
cl	100%	100%	100%
wl	0%	14.3%	3.5%
q_Σ	1.00	0.92	0.94
DPG_2 (200 replications)			
ν	13	19.89	17.15
cl	100%	69.2%	52.0%
wl	0%	30.7%	27.1%
q_Σ	1.00	1.16	0.99
DPG_3 (100 replications)			
ν	21	15.12	13.06
cl	100%	27.8%	57.7%
wl	0%	25.1%	2.8%
q_Σ	1.00	1.65	1.08

overfitting for the 'take all up' approach and – to a smaller extent – for the 'holes' method. For the other DGPs no overfitting is indicated by this measure, but the 'holes' approach results in better fitting models with a determinant of the residual covariance matrix close to that of the true DGP. For DGP_2, the share of relevant lags identified by the optimization heuristic is smaller than for the 'all' heuristic, which is surprising at first sight given the larger search space. This result deserves further attention. Nevertheless, it is remarkable that the optimization heuristic seems to identify those lags allowing for a correct estimation of the cointegration rank more often than the 'all' heuristic (see Table 9.4). Finally, for DGP_3, the optimization heuristic is much more successful in selecting the relevant lags and avoiding the inclusion non-relevant ones. Nevertheless, this advantage in the modelling of the dynamic part does not show up in a dramatic improvement in selecting the right cointegration rank. Again, our first results support earlier findings that the performance of model selection procedures in the context of cointegration depends heavily on the specific DGP. In particular, as stated by Gredenhoff and Karlsson (1999, p. 184) we might conclude that 'choosing the lag-length in VAR-models is not an easy task'. Consequently, more research is needed to identify the features of DGPs affecting the performance of different model selection methods.

9.5. Conclusion

In this chapter, we discuss the model selection issue in the context of non-stationary VAR-models with stationary cointegration relationships. Our reading of the literature suggests that the modelling of the dynamic part of these VEC-models is crucial for a correct rank identification. We compare different methods for model selection in an MC simulation including methods based on information criteria and a two-step procedure employing Johansen's testing strategy. Furthermore, we introduce a discrete optimization heuristic allowing for the selection of lag structures out of a much larger search space than the usual 'take all up to the kth lag' approach. Again, an MC simulation is used to assess the relative performance of this algorithm.

Our findings support the view that the results of methods aiming at identifying the cointegration rank of a VECM depend heavily on the modelling of the dynamic structure. In contrast to earlier studies and in accordance with more recent findings, already a very small set of DGPs indicates that this effect might differ markedly for different DGPs. In particular, the practical guideline rather to include too many lags is not supported for all DGPs by our findings. However, we find that the optimization heuristic approach in combination with a modified BIC performs relatively well as compared to the 'take all up to the *k*th lag' approach.

Given the small set of DGPs considered in this chapter and the restriction to a single model selection procedure in the optimization context points directly towards future research. First, we have to apply our method to a much larger set of different DGPs in order to find out how robust our results are and which factors might be responsible for differences in the (relative) performance. Second, we want to include other procedures in our approach, in particular the modified PIC suggested by Chao and Phillips (1999) and Johansen's procedure. Finally, we have to improve the performance of the estimation step in the optimization heuristic in order to allow for a larger number of iterations for a given problem in order to have more reliable results from the optimization method.

Despite our limited and preliminary results the tentative conclusion seems admitted that employing a more refined method for identifying the dynamic structure of a VECM might improve the performance in terms of rank order identification.

Acknowledgements

We are indebted to D. Hendry, S. Johansen, K. Juselius, H. Lütkepohl, M. Meyer, and participants of the Macromodels' 2003 conference in Warsawa for helpful comments on an earlier draft of this chapter. All remaining shortcomings lie solely with the authors.

References

Ahking, F.W. (2002), "Model mis-specification and Johansen's co-integration analysis: an application to the US money demand", *Journal of Macroeconomics*, Vol. 24, pp. 51–66.

Ahn, S.K. and G.C. Reinsel (1990), "Estimation for partially nonstationary multivariate autoregressive models", *Journal of the American Statistical Association*, Vol. 85(411), pp. 813–823.

Bahmani-Oskooee, M. and T.J. Brooks (2003), "A new criteria for selecting the optimum lags in Johansen's cointegration technique", *Applied Economics*, Vol. 35, pp. 875–880.

Bewley, R. and M. Yang (1998), "On the size and power of system tests for cointegration", *The Review of Economics and Statistics*, Vol. 80(4), pp. 675–679.

Brüggemann, R., H.-M. Krolzig and H. Lütkepohl (2003), *Comparison of Model Reduction Methods for VAR Processes*, Tech. Rep. 2003-W13, Economics Group, Nuffield College, University of Oxford.

Campos, J., D.F. Hendry and H.-M. Krolzig (2003), "Consistent model selection by an automatic gets approach", *Oxford Bulletin of Economics and Statistics*, Vol. 65(s1), pp. 803–820.

Chao, J.C. and P.C.B. Phillips (1999), "Model selection in partially nonstationary vector autoregressive processes with reduced rank structure", *Journal of Econometrics*, Vol. 91, pp. 227–271.

Cheung, Y.-W. and K.S. Lai (1993), "Finite-sample sizes of Johansen's likelihood ratio test for cointegration", *Oxford Bulletin of Economics and Statistics*, Vol. 55, pp. 313–328.

Fogel, D. (2001), *Evolutionary Computation: Toward a New Philosophy of Machine Intelligence*, 2nd edition, New York, NY: IEEE Press.

Gatu, C. and E.J. Kontoghiorghes (2003), "Parallel algorithms for computing all possible subset regression models using the QR decomposition", *Parallel Computing*, Vol. 29(4), pp. 505–521.

Gonzalo, J. and J.-Y. Pitarakis (1999), "Lag length estimation in large dimensional systems", *Journal of Time Series Analysis*, Vol. 23(4), pp. 401–423.

Gredenhoff, M. and S. Karlsson (1999), "Lag-length selection in VAR-models using equal and unequal lag-length procedures", *Computational Statistics*, Vol. 14, pp. 171–187.

Hansen, B.E. (1999), "Discussion of 'data mining reconsidered' ", *Econometrics Journal*, Vol. 2, pp. 192–201.

Hendry, D.F. and H.-M. Krolzig (2001), *Automatic Econometric Model Selection*, London: Timberlake Consultants Press.

Hendry, D.F. and H.-M. Krolzig (2003), *Automatic Model Selection: A New Instrument for Social Science*, Tech. rep., Economics Department, Oxford University.

Ho, M.S. and B.E. Sørensen (1996), "Finding cointegration rank in high dimensional systems using the Johansen test: an illustration using data based Monte Carlo simulations", *The Review of Economics and Statistics*, Vol. 78(4), pp. 726–732.

Hoover, K.D. and S.J. Perez (1999), "Data mining reconsidered: encompassing and the general-to-specific approach to specification search", *Econometrics Journal*, Vol. 2, pp. 167–191.

Jacobson, T. (1995), "On the determination of lag order in vector autoregressions of cointegrated systems", *Computational Statistics*, Vol. 10(2), pp. 177–192.

Johansen, S. (1988), "Statistical analysis of cointegration vectors", *Journal of Economic Dynamics and Control*, Vol. 12, pp. 231–254.

Johansen, S. (1991), "Estimation and hypothesis testing of cointegration vectors in gaussian vector autoregressive models", *Econometrica*, Vol. 59(6), pp. 1551–1580.

Johansen, S. (1992), "Determination of cointegration rank in the presence of a linear trend", *Oxford Bulletin of Economics and Statistics*, Vol. 54(3), pp. 383–397.

Johansen, S. (1995), *Likelihood-Based Inference in Cointegrated Vector Autoregressive Models*, Oxford: Oxford University Press.

Johansen, S. (2002), "A small sample correction for the test of cointegration rank in the vector autoregressive model", *Econometrica*, Vol. 70(5), pp. 1929–1961.

Krolzig, H.-M. and D.F. Hendry (2001), "Computer automation of general-to-specific model selection procedures", *Journal of Economic Dynamics and Control*, Vol. 25, pp. 831–866.

Lütkepohl, H. (1993), *Introduction to Multiple Time Series Analysis*, 2nd edition, Berlin: Springer.

Maringer, D. and P. Winker (2003), *Portfolio Optimization under Different Risk Constraints with Memetic Algorithms*, Tech. Rep. 2003-005E, Staatswissenschaftliche Fakultät, Universität Erfurt.

Moscato, P. (1999), "Memetic algorithms: a short introduction", pp. 219–234 in: D. Corne, M. Dorigo and F. Glover, editors, *New Ideas in Optimization*, London: McGraw-Hill.

Omtzigt, P. (2002), *Automatic Identification and Restriction of the Cointegration Space*, Tech. Rep. 2002/25, Faculty of Economics, University of Insubria, Varese.

Pötscher, B.M. (1991), "Effects of model selection on inference", *Econometric Theory*, Vol. 7, pp. 7–67.

Winker, P. (1995), "Identification of multivariate AR-models by threshold accepting", *Computational Statistics and Data Analysis*, Vol. 20(9), pp. 295–307.

Winker, P. (2000), "Optimized multivariate lag structure selection", *Computational Economics*, Vol. 16, pp. 87–103.

Winker, P. (2001), *Optimization Heuristics in Econometrics: Applications of Threshold Accepting*, Chichester: Wiley.

Subject Index

AR formulation, 86
ARCH model, 11
augmented Dickey–Fuller test, 111

Bartlett correction, 51, 90
BEKK, 180, 185
BEKK representation, 3
bootstrapping impulse responses, 135
Brownian motion, 50

Cagan's model, 79
causal inference, 31
causality, 27, 28
causality in forecasting, 36
causality in economics, 30
Chow tests, 129
CI(2,1) relations, 85
CI(2,2) relations, 87
co-breaking, 40
co-integration rank, 89, 116
co-integration relations, 36, 115
conditional correlation, 5, 9, 183
conditional density, 149, 150
conditional factorisation, 38
conditional variance, 4
conditional/marginal factorization, 164
congruence, 153
Constant Conditional Correlation (CCC)
    model, 180
cumulated nominal shocks, 76
cumulated real shocks, 76
cumulated temporary shocks, 74, 158
cycle, 73, 74
cyclical component, 74, 76

Data Generation Process (DGP), 22, 108, 148
deterministic component, 88
deterministic components in I(2) model, 71,
    88
deterministic trends, 74
DGP, 23, 149
diagnosing I(2), 80, 82

double unit roots, 71
dynamic multipliers, 165, 166

econometric model, 24
empirical Granger non-causality, 34, 150
encompassing, 154
exchange rate, 9
exclusion restrictions, 127
explosive root, 98

fractional integration, 141
forecast error, 138
forecast error variance decomposition, 138
forecasting in open models, 166
foreign direct investment, 9

GARCH model, 3
generalised impulse response, 12
generalised impulse response method, 14
Granger causality, 33, 150
Granger representation theorem, 10

heuristic optimisation techniques, 215
hyper-inflation, 70

I(2) model, 85, 88
identification, 204
identification of structural Vector Equilibrium
    Correction Model (VEqCM), 203
impulse response, 13, 14, 15, 17, 34, 40, 41, 42,
    43, 107, 108, 128, 133, 134, 135, 136, 137,
    138, 140, 148, 158, 159, 160, 164, 165, 168,
    198, 224
impulse response analysis, 12, 41, 133, 157
impulse response function, 13
impulse response in closed systems, 159, 165
impulse responses in open systems, 159
inflation rate, 74
information criterion, 214
interpreting the I(2) structure, 91
invariance, 151
irregular component, 73

joint density, 149

Keynesian-type model, 9

labour productivity , 203
labour productivity equation, 203
labour productivity function, 197, 203, 209
Likelihood Ratio (LR) test, 115
local Data Generation Process (DGP), 24, 25,
    148, 149
long-run stochastic $I(2)$ trends, 78
LR tests, 116
Lucas critique, 10, 167

marginal data density, 179
Markov Chain Monte Carlo (MCMC)
    methods, 180
Maximum Likelihood (ML) estimation, 3, 108,
    156, 178, 208, 209
Memetic algorithms, 219
Metropolis–Hastings algorithm, 179
Metropolis–Hastings Markov chains, 179
misspecification tests, 207
ML estimation, 120
model, 13
model reduction, 127
models nested in t-VECH, 183
money demand, 109, 126
money stock, 79, 109
money supply/demand, 71
money velocity, 79
Monte Carlo simulation, 220
moving average representation, 87

near unit roots, 83

order of integration, 110
orthogonal GARCH model, 4, 15
orthogonalized impulse responses, 134
over-identifying restrictions, 124

panel data study, 11
Pantula principle, 111
parameter constancy analysis, 130
permanent shocks, 74
policy analysis, 39
policy instruments, 40, 148
polynomial co-integration, 100

price homogeneity, 78, 94
price mark-up function, 203
principal component representation, 4

reduced form Vector Autoregression model
    (VAR), 13
response analysis, 157
response analysis in closed models, 159
response analysis in open models, 163

second-order stochastic trends, 75
size distortions, 55, 118
standard percentile interval, 135
stochastic, 73, 74, 75, 76, 77, 78, 79, 88, 91, 92,
    93, 94, 206
stochastic trend, 73, 74, 75, 76, 77, 78, 79, 88, 91,
    92, 93, 94, 206
strong exogeneity, 26
structural breaks, 39
structural Vector Autoregression model (VAR),
    12, 41, 134, 203, 215
structural Vector Equilibrium Correction
    Model (VEqCM), 203
super exogeneity, 26, 35, 151

target variables, 39, 147
tests for parameter constancy, 131
Threshold Accepting (TA) algorithm, 219
time varying covariance matrix, 13
transitory shock, 74
trend-cycle formulation, 76
two-step estimator, 123

unit root tests, 112, 113, 114
unit root tests structural breaks, 112

VechGARCH models, 180, 185
Vector autoregression model (VAR), 155, 158,
    217
Vector autoregression process, 2, 158
Vector error-correction model (VECM), 115, 217
Vector equilibrium correction model (VEqCM),
    156, 158, 198

wage function, 201
weak exogeneity, 25
Wold representation, 161